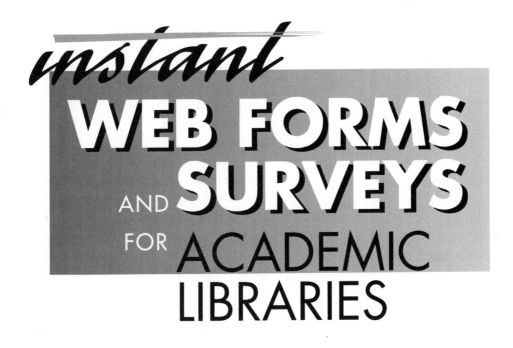

GAIL JUNION-METZ AND DERREK L. METZ

NEAL-SCHUMAN NETGUIDE SERIES

NEAL-SCHUMAN PUBLISHERS, INC.
NEW YORK   LONDON

Published by Neal-Schuman Publishers, Inc.
100 Varick Street
New York, NY 10013

Library of Congress Cataloging-in-Publication Data

Junion-Metz, Gail, 1947–
    Instant Web forms and surveys for academic libraries [computer file] / [Gail Junion-Metz and Derrek L. Metz].
    1 computer optical disc ; 4 3/4 in. + 1 manual. — (Neal-Schuman netguide series)
    System requirements: PC; Windows; CD-ROM drive.
    Title from disk label.
    Audience: Librarians.
    Summary: Contains twenty-four customizable public library forms and surveys in HTML format. Includes matching Perl scripts and tutorial.
    ISBN 1-55570-412-3
    1. Academic libraries—Forms. 2. Library surveys. 3. Library information networks. I. Metz, Derrek L. II. Title. III. Series.
Z715
027.7—dc13

2001041194

Instant Web Forms & Surveys

Contents

SECTION 2 — FORMS, SURVEYS, AND SCRIPTS

Preface

Designing usable and effective paper-based library forms and surveys has always been a challenge. As online technologies change both the higher education and academic library landscape, most libraries now have the capability to add online forms and surveys to their Web sites in order to serve both on-campus and remote patrons. We created *Instant Web Forms and Surveys for Academic Libraries* to help you upgrade your Web site . . . without spending hundreds of hours doing it . . . by providing you with many of the most popular and useful academic library forms and surveys in a ready-to-use format. Our major goal is to take the expense, work, and uncertainty out of online form and survey design and upload, and make it simple for community college and smaller college/university libraries to add these nifty tools to their Web sites.

The toolkit consists of the CD with ready-to-use forms and an accompanying manual with step-by-step instructions for using them.

The CD contains:

- 24 ready-to-use online forms and surveys in HTML format.
- 24 fully-tested and matching Perl scripts.
- A library of ready-to-select form/survey graphics in two different fonts (Times-Roman and Arial) and four different colors (red, blue, white, black) that will help you "blend" the forms with your existing Web pages.
- A step-by-step tutorial that makes it simple to preview, select, and download just the right form/survey to your computer's desktop.
- Simple instructions for adding your library's unique information to each form and its matching script.
- Step-by-step instructions for testing the forms and scripts both before and after you upload them to your library's Web server.
- A backup copy of the printed manual instructions in PDF format . . . just in case you misplace it or need an extra copy.

The accompanying manual contains:

- Step-by-step instructions for adding your library's information to each form and the matching script.
- Step-by-step instructions for making simple (and optional) modifications to each of the forms and scripts.
- Step-by-step instructions for testing the forms and scripts both before and after you upload them to your library's Web server.
- Printed copies of each of the 24 online forms and surveys
- Printed copies of each of the 24 Perl scripts

The forms and surveys in *Instant Web Forms and Surveys for Academic Libraries* include "Ask a Reference Question," "Course Reserve Request," "ILL Request," "Media / Equipment Request," "Renew/Recall/Hold" and many more. For a complete list be sure to read the next two sections: "What's On the CD?" and "What's In the Accompanying Manual?"

It's fascinating to receive feedback, opinions, and information from patrons by adding online forms and surveys to your library's Web site. You will be surprised to discover how quickly you can preview, select, and download a form or survey to your computer's desktop. Without becoming an HTML expert you can add up to 24 online forms and surveys to your library's Web site. Patrons can easily complete each form and survey and e-mail the form's information to the appropriate staff member. Each form or survey automatically sends a "thank you" e-mail and screen message to the patron who took the time to fill out the form or survey.

Academic libraries are the focus of our second CD. (Volumes for public libraries and children's and young adult services and school librarians are also available.) Like other publications in Neal-Schuman's "How To" and "NetGuide" series, *Instant Web Forms and Surveys for Academic Libraries* is designed for dedicated but busy library administrators, library professionals, and support staff. Our "instant" approach to online forms and script is evident throughout the CD and manual. Instead of teaching *you* how to create HTML forms and Perl scripts from scratch, *we* provide you with 24 fully-tested and functional forms and scripts that you can quickly and easily add to your library's Web site. You can choose to use the forms or surveys "as is" or make a few simple, optional modifications.

Perhaps you are not responsible for uploading the forms and surveys to your Web site, but you must converse with, and understand, the people who will do the job. You can use the toolkit to provide you with background information and instructions so you can work together more productively (and happily) with your technical staff.

This manual and CD grew out of the authors' differing, but in some ways also similar, experiences with the Web and Web sites. Gail is a former academic librarian and now full-time Web/Net trainer. Derrek is a college student and real-life "techie" who designs and creates Web sites both for business and pleasure. While researching this CD we looked at lots of community college and small college and university library Web sites and noticed that only a few provide their patrons with online forms and surveys. We e-mailed many small college library Webmasters about why this was so and got the same answers again and again: All wanted to add forms and surveys to their Web sites, but few had the time and many did not possess the technical skills. By solving these two problems with *Instant Web Forms and Surveys for Academic Libraries*, we hope it will be possible for more community college and small college and university libraries to easily access the views of their patrons by adding online forms and surveys to their Web sites.

What's On the CD?

The CD contains twenty-four forms and twenty-four surveys. It also contains a step-by-step tutorial that will let you preview and select just the right form from many different options. Finally, the CD contains a PDF version of this manual . . . just in case you need an extra copy. Read on to learn a few more details about what's on the CD.

The forms and surveys contained on the CD, and reproduced in the pages that follow, have been designed especially for academic libraries. They're arranged on the CD, and in the manual, in eight general categories. Each of the forms and surveys are described below.

Reference Forms / Surveys

Ask a Reference Question form
If students, faculty, or staff need an answer to a factual reference question, they can e-mail it to your reference staff. Place a link to this form on many of your Web pages.

Research Help Request form

Do students need help with class assignments, research papers, or personal research projects, but don't have time to meet with your staff? Now you can receive students' requests for information sources and factual information, as well as requests for research and citation help, via e-mail. Put a link to this form on your Reference Web page.

Library Use Survey

Add this survey to your library's Web site if want to find out how and why students, faculty, and staff use your library, how to improve your services, collections, building, and equipment, and how your patrons feel about the services/resources you currently provide. Place a link to this survey periodically on your library's homepage.

Comments, Suggestions form

Use this form to encourage students, faculty, and staff to comment about, and make suggestions for, improving your library and its resources/services. Include the link to this form on most of your library's Web pages.

Complete Citation Request form

Students and faculty often struggle to locate the information they need to create a complete and accurate citation for sources they want to cite in a research paper, thesis, or article they will be submitting for publication. Put a link to this form on your ILL or Reference Web page so that patrons can e-mail you the information they have already located. Your staff can research the missing information and e-mail it back to them.

Library Instruction Forms / Surveys

Meet with a Librarian form

Do students need help with class assignments? Do faculty members need help with research projects, but you often don't have the time to spend with them when they show up at your reference desk? Students and faculty can use this form to arrange, via e-mail or phone, to meet with you or another librarian when it's convenient for both of you. Put a link to this form on your homepage and reference pages.

Library Instruction / Program Survey

Encourage faculty, students, and staff to fill out this brief survey to help you get an idea how effective your current library instruction sessions and programs are. You'll also be able to find out if there are any new instruction sessions and programs that patrons would like you to develop and when they'd like the programs/classes offered. Finally, you can find out how faculty, students, and staff learn about currently offered library instruction sessions/programs as well as how you can notify them of such opportunities in the future. Place a link to this survey periodically on your library instruction and reference Web pages.

Library Instruction Request form

Make it easy for faculty and teaching assistants to ask library staff members to speak to their classes, present subject-related research instruction, or provide any other type of library instruction. Post this form on your library's homepage so that faculty can simply e-mail you a request.

Library Computers Forms / Surveys

Reserve a Library Computer form

Do students, faculty, and staff hate to wait in line to use one of your library's computers? Provide them with this form so that they can place an online reservation for a computer on a specific date and at a specific time. Place a link to this form on your homepage and/or technology pages.

Library Web User Survey

If you have students, faculty, and staff who primarily use your library's computers to access the Internet, and you'd like to know more about them so that you can help them better use your computers, the Internet, and your library's Web site, make sure to place a link to this survey periodically on your Web site.

Off-Campus Web User Survey

If you have faculty, students, and staff who use an Internet-connected computer at their off-campus residence or work, have them complete this brief survey so that you can learn how they use the Internet and your Web site when they're not in your library. Place a link to this survey periodically on your library's homepage.

Library Classroom I Lab Request form

If your library has classrooms, conference rooms, or computer labs that faculty and teaching assistants can reserve on an "as needed" basis, place a link to this online form on your Web site to make it simple for them to request a room, time, and date via e-mail.

Library Web Site Forms / Surveys

Suggest a New Web Link form

Encourage students, faculty, and staff to take a few minutes to recommend a new Web link they've found. Patrons can provide you with the site's URL, why they think you should add it your Web site, and even where on your site they think it should be located. Make the link to this form widely available on your Web site.

Report Broken Link or Problem form

It's a time-consuming job keeping all of your Web site links current. Faculty, staff, and students can help by reporting any broken or changed links they find while using your Web site, any graphics/images that don't load properly, or any plug-ins that you need to update and/or acquire. Patrons can also let you know if they notice any typos or grammatical errors on your site. Make the link to this form widely available on your Web site

Library Web Site Survey

If you'd like to know what local students, faculty, and staff as well as long-distance Web visitors think of your library's Web site, have them complete this brief survey. Place this survey periodically on your library's homepage.

Collection Development Forms

Library Purchase Request form

Make it easy for faculty, staff, and students to suggest a specific book, videocassette, DVD, audiotape, CD, etc., that they want you to purchase for the library collection. All patrons have to do is fill out the item's title, author/artist, publication information, and why they think the library should purchase it, and then send it to your staff via e-mail. Place a link to this form on many of your library's Web pages.

InterLibrary Loan Forms

InterLibrary Loan Request form

If faculty, students, or staff need the library to obtain a book, magazine, or newspaper article, or any other resource for them via InterLibrary Loan (ILL), they can fill out the item or article title, author/artist, and publication and/or magazine/newspaper information provided on the form and send an e-mail request to one of your ILL staff members. Place a link to this form on your ILL Web page.

InterLibrary Loan Renewal form

If faculty or students have received a book, magazine, or newspaper article, or any other resource via InterLibrary Loan, and they need/want to renew it, all they have to do is fill out this form. Place a link to this form on your ILL Web page.

Circulation Forms

Library Card Application form

Whether patrons are new to your campus or haven't found the time to come to the library to get a library card, now they can apply for one online. Place a link to this form on your circulation Web page.

Hold / Recall / Renew form

Faculty and students can extend the due-date of an item they've already checked out from the library, ask that an item checked out by another library patron be returned to the library, or place a reservation on an item that has just been returned by another library patron. Place a link to this form on your circulation page.

Missing Item Report form

Despite our every effort, some items get misshelved or stolen. Faculty, staff, and students can inform you about an item that is missing and at the same time tell you where they looked for it. Place a link to this form on your library's homepage and circulation page.

Course Reserve Request form

Each academic year faculty members place hundreds of books and journal articles on course reserve. Make the process simpler for faculty (and your staff) by placing a link to this online form on your circulation Web page so that faculty can e-mail you their requests for the materials they want you to put on reserve for their students.

Miscellaneous Forms

Media / Equipment Request form

If your library has purchased DVDs, videos, sound recordings, and software that circulate to faculty and students OR if your library has a collection of AV and computing equipment that it loans out to faculty and teaching assistants, place a link to this form on your media Web page so that faculty can reserve a video and VCR or program and traveling laptop via e-mail.

Strategic Planning Survey

Get student, faculty, and staff input on the materials you should be purchasing, the services you should be providing, and spaces you should be creating/updating in your library. Post this survey periodically on your library's homepage to see how you can do a better job serving your patrons.

The Preview/Selection Tutorial

Once you decide which of the forms or surveys you want to add to your Web site, use the step-by-step tutorial on the CD to:

1. Preview the forms so that you can see what they will look like when they're on your Web site.
2. Select a form to download to your computer's desktop.
3. Preview the two possible form fonts (Arial or Times-Roman).
4. Select the form font.
5. Preview the four different form color choices (black, blue, red, and white).
6. Select the form color.
7. Review the selections you've made and preview the form you've selected.
8. Download the form (along with its matching Perl script) to your computer's desktop.

If you want to exit the tutorial, click on the "Back to Table of Contents" link at the bottom of many of the tutorial screens.

The PDF Files

In addition to the printed manual that accompanies the CD, there is also an Acrobat (PDF) copy of Section 1 of the manual on the CD. If you misplace your manual, or if you need an additional copy for your library's technical person, all you have to do is print a copy from the CD.

You will find hypertext links to each of the PDF manual sections on the CD version of this page. To view and print the manual, you must have the Adobe Acrobat reader installed on your computer. If you need to download the free reader software, connect to *www.adobe.com/*.

What's In the Accompanying Manual?

The manual is available in three formats. There is a printed version that accompanies the CD. There is an abbreviated and linked version on the CD, and there is an Acrobat (PDF) version of the printed manual on the CD.

Overviews, Introductions

Included in the manual is a brief introduction to HTML form tags. We've also included an introduction to Perl scripts. These basic introductions should suffice to get you started if you've never worked with HTML form tags or Perl scripts before.

Step-By-Step Instructions

Once you've used the CD's preview/selection tutorial to download an HTML form and its matching Perl script to your computer's desktop, you'll want to use the manual's step-by-step instructions to help you:

1. Fill in the required information on both the form and script.
2. Optionally, customize the form and script.
3. Test the form and script before you upload them to your server.
4. Test how the form/script pair works together after you've uploaded both files to your server.

Printed Forms / HTML Documents / Perl Scripts

We've included printed examples of every form in the printed manual. All examples use the Arial (sans-serif) font. If you want to see what a form looks like with the Times-Roman (serif) font, use the preview/selection tutorial and view the form when you get to the "Review the Selections You've Made" step at the end of the tutorial. Use the printed form examples to help you:

1. Decide which form(s) to add to your Web site.
2. Examine the individual form fields included on each form.
3. Decide which form features you might want to modify.
4. Test the form before you upload it to your server.
5. Test the form after it's uploaded to your Web server.

We also included printed examples of every form's HTML code. Use the code examples to help you:

1. Learn about HTML form tags, element types, and attributes.
2. Complete the required information in each form.
3. Optionally, modify the form.
4. Test the form before you upload it to your server.
5. Test the form/script pair after it's uploaded to your server.

Finally, we included printed examples of the Perl scripts that match the forms. Use the printed Perl script examples to help you:

1. Identify the different part of a Perl script.
2. Complete the required information in each script.
3. Optionally, modify the script.
4. Test the script before you upload it to your server.
5. Test the form/script pair after it's uploaded to your server.

Sources For Further Help

Books

Castro. Elizabeth. 1998. *Perl and CGI for the World Wide Web*. Visual Quickstart Guide. Berkeley, CA: Peachpit Press.

Castro, Elizabeth. 2000. *HTML 4 for the World Wide Web*. Visual Quickstart Guide. Berkeley, CA: Peachpit Press.

Guthrie, Malcolm. 1998. *Forms: Interactivity for the World Wide Web*. San Jose, CA: Adobe Press.

Hoffman, Paul. 2000. *Perl for Dummies (with CD-ROM)*. 3rd ed. New York: Hungry Minds.

Levine, John R., and Margaret L. Young. 1998. *UNIX for Dummies*. 4th ed. New York: Hungry Minds.

Multer, Kent. 2000. *The Official Miva Web-Scripting Book.* Lakewood, CO: Top Floor Publishing.

Oliver, Dick. 1999. *Sams Teach Yourself HTML 4 in 24 Hours.* Indianapolis, IN: Sams.

Tittel, Ed, Mary Madden, and James Michael Stewart (contributors). 1999. *Windows NT Server 4 for Dummies.* New York: Hungry Minds.

Web Sites

Acrobatics: A Tutorial on Adobe Acrobat and the Portable Document Format (PDF) [Online]. Available: scout.cs.wisc.edu/addserv/toolkit/enduser/archive/1997/euc–9712.html

Bare Bones Guide to HTML [Online]. Available: werback.com/barebones/

Carlos' Forms Tutorial [Online]. Available: robot0.ge.uius.edu/~carlosp/cs317/sft.html

CuteFTP [Online]. Available: www.cuteftp.com/

Fetch [Online] Available: www.dartmouth.edu/pages/softdev/fetch.html

FTPplanet.com [Online]. Available: www.FTPplanet.com/

HTML Form Testing Home Page [Online]. Available: server3.pa-x.dec.com/nsl/formtest/home.html

HTML Goodies [Online]. Available: htmlgoodies.earthweb.com/

The HTML Station [Online]. Available: www.december.com/html/

HTML Tag List [Online]. Available: utopia.knoware.nl/users/schluter/docs/tags/

Multimedia File Formats on the Internet [Online]. Available: www.lib.rochester.edu/ multimed/contents.htm

Perl Language Home Page [Online]. Available: www.perl.com/

Two4U's Color Page [Online]. Available: www.two4u.com/color/

UNIX Help For Users [Online]. Available: www.mcsr.olemiss.edu/unixhelp/

UNIX Reference Desk [Online]. Available: geek-girl/com/unix.html

Unix Wizards [Online]. Available: www.unix-wizards.com/

WDVL: The Illustrated Encyclopedia of Web Technology [Online]. Available: wdvl.internet.com/

Web Builder's Toolkit [Online]. Available: home.hiwaay.net/~crispen/kellys-place/web_tools/html

Web Diner Forms Tutorial [Online]. Available: www.webdiner.com/annexe/forms/wdform1.htm

Webmaster's Reference Library [Online]. Available: www.webreference.com/

Web Page Design Guidelines for Public Libraries [Online]. Available: www.tiac.net/users/ mpl/guidelines.html

Writing for the Web: A Primer for Librarians [Online]. Available: bones.med.ohio-state.edu/eric/papers/primer/webdocs/html

Acknowledgments

We would both like to thank the following people who helped us complete the book:

Ray Metz for putting up with both of us while we were creating this CD and manual.
Keelan Cleary for helping us set up the Perl scripts correctly.
Kevin Cottrill for helping us test the forms and scripts on an NT server.

Finally, we'd both like to thank Charles Harmon for his patience (and tenacity) in making sure the CD and its manual meet the needs of academic librarians everywhere.

Introduction

This section will give you an idea of who can, and should, use this CD and its accompanying manual. It will also provide you with brief introductions to servers and to the two types of files that are found on the CD and printed in the manual.

*   *   *   *   *

Thank you for purchasing *Instant Web Forms and Surveys for Academic Libraries.* We hope you'll find working with the CD's preview/selection tutorial, the printed and online manuals, and the forms and scripts themselves, relatively simple and straightforward.

We've done everything we can to make the CD and its manual as non-technical as possible; however, there are a few unavoidable technical details that require you, or your library's technical person, to have some basic skills.

Needed Skills

Here are some of the assumptions we've made about you and your library's technical person, and the skills you both need to possess to successfully use this product.

We assume that you are involved with creating and maintaining your library's Web site.

We assume that you have a working knowledge of HTML and have either created a homepage from scratch or used an HTML editing program like FrontPage, PageMill, or DreamWeaver, and have had experience with editing HTML documents to resolve problems and to fix broken links.

We assume that you've enhanced your Web site to the extent that you've added some graphics, tables, imagemaps, or frames to individual Web pages, and are now ready to take the next step and get involved in the world of HTML forms and Perl scripts. (You may even have a little form/script experience . . . if you do, this CD and manual will probably seem basic.)

We assume that either you are one of two people: you are a staff member who works closely with your library's technical person or you are the library's technical/Web/Internet person.

If you are the staff member who works closely with your library's technical person, you should be able to save files, rename files, and have some experience transferring files either to/from your server, or to/from another site. (In order to get the files from the CD to your computer you, or your technical counterpart, will need to download files to your computer's desktop, modify them minimally, save/archive them, then upload them to your server.)

If you are the library's technical/Web/Internet server person you should have a basic knowledge of either UNIX or NT (depending on your server type), be familiar with your server's directory structure and be able to locate the directory paths to your e-mail system, cgi-bin directory, and Perl interpreter. (If your server doesn't have a Perl interpreter you must have the skills to download a version from the Web and install it on your server.) You also must be able to access your server's directories, make directories, and set up server/directory permissions for staff members who will be adding, editing, and deleting HTML forms and Perl scripts on your server.

This list of assumptions might, at first glance, seem a bit daunting. Before you give up before you've even started — or before you start previewing, selecting, downloading, editing, and uploading the files on this CD — we strongly recommend that you meet with any/all staff who possess any of the above-listed skills to see who can/will do what.

If after you've met, you still find that you lack some of the technical skills necessary to successfully use this product, we recommend that you locate an outside person (perhaps a technical expert from your city or county government, a local company technical person, or a school district technology coordinator) who can help you with the technical preparations and steps that you can't handle yourself.

File Servers — A Brief Checklist

Servers are computers that store different types of files. The forms and scripts on this CD must be loaded onto a server to make them work. Generally, technical staff handles the details that are necessary to get and keep a server up and running. Therefore if you are a staff member who works with your library's technical/server person, now might be a perfect time to meet with him/her and get an introduction to your server and some of its basic technical details.

Since you already have a Web site, we assume that you either own a server or have access to someone else's Web server. Either way, you already have individual HTML documents stored in some identifiable directory on your/someone else's server.

The forms and scripts on this CD will eventually wind up in different directories on your server. You'll load the HTML forms into the same directory that contains your Web site's other HTML documents. You'll load the Perl scripts into a separate cgi-bin directory that is designed especially for such programs.

The following are things you should know in advance about your library's server:

If your library has its own server you, or your local technical person, probably already know what type of server it is. If you have your Web site's files stored on someone else's computer, you may or may not know whether it is a UNIX or NT server — now is the time to find out.

Find out if the server has a cgi-bin directory already set up on it. If not, your technical person will need to create one.

Find out if the server has a Perl interpreter program already stored somewhere on it. If not, you or your technical person will need to download and install one. (Later we list a Web site where you can download the correct Perl interpreter program for your server type.)

Locate and note the directory paths to your library's e-mail system, to its Perl interpreter program, and to your server's cgi-bin directory.

Find out who has "permissions" to access the different areas of the server. ("Permissions" are virtual keys that give or deny access to different server directories and functions. Check with the technical person in charge of your server to get a list of permissions related to the e-mail and cgi-bin directories.

HTML Forms — A Brief Overview

There are 24 different HTML forms on this CD. We designed them so that you'll only need to change a few things to get them to work when online and match your other Web site content.

The CD-ROM will allow you to use the forms in two ways. You can use them "as is"(adding only the required information to make them work), making only cosmetic textual changes (editing the introductory paragraphs or slightly rewording the form's questions/statements, or modifying the form's colors and fonts). We designed the CD and manual to be used primarily this way.

You can also, if you choose, add new elements to the forms or reorder the fields. However, this will require you to also modify the matching Perl script. We don't recommend you do this unless you are already familiar with script coding. Remember that these forms/scripts were designed as a simple/quick/ non-technical alternative for librarians who may not have the time/expertise to create their own forms and matching scripts.

If you are not already familiar with HTML form tags, please take a few minutes to read the following brief introduction. It will familiarize you with the tags that you'll find on each of the forms.

Form Basics

Standard Web page HTML documents can function independently of any/all other HTML documents. Form HTML documents won't function unless there is a matching Perl script also loaded somewhere on the same server. This pairing of two interrelated, but differently formatted files makes creating and working with HTML forms/Perl scripts more challenging and also more fun.

When you visit a Web site and fill in an online form you're only interacting with the HTML form document until you press the "Submit Form" button . . . then you're interacting with the form's matching script that handles/responds to the information patrons submit via the HTML form.

The <form> Tag

The <form> tag is the first tag in every form and the </form> tag is the last tag. Inside the opening tag are the two tag attributes, method= and action=. The method= attribute tells a patron's computer how to send the form's information to your library's Web server. The action= attribute tells a patron's computer where the form's matching Perl script is located on your Web server, so that the script can process and react to the information submitted via the HTML form.

<form method="post" action="http://www.yourLibrary.com/cgi-bin/prg4.pl">

Form Tag Elements

All forms are made up of elements and most form elements have two attributes name= and type= (see below for examples of the name= and type= attributes). Form elements identify the form's different types of information and methods for delivering information. Each form element must have a unique name so that a Web server will be able to identify every piece of form information. Form element names are also case sensitive and shouldn't include spaces or punctuation marks (other than an underscore character).

Every form on the CD uses one or more of the following types of form elements. There are additional form element types besides the ones listed below, but since they are not used on any of the forms, we didn't include them. For a complete list and description of every possible form element type, see any of the HTML texts listed in the bibliography at the end of this manual.

Form element types provide patrons with different methods for getting their questions, requests, comments, and personal/contact information to you and your staff. Some form element types allow patrons to type text information into an open text area, while other form elements allow patrons to select from a number/variety of pre-structured responses. To learn about the various elements you'll see on every form, read on. If you'll be customizing the CD's forms or creating your own forms from scratch, the following brief explanation will serve to get you started.

SINGLE LINE TEXT BOX
This element produces a text box that allows patrons to enter a single line of text.

input type= set to "text"
size= the number of characters (size=10 will hold 10 characters and/or spaces)

name= name of the form element

```
<input type ="text" name="state" size=10>
```

Name (last, first)

Street address   **City**   **State** **Country**

USA

E-mail   **Phone/Fax** (+ area code)

MULTIPLE-LINE TEXT BOX

This element produces a text box that allows patrons to enter more than one line of text.

opening <textarea> tag
name= of your text area
number of cols (columns) and rows
text that will appear inside the box
closing </textarea> tag

```
<textarea name="zip_code" cols=40 rows=5>Your zip code</textarea>
```

Subject of your message

RADIO BUTTON

This element produces a yes/no, multiple-choice button feature.

input type= set to "radio"
name= all answer choices for the same question have the same name
value= either yes or no

```
<input type="radio" name="type" value="comment">
<input type="radio" name="type" value="suggestion">
```

Type of your message
○ Comment   ○ Suggestion   ○ New idea   ○ Compliment   ○ Complaint

CHECK BOX
This element produces a square box that a patron can select by clicking in it.

input type= set to "checkbox"
name= of the form element
value= either on or off

> Books<input type ="checkbox" name ="books" value="on">
> Magazines<input type ="checkbox" name ="magazines" value=on">
> Newspapers<input type ="checkbox" name ="newspapers" value="on">

Which three library resouces do you use the most? (check 3)

☐ Books ☐ Magazines ☐ Newspapers ☐ Audiotapes/CDs

☐ Videos/DVDs ☐ Reference materials ☐ The Web

SUBMIT BUTTON
This element sends the information in the form to your Web server.

input type= set to "submit"
value= text that shows up on the face of the button

> <input type="submit" value="Send Message">

> Send Message

RESET BUTTON
This element puts of all your form's fields back to the way they were before a patron started to fill out the form.

input type= set to "reset"
value= text that shows up on the face of the button

> <input type="reset" value="Clear Form">

> Clear Form

HIDDEN FORM FIELDS
Hidden form fields hold the behind-the-scenes instructions that are sent to the script along with the information/selections that a patron provides you via a form/survey. Below is an example of the three hidden

fields that can be found in each of the HTML form documents. You must add information to two of the three hidden fields in order for them to work.

input type= set to "hidden"
name= name of the form element
value= your e-mail address, the URL of your homepage, the name of the form/survey

```
<input type="hidden" name="LibraryEmail" value="you@yourLibrary.com">
<input type="hidden" name="LibraryURL" value="http://www.yourLibrary.com">
<input type="hidden" name="Form" value="Ask a Reference Question">
```

Sample Form

We've highlighted some form fields in a form so that you can familiarize yourself with what the fields look like. The bold printed text below explains the form elements immediately following them.

```
<html>
<head><title>Comments, Suggestions</title></head>
<body bgcolor="#FFFFFF">
<table width="700" border="0" height="85" bgcolor="#003399">
<tr valign="middle" align="center"><td>
<p><font halign=center color="#FFFFFF" face="Arial, Helvetica, sans-serif" size="+3"> <b><i>Comments,
Suggestions </i></b></font></p>
</td></tr></table>
```

Here is the HTML code for the start of the form. Note the attributes method= and action=

```
<form method="post" action="http://www.yourLibrary.com/cgi-bin/prg4.pl">
```

```
<p> </p>
<p><font face="Arial, Helvetica, sans-serif" size="2"><b>Please take a few minutes to send us your comments
about, and suggestions for, improving our library <br>and its resources/services. We'd also like to know what you
think of our Web site and Web links.</b></font></p>
<p> </p>
```

Here is the HTML code for the hidden elements of the form that communicate with the script

```
<input type="hidden" name="LibraryEmail" value="you@yourLibrary.com">
<input type="hidden" name="LibraryURL" value="http://www.yourLibrary.com">
<input type="hidden" name="Form" value="Comments, Suggestions"></p>
```

```
<table width="500" border="0" cellspacing="4" cellpadding="1">
<tr> <td width="187">
<b><font face="Arial, Helvetica, sans-serif" size="2">Name</font></b>  <font size="1" face="Arial,
Helvetica, sans-serif">(last, first)</font><br><font face="Arial, Helvetica, sans-serif" size="2"><input type="text"
name="Name" size="25"></font></td>
```

```
<td width="121"> </td><td width="33"> </td><td width="131"> </td></tr>
<tr><td width="187">
```

Here is the HTML code for a single text box. Note the input type="text" and the matching name= field.

```
<b><font face="Arial, Helvetica, sans-serif" size="2">Street address<br></font></b>
<font face="Arial, Helvetica, sans-serif" size="2"><input type="text" name="StreetAddress" size="25"></font></td>
```

```
<td width="121">
<b><font face="Arial, Helvetica, sans-serif" size="2">City<br></font></b><font face="Arial, Helvetica, sans-serif" size="2"><input type="text" name="City" size="10"></font></td>
<td width="33">
<b><font face="Arial, Helvetica, sans-serif" size="2">State<br></font></b><font face="Arial, Helvetica, sans-serif" size="2"><input type="text" name="State" size="2" maxlength="2">
</font></td>
<td width="131">
<b><font face="Arial, Helvetica, sans-serif" size="2">Country <br></font></b><font face="Arial, Helvetica, sans-serif" size="2"><input type="text" name="Country" size="5" value="USA">
</font></td></tr>
<tr><td width="187">
<b><font face="Arial, Helvetica, sans-serif" size="2">E-mail<br></font></b><font face="Arial, Helvetica, sans-serif" size="2"><input type="text" name="Email" size="25"></font></td>
<td colspan="3">
<b><font face="Arial, Helvetica, sans-serif" size="2">Phone/Fax</font></b>  <font size="1" face="Arial, Helvetica, sans-serif">(+ area code)</font><br><font face="Arial, Helvetica, sans-serif" size="2"><input type="text" name="Phone/Fax" size="24"></font>
</td></tr></table>
<p>
```

Here is the HTML code for a series of radio buttons. Note that the name= tag is the same for each option, but the value= tag for each option is different.

```
<b><font face="Arial, Helvetica, sans-serif" size="2">Type of your message<br></font></b>
<font face="Arial, Helvetica, sans-serif" size="2">
<input type="radio" name="Type" value="Comment">Comment    
<input type="radio" name="Type" value="Suggestion">Suggestion    
<input type="radio" name="Type" value="New idea">New idea   
<input type="radio" name="Type" value="Compliment">Compliment   
<input type="radio" name="Type" value="Complaint">Complaint</font></p>
```

```
<p>
<b><font face="Arial, Helvetica, sans-serif" size="2">Subject of your message </font></b>
<br><font face="Arial, Helvetica, sans-serif" size="3"><textarea name="Subject" cols="40" rows="2"></
```

textarea></font></p>
<p>

Here is the HTML code for a multi-line text box. Note the difference in tagging from the single line text box.

*<b><font face="Arial, Helvetica, sans-serif" size="2">Your message</font></b>
*
<font face="Arial, Helvetica, sans-serif" size="3"><textarea name="Message" cols="40" rows="10"></textarea></font></p>

<p> </p>
<table width="700" border="0" cellspacing="10" cellpadding="1"><tr><td width="255">
<div align="right">

Here is the HTML code for the form's submit button.

<input type="submit" name="send" value="Send Message">

</div></td>
<td width="192"> </td><td width="207"><div align="left">

Here is the HTML code for the form's reset button.

<input type="reset" name="clear" value="Clear Form">
</div></td>
</tr><tr colspan=3><td colspan=3>
<table width="500" border="0" height="2" align="center" cellpadding="0" cellspacing="0"
bgcolor="#003399"><tr><td><font size="1" color="#003399">.</font></td></tr></table>
</td></tr>
<tr><td colspan=3><div align="center">

Here is the HTML code for the form's footer information, including the URL and "mailto" link.

<font face="Arial, Helvetica, sans-serif" size="1"><b>http://</b></font>
<font face="Arial, Helvetica, sans-serif" size="1"><b>© 2001</b></font>
<font face="Arial, Helvetica, sans-serif" size="2"><a href="mailto:">
<b><font size="1">Contact Webmaster</font></b></a> </font></div>

Here is the HTML code for the end of the form.

</td></tr></table></form>

</body>
</html>

Perl Scripts — A Brief Introduction

Perl (Practical Extraction and Reporting Language) is a programming language. The scripts (or mini-programs) on the CD are written in Perl. Perl scripts look somewhat intimidating at first glance, but they're not so hard to figure out after you've seen a few. (Remember how difficult HTML documents looked when you first started to work with them?)

There are 24 different Perl scripts on the CD. As with the HTML versions of these forms and surveys, there are two ways that you can use the scripts on this CD. Firstly, you can use the scripts "as is" (adding only the required information to make them work), or you can make minor changes to them (like editing the on-screen response or e-mail message a patrons sees when s/he presses the "Submit Form" button). You can find directions for making minor changes to the scripts later in this manual.

Secondly, you can add new form elements to any of the forms. This approach will require you to add new lines of Perl code to the script. We don't recommend you do this unless you are already familiar with script coding. Remember that these forms/scripts were designed as a simple/quick/non-technical alternative for librarians who may not have the time/expertise to create their own forms and matching scripts.

If you are not familiar with Perl scripts, please take a few minutes to read the following brief introduction. It will familiarize you with a few of the "coding bits" that you'll need to locate and complete in order to get the scripts to work.

Perl Basics

HTML forms can be loaded onto your library's Web server, but they won't function unless there is a matching Perl script also loaded somewhere on the same server. This pairing of two interrelated, but differently formatted files, makes creating and working with HTML forms/Perl scripts more challenging and also more fun.

When you visit a Web site and fill in an online form you're only interacting with the HTML form document until you press the "Submit Form" button . . . then you're interacting with the form's matching Perl script.

You can write or edit Perl scripts using any simple text editor (such as WordPad or NotePad) as long as you save the script in ASCII (plain text) format. All Perl programs are case sensitive. Every Perl script has to have a .pl file extension.

Below is a brief introduction to Perl and Perl scripts. It is designed to help you understand a bit about the scripts that are included on the CD and the part of the script that you'll have to modify in order to get them to function. If you want to learn more about Perl and scripts so that you can add additional form/script fields or make major changes to the forms/scripts, you'll need to purchase one of the excellent Perl texts cited in this manual's bibliography.

PERL HEADERS

Every Perl script begins with is what is called a header. The header contains instructions that tell each Perl script how it will function and where it can locate necessary programs (like your server's Perl interpreter).

PERL VARIABLES

All the Perl scripts on the CD contain variables. Variables link to and do something with the information that a patron types/selects on a form.

When a patron submits a form by clicking the "Submit" button, it activates the matching Perl script that is stored on your Web server. The data from the HTML form, which is sent to the matching PERL script, will match up its matching script variable.

HTML Form Element	PERL variable
NAME	$in{'NAME'}
DATE	$in{'DATE'}

The following example will make this even clearer. The "Library Purchase Request" HTML form contains a single-line text box that is named "TITLE." A patron types "Geek Love" into the form text box and submits the form to the library's Web server. The Web server will receive this information and the matching script will create a variable that looks like this:

```
$in{'TITLE'} = "Geek Love"
```

THE PRINT FUNCTION

All the Perl scripts on the CD contain print functions. Print functions allow scripts to send messages to patrons automatically. The messages can either display on a patron's or your library's computer, or be sent as messages directly to a patron's e-mail address. Here are some examples that will help to familiarize you with what a print function looks like.

The PERL script below will display "Thanks for filling out our survey" on a patron's computer screen:

```
print ("Thanks for filling out our survey");
```

The bit of Perl script below will display "Thanks for recommending the title Geek Love. You'll be notified if we decide to purchase it." The first line contains the variable. Note also that each line of text is in a separate print function.

```
$in{'TITLE'} = "Geek Love";
print ("Thanks for recommending the title $in{'TITLE'.");
print ("You'll be notified if we decide to purchase it.");
```

Sample Script

We've highlighted the various sections and fields of one of the scripts so that you can familiarize yourself with what each part looks like and does.

This section of the script is called the header:

Here is where you must specify the directory path to the Perl interpreter program on your server.

#!/usr/local/bin/perl

Here are the basic instructions for how the script will interact with the form data. (The spacing/ indentions are necessary for the script to function properly.)

```
if ($ENV{'REQUEST_METHOD'}eq"GET"){$buffer = $ENV{'QUERY_STRING'};}
    elsif($ENV{'REQUEST_METHOD'}eq"POST"){
      read(STDIN,$buffer,$ENV{'CONTENT_LENGTH'});
    }
```

```
$bufferb = $buffer;
#separate the name of the input from its value.
@forminputs = split(/&/, $bufferb);

foreach $forminput (@forminputs)
{
        #separate the name of the input from its value
        ($name, $value) = split(/=/, $forminput);

        #Un-Webify plus signs and %-encoding
        $value =~ tr/+/ /;
        $value =~ s/%([a-fA-F0–9][a-fA-F0–9])/pack("C", hex($1))/eg;

        #stick them in the in array
        $in{$name} = $value;
}
print "Content-type: text/html\n\n";
```

This section of the script contains instructions for e-mailing the form information to the appropriate staff member:

Here is where you must specify the directory path to your library's e-mail program.

```
open (LMAIL, "\/usr/sbin/sendmail-t");
```

Here is a list of script fields that match the form fields. Also included are instructions for how to send the form information via e-mail to the appropriate staff member.

```
print LMAIL ("To: $in{LibraryEmail}\n");
print LMAIL ("From: $in{Email}\n");
print LMAIL ("Subject: $in{Form} —patron submission\n");

print LMAIL ("————————————\nPatron information\n\n");
print LMAIL ("Name:\n $in{Name}\n\n");
print LMAIL ("Street address:\n $in{StreetAddress}\n\n");
print LMAIL ("City:\n $in{City}\n\n");
print LMAIL ("State:\n $in{State}\n\n");
print LMAIL ("Country:\n $in{Country}\n\n");
print LMAIL ("E-mail:\n $in{Email}\n\n");
print LMAIL ("Phone / fax:\n $in{PhoneFax}\n\n");

print LMAIL ("————————————\nSubmitted information \n\n");

print LMAIL ("Type of message:\n $in{Type}\n\n");
print LMAIL ("Message subject:\n $in{Subject}\n\n");
```

```
print LMAIL ("My message:\n $in{Message}\n\n");
print LMAIL ("\n.\n");
```

This section of the script contains instructions for e-mailing a "thank you" message to the patron who filled out the form/survey:

Here is where you must specify the directory path to your library's e-mail program.

```
open (MAIL, "\/usr/sbin/sendmail-t");
```

Here is the text of the "thank you" e-mail message that will be sent to the patron. Also included in the script are instructions for how to send the message. (You may modify the text of this message if you wish.)

```
print MAIL<<toEnd;
To: $in{Email}
From: $in{LibraryEmail}
Subject: $in{Form}

Thanks for sending us your comments and suggestions.\n\n
We are always looking for new ideas and ways we can make the library better!

toEnd
 print MAIL ("\n.\n");
```

This section of the script contains instructions for displaying a "thank you" screen message to the patron who filled out the form/survey and a link back to your Web site:

Here are instructions for setting up the display on the patron's computer screen.

```
print ("<html><head><title>$in{Form}</title></head>");
print ("<body bgcolor=\"ffffff\">");
```

Here is the text of the "thank you" message that will display after a patron has submitted the form. Also included in the script are instructions for how to send the message. (You may modify the text of this message if you wish.)

```
print ("Thanks for sending us your comments and suggestions.<p>
We are always looking for new ideas and ways we can make the library better!");
```

Here is the text of the hypertext link that will display after a patron has submitted the form. (You may modify the text of the link if you wish.)

```
print ("<p><center><a href=$in{LibraryURL}>Return to our main page.</a></center>");
```

This is the end of the script.

print ("</body></html>");

SECTION 1
How to Use
the CD-ROM

How to Use the CD-ROM

Preview and Select a Form / Survey

Once you decide which of the forms or surveys you want to add to your Web site, use the simple, step-by-step tutorial on the CD to:

1. Preview all the forms, so that you can know what they'll look like when they're on your Web site.
2. Select a specific form to download.
3. Preview the two possible form fonts (Arial or Times-Roman).
4. Select the form's font.
5. Preview the four different form color choices (black, blue, red, and white).
6. Select the form's color.
7. Review the selections you've made and preview the form you've selected.
8. Download the form (along with its matching Perl script) to your computer's desktop. (We've included step-by-step instructions for both Windows PC and Macintosh users.)

To start using the preview/selection tutorial, launch the CD. When you get to the "Table of Contents" page, click on the link that says "Preview and Select a Form/Survey."

If you want to exit the tutorial, click on any of the "Back to Table of Contents" links that can be found at the bottom of many of the tutorial screens.

After You Download the Files to Your Desktop

This section will provide you with step-by-step instructions to help you edit the HTML forms and Perl scripts so that they will work when placed on your library's server. There are eight steps (five are required and three are optional). Every task is explained in detail and includes examples from the forms/scripts.

This section will also provide you with instructions to help you modify, in a limited way, the HTML forms and Perl scripts. Every modification step is explained in detail and includes examples from the forms/scripts.

Step 1 — Save the Downloaded Files

The first thing you must to do after you've finished downloading the HTML form and the Perl script to your desktop is to save/archive them so that you don't lose them. (We assume you already know how to save files.) We suggest that you make multiple saved copies. First, save both files somewhere on your computer's hard drive. Next, save both files to a floppy/Zip disk.

After saving the files, store the floppy disk or Zip disk in a safe place, take it home, or give it to a colleague to ensure that if something happens to your office area, or to your library, you still have the files. (Consider archiving the rest of your Web site's HTML documents offsite, if you haven't already done so.)

Step 2 — Check to See If Your Server Has a Perl Interpreter

In order to get the Perl scripts to function, your server must have a Perl interpreter program loaded on it. With any luck, your server already has a Perl interpreter on it. Follow the instructions below to see if a Perl interpreter is already installed on your server.

UNIX servers   At the command prompt type which perl
NT servers   At the command prompt type dir /s perl.exe

If your server doesn't currently have a Perl interpreter program loaded on it, don't despair. You or a technical staff member can easily FTP a free copy of the interpreter software from one of two Web sites.

     If you need a UNIX/Linux Perl interpreter, connect to *www.perl.org/* and download the version appropriate for your version of UNIX or Linux. If you need an NT Perl interpreter, connect to *www.activestate.com/* and download the version appropriate for your NT server.

Step 3 — Get the Paths To Your Server's E-mail Program and Perl Interpreter

In order to complete the required information on the forms and scripts you'll need to locate two directory paths on your Web server.

UNIX SERVERS

At the command prompt:

Type which perl to locate the path to your Perl interpreter. If you don't have an interpreter program yet, have a technical staff person provide you with its directory path.

Type which sendmail (or the name of another UNIX e-mail program). The server will display its directory path.

NT SERVERS

You can search for an e-mail program and its directory path on an NT server the same way you search for a program and its directory path on any Windows PC. Just open up Windows NT Explorer and browse through the menu structure until you locate your server's e-mail program and its Perl interpreter. Once you locate them, the directory path should display in the dialog window at the top of the Explorer screen. Copy it down and you're all set!

Step 4 — Complete the Required Form Information

In order to get the forms to function you *must* add a few pieces of information to each form that you download. The simple instructions and HTML code samples that follow will make this process easy and fast.

LINK UP THE FORM AND SCRIPT

You *must* link up the HTML form with its Perl script. Below (in bold text) is where you'll add the URL for your library's Web server and the path through your server's directories to the cgi-bin directory where the form's matching Perl script is stored.

Note: The text you need to change on the actual forms will not be in bold.

```
<font halign=center color="#FFFFFF" face="Arial, Helvetica, sans-serif" size="+3">
<b><i>Reserve a Library Computer</i></b></font></p>
</td></tr></table>
<form method="post" action="http://www.yourLibrary.com/cgi-bin/plc1.pl"><p> </p>
<p><font face="Arial, Helvetica, sans-serif" size="2"><b>Do you hate to wait in line to use one of the library's
computers? Just fill out the form below to reserve <br>a computer on a specific date and at a specific time. All
reservations must be made in advance and <br>dates/times are assigned on a first-come-first-serve basis. We'll
call or send you an e-mail message <br>
letting you know if a computer is available when you want/need it.</b></font></p>
```

COMPLETE THE LINK BACK TO YOUR LIBRARY'S HOMEPAGE

You *must* provide a way for patrons to return to your Web site after they've sent you a form or survey. Below (in bold text) is where you'll add the URL for the link that will return patrons back to a specified Web page (like your library's homepage) after they've filled out a form/survey.

Note: The text you need to change on the actual forms will not be in bold.

```
<p> </p>
<input type="hidden" name="LibraryEmail" value="you@yourLibrary.com">
<input type="hidden" name="LibraryURL" value="http://www.yourLibrary.com">
<input type="hidden" name="Form" value="Reserve a Library Computer"></p>
<table width="500" border="0" cellspacing="4" cellpadding="1">
<tr><td width="187">
```

SPECIFY THE E-MAIL ADDRESS OF THE PERSON WHO'LL RECEIVE THE FORM INFORMATION

You *must* provide the e-mail address of the staff member whose job it is to collect/process the information submitted by patrons via the form/survey. (If you wish, circulation forms can be e-mailed to circulation staff, and reference forms can be e-mailed to reference staff.) Below (in bold text) is where you add a staff e-mail address to the HTML code.

Note: The text you need to change on the actual forms will not be in bold.

```
<p> </p>
<input type="hidden" name="LibraryEmail" value="you@yourLibrary.com">
<input type="hidden" name="LibraryURL" value="http://www.yourLibrary.com">
<input type="hidden" name="Form" value="Reserve a Library Computer"></p>
<table width="500" border="0" cellspacing="4" cellpadding="1">
<tr><td width="187">
```

ADD THE URL FOR THE FORM

It's good Web design and a good idea to include the URL for every Web page in the footer information. (That way patrons can make a note of it so they can return to it again. Also when/if patrons print the page, the URL always prints on the page.) Below (in bold text) is where you *must* add the URL to the HTML code.

Note: The text you need to add to the actual forms will not be in bold.

```
<font face="Arial, Helvetica, sans-serif" size="1"><b>http://</b></font><br>  <font face="Arial, Helvetica,
sans-serif" size="1"><b>&copy; 2001</b></font>
<font face="Arial, Helvetica, sans-serif" size="2"><a href="mailto:">
<b><font size="1">Contact Webmaster</font></b></a> </font></div>
</td></tr></table></form>
</body>
</html>
```

ADD A "MAILTO" LINK TO YOUR WEBMASTER

It's also good Web design and a good idea to include an e-mail link to your library's Webmaster on every page so that patrons have a way to let him/her know about broken links or any other errors that might be found on your Web site. To get the mailto link to work, you *must* add the e-mail address of your Webmaster after the colon and before the closing quotation marks (in bold text). Optionally, you can rename the text of the link, just change the bold text below.

Note: The text you need to add to/change on the actual forms will not be in bold.

```
<font face="Arial, Helvetica, sans-serif" size="1"><b>http://</b></font><br>  <font face="Arial, Helvetica,
sans-serif" size="1"><b>&copy; 2001</b></font>
<font face="Arial, Helvetica, sans-serif" size="2"><a href="mailto:">
<b><font size="1">Contact Webmaster</font></b></a> </font></div>
```

Step 5 — Complete the Required Script Information

In order to get the scripts to function, you *must* add a few pieces of information to each script you download. The simple instructions and Perl code samples that follow will make this process simple and fast.

SPECIFY THE PATH TO YOUR SERVER'S PERL INTERPRETER

You *must* tell the Perl script where the Perl interpreter is located on your Web server. Below (in bold text) is where you add the path through your server's directories to where the Perl interpreter is stored.

Note: The text instructions below are included in each Perl script so that you can more quickly and easily locate the correct line of coding to complete. However, the text to change in the actual scripts is not bold.

```
#!/usr/local/bin/perl

# ****************************************************************
# ABOVE is where you MUST specify the path to your
# perl interpreter on your Web server.
# Replace /usr/local/bin/perl with your path.
# ****************************************************************
#
```

SPECIFY THE PATH TO YOUR SERVERS' E-MAIL PROGRAM (SO THAT YOU CAN GET FORM INFORMATION E-MAILED TO YOU)

You *must* tell the Perl script where your library's e-mail program is located on your server so that the script will be able to locate the e-mail program in order to e-mail the form information to the staff member whose job it is to collect/process it. Below (in bold text) is where you add the path through your server's directories to where your e-mail program is stored.

Note: The text instructions below are included in each Perl script so that you can more quickly and easily locate the correct line of coding to complete. However the text to change in the actual scripts is not bold.

```
# ********************************************************************
# Here's where you MUST specify the path to your
# email program (probably sendmail) ON your Web server.
# Replace /usr/sbin/sendmail with your path.
# ********************************************************************

open (LMAIL, "I/usr/sbin/sendmail -t");
```

SPECIFY THE PATH TO YOUR SERVERS' E-MAIL PROGRAM (SO THAT THE SCRIPT CAN SEND AN E-MAIL RESPONSE TO THE PATRON)

You *must* tell the Perl script where your library's e-mail program is located on your server so that the script will be able to locate the e-mail program in order to send an e-mail "thank you" message to the patron who filled out the form/survey. Below (in bold text) is where you add the path through your server's directories to where your e-mail system is stored.

Note: The text instructions below are included in each Perl script so that you can more quickly and easily locate the correct line of coding to complete. However, the text to change in the actual scripts is not bold.

```
# ********************************************************************
# Here's where you MUST specify the path to your
# email program ON your Web server.
# Replace /usr/sbin/sendmail with your path.
# ********************************************************************

open (MAIL, "I/usr/sbin/sendmail-t");
```

Step 6 (Optional) — Modify the HTML Forms

If you wish, you can make the following changes to any/all of the forms. All the changes below are very basic and only affect the HTML forms. (In other words, they don't involve making major changes to any of the HTML documents nor do they require that you make any changes to the matching Perl scripts.)

If you want to make changes to the forms that also require you to change the Perl scripts (like renaming form element names), you'll need more knowledge about Perl scripts than we assume you have. Please make sure you get, and read, one of the Perl script texts that are cited in the bibliography at the end of this manual before you make any changes other than those listed below.

MAKE MINOR CHANGES TO FORM TEXT

You can make minor changes to the text that displays on the form. Limit your editing to minor changes in wording, not changes in meaning. For instance, if you want to change the text " Junior High" to "Middle School" edit the bold text below.

What a patron will see on the form will then be "Middle School," but the e-mail form response that your staff member receives will still say "Junior High." (To make the text the same on the form and e-mail message, you would have to also change the HTML form value and the matching variable on the Perl script.)

Note: The text you need to change on the actual forms will not be in bold.

```
<input type="radio" name="EducationLevel" value="Elementary">Elementary    
<input type="radio" name="EducationLevel" value="Junior High">Junior High    
<input type="radio" name="EducationLevel" value="High School">High School    
```

CHANGE THE FORM FONTS

We've provided you with forms that contain the two most common Web site fonts, a serif font (Times-Roman) and a sans-serif font (Arial). If your Web site uses another font, you can change the fonts on any/all of the forms/surveys so that they blend in with your other Web pages. First, you'll need to decide which font you want to substitute (by looking at the HTML code on your Web pages), then you'll have to change all of the font tags on the form . . . there are lots of them!

Tip: Use the "find/replace" feature of any full-featured word-processing package to quickly make all the changes.

Note: The text you need to change on the actual forms will not be in bold.

```
<p><font face="Arial, Helvetica, sans-serif" size="2"><b>Would you like help searching the Internet/Web for information and facts? Do you retrieve either too <br>many or too few results from the Web? Would you like our librarians to suggest ways you can focus your <br>Web searches to retrieve highly relevant results? We'll send you an e-mail message or call you to help <br>you use/search the Web more effectively.</b></font></p>
```

Step 7 (Optional) — Modify the Form Colors

If you wish, you can make the following changes to any/all of the forms. All the changes below are very basic and only affect the HTML forms. (In other words, they don't involve making major changes to any of the HTML documents nor do they require that you make any changes to the matching Perl scripts.)

CHANGE THE COLOR OF THE HEADER AND BOTTOM LINE

You can easily change the background colors of the colored header and the bottom line on each form/ survey to match your Web site colors. All you need to do is locate a list of browser-safe, six-digit/character hexadecimal color codes (connect to *www.two4u.com/colors/* for an online list). Once you've found a color you like (or a color that matches the graphics you use already on your Web site) and you've determined what its hexadecimal color code is, just substitute the new color code for the two color codes below (in bold text).

Tip: Please be aware that colors display differently on PC and Macintosh computers. Be sure to check to see that the color you've selected looks good on both types of machines.

Note: The text you need to change on the actual forms will not be in bold.

HEADER GRAPHIC

```
<html>
<head><title>Internet Search Help</title></head>
<body bgcolor="#FFFFFF">
<table width="700" border="0" height="85" bgcolor="#003399">
<tr valign="middle" align="center"><td>
<p><font halign=center color="#FFFFFF" face="Arial, Helvetica, sans-serif" size="+3">
```

BOTTOM LINE

```
<tr colspan=3> <td colspan=3>
<table width="500" border="0" height="2" align="center" cellpadding="0" cellspacing="0"
bgcolor="#003399"><tr><td><font size="1" color="#003399">.</font></td></tr></table>
</td></tr>
```

CHANGE THE COLOR OF THE HEADER TEXT

You also can easily change the color of the text inside the colored header on each form/survey. (For instance, you might want to switch from white text to black text.) Once you've found a color you like (or a color that matches the text you use already in your Web site graphics) and you've determined what its hexadecimal color code is, just substitute the new color code for the color code below (in bold text).

Tip: Please be aware that colors display differently on PC and Macintosh computers. Be sure to check to see that the color you've selected looks good on both types of machines.

Note: The text you need to change on the actual forms will not be in bold.

```
<table width="700" border="0" height="85" bgcolor="#003399">
<tr valign="middle" align="center"><td>
<p><font halign=center color="#FFFFFF" face="Arial, Helvetica, sans-serif" size="+3">
```

Step 8 (Optional) — Modify the Perl Scripts

If you wish, you can make the following changes to any/all of the scripts. All the changes below are very basic and only affect the Perl scripts. (In other words, they don't involve making major changes to any of the scripts nor do they require that you make any changes to the matching HTML forms.)

RE-WORD THE "THANK YOU" SCREEN MESSAGE

We've included an appropriate and patron-friendly screen message with each form. If you like, you can change the wording of the screen message . . . just edit the text (displayed in bold).

Note: The text instructions below are included in each Perl script so that you can more quickly and easily locate the correct line of coding to complete. However, the text to change in the actual scripts is not bold.

```
# *************************************************************
# Here's where you MAY change the screen response
# the user sees after submitting the form. You may
# reword the message.
# *************************************************************
```

print ("**Thanks for sending us a library computer reservation.<p>
A librarian will contact you in the next couple of days to let you know if a computer
is available on the day and at the time you requested.**");

RE-WORD THE "THANK YOU" E-MAIL MESSAGE

We've also included an appropriate e-mail message with each form (it's identical to the screen message). If you like, you can change the wording of the e-mail message . . . just edit the text (displayed in bold).

Note: The text instructions below are included in each Perl script so that you can more quickly and easily locate the correct line of coding to complete. However the text to change in the actual scripts is not bold.

```
# *************************************************************
# Here's where you MAY customize the email
# response to the user. You may change any wording
# on the two lines
# *************************************************************
```

print MAIL<<toEnd;
To: $in{Email}
From: $in{LibraryEmail}
Subject: $in{Form}

Thanks for sending us your comments and suggestions.\n\n
We are always looking for new ideas and ways we can make the library better!
toEnd
 print MAIL ("\n.\n");

RE-WORD THE LINK BACK TO YOUR LIBRARY'S HOMEPAGE

We've included a generic "Return to Our Main Page" link with each form. If you like, you can change the wording of the link . . . just edit the text (displayed in bold).

Note: The text instructions below are included in each Perl script so that you can more quickly and easily locate the correct line of coding to complete. However, the text to change in the actual scripts is not bold.

```
# *************************************************************
# Here's where you MAY change the wording of the link
# back to your main page. You may replace "Return
# to our main page" with your own wording.
# *************************************************************
```

```
print ("<p><center><a href=$in{LibraryURL}>Return to our main page.</a></center>");
print ("</body></html>");
```

Before You Upload the Files to Your Server

This section will provide you with step-by-step instructions and lists of the things to check when you test the forms and scripts prior to uploading them to your server. It will remind you to create the necessary directories to hold the Perl scripts and your HTML forms. In addition, it will help you set up your library's computers so that the forms/scripts will look their best when patrons view them.

Step 1 — Test the Files Before They're Uploaded

Once you've finished adding the required information to both the forms and scripts, you *must* test them before you upload them to your server. Below are instructions for testing your forms and scripts (and lists of the things that need to be tested).

How to test an HTML form

To test the forms, start your library's Web browser (Internet Explorer or Netscape). If your library provides both browsers to staff and patrons, start both and check your HTML on each one.

First, you'll need to see if the *visible* changes you made to the form are correct. To do this:

1. Click on word "File" which is located in the top left corner of both browsers.
2. If you are using Netscape, select and click on the "Open Page" option. If you are using Internet Explorer, select and click on the "Open" option.
3. Use the "Browse" button and the directory dialog boxes to locate your computer's desktop. Then click until the files for that directory display . . . one of them should be your form.
4. Once you've located the form, highlight it, and then click on it.
5. Both Netscape and Internet Explorer will then ask you if you want to open the form. Confirm that you do by clicking on the "Open" or "OK" button.
6. You should now be viewing the form from your desktop.

Here is a list of the visible text on a form that you should check:

Check to see that the page URL in the footer displays correctly.
Check to see that the "mailto" link in the footer goes to the correct address (click on it).
If you've modified any of the form text (the introduction, any minor re-wording of form element text), check to see it displays correctly.
If you've modified the color of the form header (and/or the color of the header text) and color of the bottom line, check to see it displays correctly.
If you've modified the fonts, check to see that the whole form displays in the new font.

Next, you'll need to see if the changes you made, that are *not visible*, are correct. To do this:

1. If you are using Netscape or Internet Explorer, click on the "View" menu and click on either the "Page Source" or "Source" option from the pull-down menu.
2. An additional window with the HTML coding for your form will appear on your screen.

3. Use this display to make sure that the hidden HTML coding changes you made are correct. (When you are finished checking the form, click on the "X" box in the upper right corner of the screen, if using a PC, or the square in the upper left corner of the screen, if using a Macintosh.)

Here is a list of the coding-level HTML on a form that you should check:

Check to see that the form action contains the correct URL and directory path to where you will be storing the Perl script once you upload it.
Check to see that there is a link in one of the hidden fields to your homepage (or whichever page you want a patron to return to after they've finished filling out a form or survey).
Check to see that you've also put the correct e-mail address into one of the hidden fields.

HOW TO TEST A PERL SCRIPT

To test the scripts, open a simple word-processing program. If you are using a PC, open either NotePad or WordPad. If you are using a Macintosh, open SimpleText. Don't use a full-featured word-processing program like Word, WordPerfect, ClarisWorks, or Microsoft Works, as they can add unwanted formatting to the script.

To test a script:

1. Open either NotePad, WordPad, or SimpleText.
2. Click on the "File" option in the upper left corner of the window, and then click on the "Open" option.
3. Use the "Browse" button and the directory dialog boxes to locate your computer's desktop. Then click until the files for that directory display . . . one of them should be your script.
4. Once you've located the script, highlight it, and then double click on it.
5. You should now be viewing the script from your desktop.

Here is a list of script items that you should check:

Check to see that the correct path to your Web server's Perl interpreter is in the first line of code.
Check to see that the correct path to your Web server's e-mail program is in the script in two places.
Check to see that the e-mail address of the person who'll receive the e-mailed form input is correct.
If you re-worded the screen response message, check to see that it is correct.
If you re-worded the e-mail response message, check to see that it is correct.
If you re-worded the "Return to Your Main Page" link, check to see that it is correct.

Step 2 — Create Directories On Your Server To Hold the Forms/Scripts

Before you upload the first Perl script to your Web server, you must have, or must create, a cgi-bin directory. If your Web server does not already have a cgi-bin directory, ask the person in charge of your server to create one. (This is not generally something you can do, not because it is so difficult, but because you probably don't have "permission" to make this type of directory on your server.) Make sure your technical person provides you with the path to the cgi-bin directory and sets up the server's permissions so that when you are ready to upload the script to the server you can go ahead and put it in the correct directory. Once you've found your server's cgi-bin directory or created one, make a note of the directory path so that you can load any other of the CD's Perl scripts into it.

If you already have a Web site, you've probably created a directory for your Web page HTML files. You don't have to create a new directory to hold the forms and scripts, just put them into the directory with your other Web HTML documents. (You might want to make a note of the directory path to your HTML files, so that when you get ready to upload the forms or scripts you'll know right where they go.)

Step 3 — Set Up Your Computers To View the Forms

All of the forms on the CD are designed for computer monitors with a screen resolution set to 800×600 pixels. This is so that the formatting of each form remains consistent from one monitor setting to another. If your monitor resolution is set at 640×480 pixels, the forms may appear a bit large for the screen. This means that patrons might have to use the horizontal scroll bar, located at the bottom of your Web browser's window, to view all of the form's content. If your monitor resolution is set at 1024×768 pixels the forms will probably not fill up the whole screen and will not be centered on screen.

CHANGING MONITOR RESOLUTIONS — WINDOWS PC

If you don't know the resolution setting of the computer monitors in your library, or if you wish to change the resolution to the optimal 800×600 setting, just follow these simple instructions:

1. Click on the "Start" button in the bottom left corner of your computer screen.
2. Locate the "Settings" option from the pop-up menu. (If you are using a computer that is connected to an NT server, this option may or may not appear on the pop-up menu. If it does not appear, contact your NT technical person so that they can change the monitor resolution for you.)
3. Select on the "Settings" option and then click on the "Control Panel" option from the additional menu that pops open.
4. A free-floating "Control Panel" window will open up. Locate and click on the "Display" icon and double click on it.
5. You will see a window display with a number of tabs at the top of the screen. What exactly you will see will depend on which version of Windows you are using (95/98/NT). Locate the "Settings" tab and click on it
6. Somewhere on the screen you will see what your current screen resolution is. It should look something like 640×480 (but may actually be another set of numbers). Using the method supplied on the screen (either a movable tab or pull-down menu), select the 800×600 pixels option.
7. To apply this change to the monitor resolution you will need to restart your computer. Just click on "Yes" when Windows asks you if you want to restart.

CHANGING MONITOR RESOLUTIONS — MACINTOSH

If you don't know the resolution setting of the computer monitors in your library, or if you wish to change the resolution to the optimal 800×600 setting, just follow these simple instructions:

1. Click on the apple icon on the top left corner of your computer screen.
2. Click on the "Control Panel" option from the pull-down menu.
3. Click on either the "Monitors" or "Display" or "Appearance" option (the name will depend on which version of MacOS your computer is running).
4. Somewhere on the screen that pops up you will see what your current screen resolution is. It should look something like 640×480 (but may actually be another set of numbers). Using the method supplied on the screen (either a movable tab or a pull-down menu), select the 800×600 pixels option.

To apply the change to the monitor resolution you will need to restart your computer. Depending on your version of MacOS, your computer may or may not ask you if you want it to restart itself. If it doesn't, be sure you manually shut down and restart.

INTERNET-BASED LIBRARY PATRONS

It's also important that you let your patrons with home/school/business computers know that to optimally view the forms they might want to reset their monitors to 800 × 600 pixels. Consider putting a brief message to this effect on your homepage and also on any page that contains a link to one of the forms or surveys.

Step 4 — Save the Files One Last Time . . . Just In Case

Once you've selected and downloaded a form/script pair to your desktop and once you've taken the time to complete/modify the form and script, you'll want to save them one last time. (We recommend saving copies on floppy or Zip drive and storing one copy offsite.)

Upload the Files to Your Server

The next-to-last stage involves transferring (uploading) the files from your desktop to your library's server. If you're not familiar with file transfer (FTP), we've included a brief overview to help you get started or to help you understand better what your technical staff member will need to do to upload the files. The last stage involves testing the forms and scripts one more time. This time, though, you'll be checking to make sure that the form and script work together properly.

FTP (File Transfer) — A Brief Overview

To get the forms/surveys onto your Web server, you'll have to FTP (upload) them. Transferring files used to be a complex task; nowadays, all you have to do to transfer a file is:

1. Locate your FTP software, download free FTP software, or purchase FTP software.
2. Get the permissions set up on your server so that you can upload (FTP) files to them.
3. Know a bit about how the directories and files are arranged on your server.
4. Know a tiny bit about file extensions.
5. Know how to use your FTP software to actually transfer (upload) the forms and scripts to your Web server.

If the above list of what you need to do/know in order to transfer the files to your server is a bit overwhelming, consider asking your technical counterpart to set up the required server directories and do the file transfers for you.

If your technical staff person will be handling the directory setup and uploading tasks . . . all *you'll* have to do is:

1. Select a form or survey using the Preview/Selection Tutorial on the CD.
2. Download it to your computer's desktop.
3. Complete the required parts on each HTML form and Perl script and/or modify it.
4. Save the form and script to a floppy disk.
5. Hand the floppy to your technical person so they can upload the files for you!

Step 1 – Locate an FTP Program and Learn the FTP Basics

The first thing you must do is to locate or purchase a copy of some FTP software. If you need FTP software and you use a Windows PC (or have an NT server), there should be a generic FTP program (with the filename FTP) located in the Windows directory on your computer's hard drive. It's not the most user-friendly piece of software, but with a little reading and practice you can master it fairly quickly. If you don't have FTP software and want some that is easy to learn and use, try either CuteFTP, if you're a Windows user, or Fetch, if you're a Macintosh user. You can either download free/demo versions of them or download/purchase them.

Computers store individual files (like the CD's individual HTML and Perl script files) in directories and sub-directories. Depending on the FTP software you use, a directory will either look like a folder icon, or it will indicate by code/word that it is a directory. Clicking on a folder icon (or supplying the correct keystroke/command) will "open" a folder so that you can see the files and/or sub-directories inside it. Files look either like pieces of paper with different things written on them, or they are identifiable as files by their textual file extensions.

File extensions let you know a file's format and probable content. There are only three file extensions you'll need to learn and work with. The extensions are:

.htm	HTML file
.pl	Perl script
.pdf	PDF (Acrobat) file

All the forms on the CD have an .htm file extension. All the Perl scripts have a .pl file extension. All the Acrobat-formatted sections of this manual have a .pdf file extension.

Step 2 — Transfer the Files to Your Web Server

Which keys you press or commands you type to transfer (upload) the forms and scripts to your server depend entirely on the FTP software program you use. Since there are so many possible variations/looks to the actual transfer process and so many different types/brands of FTP software, we cannot explain how you will actually transfer the files from your computer's desktop to your Web server.

If your technical staff person will transfer the files for you, you don't have to worry about this step at all. If you are the person who will be transferring the files and you don't have much experience doing it, we recommend that you read the help/readme files that accompany your FTP software and/or purchase a book that explains how to use your FTP software. We've listed some excellent FTP resources in the "Sources For Further Help" section of the Preface.

Step 3 — Test the Files After You've Uploaded Them

Once you've finished uploading the forms and scripts to your server you *must* test them again. This time you'll be checking to see if the HTML forms and Perl scripts work together correctly and output e-mail data to a staff member and a "Thank You" message to a patron. Below are instructions for testing your forms and scripts.

CHECK TO SEE IF THE FORM/SCRIPT PAIR WORKS TOGETHER CORRECTLY

To test the form/script pair, fire up your library's Web browser (Internet Explorer or Netscape).

1. Type in the URL for the form. It should display on your computer screen. Make sure that the URL in

the footer displays correctly. Check to make sure that the "mailto" link in the footer goes to the correct address (click on it). If you've modified any of the form text (the introduction, any minor re-wording of form element text), check to make sure it displays correctly. If you've modified the color of the form header (and/or the color of the header text) and the color of the bottom line, check to make sure it displays correctly. If you've modified the fonts, check to make sure that the whole form displays in the new font.

If the form doesn't display, you might have transferred the HTML form into the wrong directory, or you might have copied down the URL incorrectly. Check to see where the HTML form is located (and move the file to the correct directory if necessary) or copy down the correct URL/path and try typing the URL again.

If anything in the form doesn't display correctly, take out your saved copy on disk, make the necessary corrections, test it before you upload it, and then upload/overwrite the form or have your technical person upload/overwrite it for you . . . and then retest it again!

2. Once the form displays on your screen, fill out the form just like a patron would (including *your* real e-mail address) and click on the "Send" button. If the form/script are working together correctly you should see a "Thank You" message on your computer screen, along with a working link back to your library's homepage (or whatever page you designated). Make sure that the message is correct and that the link takes you back to the correct Web page.

If the message or URL is incorrect, correct the information on your server. Use a server text editor like Emacs or PICO to make the necessary changes to the message or URL. If you don't want to make the changes online, just pull out the saved copy of the Perl script, go back into NotePad, WordPad, or SimpleWrite, and change the message or URL. Then re-save the script (and back it up again), upload it, and overwrite/replace the existing script, or hand it to your techie to upload and overwrite/replace. Then test it again.

3. Once you've seen the "Thank You" message on the screen and made sure that the link below it works, it's time to check your e-mail. If the form/script is working correctly you should receive an e-mail message (depending on your e-mail system, this could take a while to receive) with the form name in the subject line. The message will be identical to the "Thank You" message that displayed on your computer screen.

If you didn't receive an e-mail message, check to see that the correct path to your e-mail program was added to the Perl script. If you did receive an e-mail but the message was incorrect, correct it. You can correct both of these errors in the Perl script by opening up a simple word processor, making the corrections, and uploading the script to your server again.

4. Finally, you should ask the staff member who is assigned to collect/process the form information if they've received an e-mail message containing the form information. (The subject line on the e-mail message will be the form name.) If they received the e-mail message, print it out and check to make sure that all the fields on the e-mail and on the form match. (The wording won't match exactly, but each form field should correspond to one on the e-mail message.)

If the staff member didn't receive an e-mail message, check to see if their correct e-mail address was added to the HTML form. If it wasn't, correct the HTML form using a simple word processor (or make the correction by using a server text editor like Emacs or PICO). If the staff member does receive an e-mail but the form data on it is incorrect, this isn't easily fixed. If this happens, find someone in your community who knows how to troubleshoot Perl scripts and ask them to change/correct it for you.

Congratulations!!!

You've just successfully added a working form to your library's Web site. If you've never done anything like this before, give yourself credit for what you've just accomplished. Now all that's left to do is to let your library patrons know that "you've got forms!"

SECTION 2
Forms, Surveys,
and Scripts

Group 1 — Reference Forms / Surveys

In this section you'll find Web-based forms that will enable students, faculty, and staff to contact library staff to get help with basic reference questions, research projects, and class assignments. Here you'll also find one form and one survey that will enable patrons to give your staff general feedback, opinions, and comments, as well as input on how they use your library's resources and services.

Ask a Reference Question

If students have a straightforward, factual question or reference question, they can fill in this form and e-mail it to your reference staff. Make sure you include a link to this form from your Web site's reference page and homepage.

Research Help Request

Do students need help with class assignments? Do faculty and grad students need help with research papers or personal research projects? Now you can receive patron requests for information sources and factual information, as well as requests for your research and citation help via e-mail and respond to them by phone, fax, or e-mail. Be sure to add a link to this form from your Web site's reference, genealogy, and homework help pages.

Library Use Survey

Add this survey to your library's Web site if you'd like to find out how and why faculty, students, and staff use your library, if you want input on how to improve your services, collections, building, and equipment, and if you want to learn how patrons feel about the services/resources you currently provide. Add a link to this survey from your library's homepage every couple of months.

Comments, Suggestions

Let members of your academic community comment about, and make suggestions for, improving your library and its resources/services. Put a link to this form right on your library's homepage.

Complete Citation Request form

Students and faculty often struggle to locate the information they need to create a complete and accurate citation for sources they want to cite in a research paper, thesis, or article they will be submitting for publication. Put a link to this form on your ILL or Reference Web page so that patrons can e-mail you the information they have already located. Your staff can research the missing information and e-mail it back to them.

Ask a Reference Question

If you'd like an answer to a straightforward, factual question fill in the form below. We will provide you with an answer (and relevant sources) via e-mail or phone. Please visit the library's reference desk in person if you need an answer in less than 48 hours.

Name (last, first middle)

Department / Major

Campus address

Campus e-mail

Campus phone

Fax / Other phone

Status

O Freshman   O Sophomore   O Junior   O Senior
O Grad Student   O Faculty   O Staff   O Other

Your question (please provide as many details as you can)

How would you like us to reply?

O E-mail   O Phone (when is the best day/time to reach you?)

I need an answer before (specify date)

O Anytime is fine

I would like to receive

O Facts / Specific information   O Information sources   O Both facts and sources

If course related...

Course number _____   Instructor _____

For sources I must / would like to use (select all that apply)

- O Books
- O Journal articles
- O Newspaper articles
- O CD-ROMs
- O Web sites
- O Online databases
- O Theses / Disertations
- O Other (please specify) [   ]

[Send Question]   [Clear Form]

Ask a Reference Question — HTML Form

```
<html>
<head><title>Ask a Reference Question</title></head>
<body bgcolor="#FFFFFF">
<table width="700" border="0" height="85" bgcolor="#000000">
<tr valign="middle" align="center"> <td>
<p>
<font halign=center color="#FFFFFF" face="Arial, Helvetica, sans-serif" size="+3">
<b><i>Ask a Reference Question</i></b></font></p>
</td></tr></table>
<form method="post" action="http://www.yourLibrary.edu/cgi-bin/arg1.pl"><p> </p>
<p>
<b><font size="2" face="Arial, Helvetica, sans-serif">If you'd like an answer to a straightforward, factual question
fill in the form below. We will provide<br></font></b><b><font size="2" face="Arial, Helvetica, sans-serif"> you
with an answer (and relevant sources) via e-mail or phone. Please visit the library's reference<br></font></
b><b><font size="2" face="Arial, Helvetica, sans-serif"> desk in person if you need an answer in less than 48
hours.</font></b></p>
<p> </p>
<input type="hidden" name="LibraryEmail" value="you@yourLibrary.edu">
<input type="hidden" name="LibraryURL" value="http://www.yourLibrary.edu">
<input type="hidden" name="Form" value="Ask a Reference Question"><p></p>
<p></p>
<table width="500" border="0" cellspacing="4" cellpadding="1">
<tr><td width="257">
<b><font face="Arial, Helvetica, sans-serif" size="2">Name </font></b><font face="Arial, Helvetica, sans-
serif" size="1"> (last, first middle)</font><br><font face="Arial, Helvetica, sans-serif" size="2"><input
type="text" name="Name" size="25"></font></td>
<td width="227">
<b><font face="Arial, Helvetica, sans-serif" size="2">Department / Major<br></font></b><font face="Arial,
Helvetica, sans-serif" size="2"><input type="text" name="Department" size="25"></font> </td></tr>
<tr><td width="257">
<b><font face="Arial, Helvetica, sans-serif" size="2">Campus address<br></font></b><font face="Arial,
Helvetica, sans-serif" size="2"><input type="text" name="CampusAddress" size="25"></font></td>
<td width="227">
<b><font face="Arial, Helvetica, sans-serif" size="2">Campus e-mail<br></font></b><font face="Arial, Helvetica,
sans-serif" size="2"><input type="text" name="CampusEmail" size="25"></font></td></tr>
<tr><td width="257">
<b><font face="Arial, Helvetica, sans-serif" size="2">Campus phone</font></b><br><font face="Arial, Helvetica,
sans-serif" size="2"><input type="text" name="CampusPhone" size="25"></font></td>
<td width="227">
<b><font face="Arial, Helvetica, sans-serif" size="2">Fax / Other phone<br></font></b><font face="Arial,
Helvetica, sans-serif" size="2"><input type="text" name="OtherPhone" size="25"></font></td></tr> </table>
<p>
<b><font face="Arial, Helvetica, sans-serif" size="2">Status</font></b><table width="550" border="0"
```

```
cellspacing="0" cellpadding="0">
<tr><td width="126" height="13">
<font face="Arial, Helvetica, sans-serif" size="2"><input type="radio" name="Status"
value="Freshman">Freshman</font></td>
<td width="117" height="13">
<font face="Arial, Helvetica, sans-serif" size="2"><input type="radio" name="Status"
value="Sophomore">Sophomore</font></td>
<td width="87" height="13">
<font face="Arial, Helvetica, sans-serif" size="2"><input type="radio" name="Status"
 value="Junior">Junior</font></td>
<td width="202" height="13">
<font face="Arial, Helvetica, sans-serif" size="2"><input type="radio" name="Status"
value="Senior">Senior</font></td></tr>
<tr><td width="126" height="9">
<font face="Arial, Helvetica, sans-serif" size="2"><input type="radio" name="Status"
value="Graduate Student">Grad Student</font></td>
<td width="117" height="9">
<font face="Arial, Helvetica, sans-serif" size="2"><input type="radio" name="Status"
value="Faculty">Faculty</font></td>
<td width="87" height="9">
<font face="Arial, Helvetica, sans-serif" size="2"><input type="radio" name="Status"
value="Staff">Staff</font></td>
<td width="202" height="9">
<font face="Arial, Helvetica, sans-serif" size="2"><input type="radio" name="Status"
value="Other">Other</font></td></tr></table>
<p>
<b><font face="Arial, Helvetica, sans-serif" size="2">Your question</font></b><font face="Arial, Helvetica, sans-
serif" size="1">  (please provide as many details as you can)</font><br>
<font face="Arial, Helvetica, sans-serif" size="3"><textarea name="Question" cols="40" rows="10">
</textarea></font></p>
<p>
<font face="Arial, Helvetica, sans-serif" size="2"><b>How would you like us to reply?</b></font><br>
<font face="Arial, Helvetica, sans-serif" size="3">
<input type="radio" name="Reply" value="Email"></font><font face="Arial, Helvetica, sans-serif" size="2">E-
mail</font>   
<input type="radio" name="Reply" value="Phone"><font face="Arial, Helvetica, sans-serif" size="2">Phone
</font>  <font face="Arial, Helvetica, sans-serif" size="1">(when is the best day/time to reach
you?)</font><font face="Arial, Helvetica, sans-serif" size="3"> <input type="text" name="BestTime"
size="10"></font></p>
<p>
<b><font face="Arial, Helvetica, sans-serif" size="2">I need an answer before  </font></b><font
face="Arial, Helvetica, sans-serif" size="1">(specify date) <font size="3"><br><input type="text"
name="NeedBefore" size="15"></font></font><font size="3">  </font>    
<input type="radio" name="TimeIssue" value="Time is not an issue"><font face="Arial, Helvetica, sans-serif"
size="2">Anytime is fine</font> </p>
```

```
<p>
<b><font face="Arial, Helvetica, sans-serif" size="2">I would like to receive<br></font></b>
<input type="radio" name="Answer" value="Facts / specific information"><font face="Arial, Helvetica, sans-serif"
size="2">Facts / Specific information   
<input type="radio" name="Answer" value="Information sources">Information sources   
<input type="radio" name="Answer" value="Both facts and sources">Both facts and sources </font></p>
  <p><b><font face="Arial, Helvetica, sans-serif" size="2">If course related...</font></b><br><font face="Arial,
Helvetica, sans-serif" size="2">Course number</font><font size="3"><input type="text" name="CourseNum"
size="15">  </font>
<font face="Arial, Helvetica, sans-serif" size="2">Instructor<font size="3"></font></font><font size="3">
<input type="text" name="Instructor" size="15"></font></p>
<p>
<b><font face="Arial, Helvetica, sans-serif" size="2">For sources I must / would like to use nbsp;</font></
b><font face="Arial, Helvetica, sans-serif" size="1">(select all that apply)</font><br>
<table width="548" border="0" cellspacing="0" cellpadding="0">
<tr><td width="93">
<font face="Arial, Helvetica, sans-serif" size="2"><input type="radio" name="B" value="Books">
Books</font></td>
<td width="157">
<font face="Arial, Helvetica, sans-serif" size="2"><input type="radio" name="JA" value="Journal articles">
Journal articles</font></td>
<td width="174">
<font face="Arial, Helvetica, sans-serif" size="2"><input type="radio" name="NM" value="Newspaper
articles">Newspaper articles</font></td>
<td width="124">
<font face="Arial, Helvetica, sans-serif" size="2"><input type="radio" name="CD" value="CDROMS">
CD-ROMs</font></td></tr>
<tr><td width="93">
<font face="Arial, Helvetica, sans-serif" size="2"><input type="radio" name="WS" value="Web sites">
Web sites</font></td>
<td width="157">
<font face="Arial, Helvetica, sans-serif" size="2"><input type="radio" name="O" value="Online indexex or
databases">Online databases</font></td>
<td width="174">
<font face="Arial, Helvetica, sans-serif" size="2"><input type="radio" name="T" value="Theses">
Theses / Dissertations</font></td>
<td width="124"> </td></tr>
<tr><td colspan="3">
<font face="Arial, Helvetica, sans-serif" size="2"><input type="radio" name="OT" value="Pictures / maps">Other
 <font face="Arial, Helvetica, sans-serif" size="1">(please specify)</font> <font size="3">  <input
type="text" name="OtherSources" size="20"></font></font></td>
<td width="124"> </td></tr></table>
<p> </p><table width="700" border="0" cellspacing="10" cellpadding="1"><tr><td width="247">
<div align="right"><input type="submit" name="send" value="Send Question"></div></td><td
width="200"> </td><td width="207">
```

```
<div align="left"><input type="reset" name="clear" value="Clear Form"></div></td></tr>
<tr colspan=3><td colspan=3>
<table width="500" border="0" height="2" align="center" cellpadding="0" cellspacing="0"
bgcolor="#000000"><tr><td><font size="1" color="#000000">.</font></td></tr></table></td></tr>
<tr><td colspan=3><div align="center">
<font face="Arial, Helvetica, sans-serif" size="1"><b>http://</b></font><br><font size="2"> 
<font face="Arial, Helvetica, sans-serif" size="1"><b>&copy; 2001</b></font></font>
<font face="Arial, Helvetica, sans-serif" size="2"><a href="mailto:">
<b><font size="1">Contact Webmaster</font></b></a></font></div></td></tr>
</table></form>
</body>
</html>
```

Ask a Reference Question — Perl Script

```perl
#!/usr/local/bin/perl


# **************************************************
# ABOVE is where you MUST specify the path to your
# perl interpreter on your Web server.
# Replace /usr/local/bin/perl with your path.
# **************************************************


if ($ENV{'REQUEST_METHOD'}eq"GET"){$buffer = $ENV{'QUERY_STRING'};}
    elsif($ENV{'REQUEST_METHOD'}eq"POST"){
        read(STDIN,$buffer,$ENV{'CONTENT_LENGTH'});
    }
$bufferb = $buffer;
#separate the name of the input from its value.
@forminputs = split(/&/, $bufferb);

foreach $forminput (@forminputs)
{
    #separate the name of the input from its value
    ($name, $value) = split(/=/, $forminput);

    #Un-Webify plus signs and %-encoding
    $value =~ tr/+/ /;
    $value =~ s/%([a-fA-F0-9][a-fA-F0-9])/pack("C", hex($1))/eg;

    #stick them in the in array
    $in{$name} = $value;
}
print "Content-type: text/html\n\n";


##############################################################
# ABOVE is the required header for a perl script         #
##############################################################


###################################################################
# (Below) Email received by library containing user-entered information #
###################################################################


# *********************************************
# Here's where you MUST specify the path to your
# email program (probably sendmail) ON your Web server.
# Replace /usr/sbin/sendmail with your path.
# *********************************************
```

```
open (LMAIL, "|/usr/sbin/sendmail -t");
print LMAIL ("To: $in{LibraryEmail}\n");
print LMAIL ("From: $in{CampusEmail}\n");
print LMAIL ("Subject: $in{Form} - patron submission\n");

print LMAIL ("------------------\nPatron information\n\n");
print LMAIL ("Name:\n $in{Name}\n\n");
print LMAIL ("Department / Major:\n $in{Department}\n\n");
print LMAIL ("Campus Address:\n $in{CampusAddress}\n\n");
print LMAIL ("Campus Email:\n $in{CampusEmail}\n\n");
print LMAIL ("Campus Phone:\n $in{CampusPhone}\n\n");
print LMAIL ("Other Phone:\n $in{OtherPhone}\n\n");
print LMAIL ("Status:\n $in{Status}\n\n");

print LMAIL ("------------------\nSubmitted information \n\n");

print LMAIL ("My question:\n $in{Question}\n\n");
print LMAIL ("My preferred reply method:\n $in{Reply}\n\n");
print LMAIL ("Best day/time to reach me:\n $in{BestTime}\n\n");
print LMAIL ("I need an answer before:\n $in{NeedBefore} $in{TimeIssue}\n\n");
print LMAIL ("I would like to receive:\n $in{Answer}\n\n");
print LMAIL ("Sources I would like:\n $in{B}, $in{JA}, $in{NM}, $in{CD}, $in{WS}, $in{T}, $in{O}, $in{OT}\n\n");
print LMAIL ("Other sources: $in{OtherSources}\n\n");
print LMAIL ("\n.\n");


######################################################
# Email received by the user confirming form submission #
######################################################


# ************************************************
# Here's where you MUST specify the path to your
# email program ON your Web server.
# Replace /usr/sbin/sendmail with your path.
# ************************************************

open (MAIL, "|/usr/sbin/sendmail -t");

# ************************************************
# Here's where you MAY customize the email
# response to the user. You may change any wording
# on the form.
# ************************************************

print MAIL<<toEnd;
To: $in{CampusEmail}
```

From: $in{LibraryEmail}
Subject: $in{Form}

Thanks for sending us your reference question.\n\n
A librarian will contact you in the next couple of days with either an answer to your question or a list of resources that will help you answer the question yourself.

toEnd
    print MAIL ("\n.\n");


```
#####################################################
# Screen response to user after submitting the form  #
#####################################################

print ("<html><head><title>$in{Form}</title></head>");
print ("<body bgcolor=\"ffffff\">");


# ************************************************
# Here's where you MAY change the screen response
# the user sees after submitting the form. You may
# change any wording between the quotation marks.
# ************************************************

print ("Thanks for sending us your reference question.<p>
A librarian will contact you in the next couple of days with either an answer to your question or a list of resources that will help you answer the question yourself. ");


# ************************************************
# Here's where you MAY change the name of the link
# back to your main page. You may replace Return
# to our main page with your own wording.
# ************************************************

print ("<p><center><a href=$in{LibraryURL}>Return to our main page.</a></center>");
print ("</body></html>");
```

Research Help Request

Do you need help with course assignments, papers, research projects, but don't have the time to meet with a librarian? We'll provide you with selected information sources and factual information, as well as help you organize your research, cite your sources correctly... via e-mail.

Name (last, first)

Department / Major

Campus address

Campus e-mail

Campus phone

Other phone (if applicable)

Status:

- ○ Freshman
- ○ Sophomore
- ○ Junior
- ○ Senior
- ○ Grad Student
- ○ Faculty
- ○ Staff
- ○ Other

Course title

Instructor

Date due

○ Anytime is fine

What type of research are you doing?

- ○ Course assignment
- ○ Undergrad paper
- ○ Honors / Grad paper
- ○ Grad / Faculty research
- ○ Casual research
- ○ Other (please specify)

Topic of your research (please provide as many details as you can)

For sources I must / would like to use (select all that apply)

- ○ Books
- ○ Journal articles
- ○ Newspaper articles
- ○ Online databases
- ○ Web sites
- ○ CD-ROMs
- ○ Other (please specify)

Type of help you need

○ I'm not quite sure how / where to start researching my topic

○ I'd like help locating specific facts / information

○ I'd like help locating relevant books / journal articles/ Web sites, etc.

○ I'd like help organizing the information I find

○ I'd like help citing my sources / creating a bibliography

○ I'd like to learn how to do academic research

○ Other (please specify)

[Send Request]   [Clear Form]

Research Help Request — HTML Form

```
<html>
<head><title>Research Help Request</title>
</head>
<body bgcolor="#FFFFFF">
<table width="700" border="0" height="85" bgcolor="#000000"><tr valign="middle" align="center"><td>
<p>
<font halign=center color="#FFFFFF" face="Arial, Helvetica, sans-serif" size="+3"><b><i>Research Help Re-
quest</i></b></font></p>
</td></tr></table>
<form method="post" action="http://www.yourLibrary.edu/cgi-bin/arg2.pl"><p> </p>
<p>
<b><font size="2" face="Arial, Helvetica, sans-serif">Do you need help with course assignments, papers, re-
search projects, but don't have <br>the time to meet with a librarian? We'll provide you with selected information
sources and <br>factual information, as well as help you organize your research, cite your sources correctly... via
e-mail.</font></b></p>
<p> </p>
<input type="hidden" name="LibraryEmail" value="you@yourLibrary.edu">
<input type="hidden" name="LibraryURL" value="http://www.yourLibrary.edu">
<input type="hidden" name="Form" value="Research Help Request"><p></p>
<p></p>
<table width="500" border="0" cellspacing="4" cellpadding="1">
<tr><td width="257">
<b><font face="Arial, Helvetica, sans-serif" size="2">Name </font></b><font face="Arial, Helvetica, sans-
serif" size="1"> (last, first)</font><br><font face="Arial, Helvetica, sans-serif" size="2"><input type="text"
name="Name" size="25"></font></td>
<td width="227">
<b><font face="Arial, Helvetica, sans-serif" size="2">Department / Major<br></font></b><font face="Arial,
Helvetica, sans-serif" size="2"><input type="text" name="Department" size="25"></font></td></tr>
<tr><td width="257">
<b><font face="Arial, Helvetica, sans-serif" size="2">Campus address<br></font></b><font face="Arial,
Helvetica, sans-serif" size="2"><input type="text" name="CampusAddress" size="25"></font></td>
<td width="227">
<b><font face="Arial, Helvetica, sans-serif" size="2">Campus e-mail<br></font></b><font face="Arial, Helvetica,
sans-serif" size="2"><input type="text" name="CampusEmail" size="25"></font></td></tr>
<tr><td width="257">
<b><font face="Arial, Helvetica, sans-serif" size="2">Campus phone</font></b><br><font face="Arial, Helvetica,
sans-serif" size="2"><input type="text" name="CampusPhone" size="25"></font></td>
<td width="227">
<b><font face="Arial, Helvetica, sans-serif" size="2">Other phone </font></b><font face="Arial, Helvetica,
sans-serif" size="1">(if applicable)</font><br><font face="Arial, Helvetica, sans-serif" size="2"><input
type="text" name="OtherPhone" size="25"></font></td></tr></table>
<p>
<b><font face="Arial, Helvetica, sans-serif" size="2">Status:</font></b><table width="550" border="0">
```

```
<tr><td width="126">
<font face="Arial, Helvetica, sans-serif" size="2"><input type="radio" name="Status"
value="Freshman">Freshman</font></td>
<td width="117">
<font face="Arial, Helvetica, sans-serif" size="2"><input type="radio" name="Status"
value="Sophomore">Sophomore</font></td>
<td width="87">
<font face="Arial, Helvetica, sans-serif" size="2"><input type="radio" name="Status"
value="Junior">Junior</font></td>
<td width="202">
<font face="Arial, Helvetica, sans-serif" size="2"><input type="radio" name="Status"
value="Senior">Senior</font></td></tr>
<tr><td width="126">
<font face="Arial, Helvetica, sans-serif" size="2"><input type="radio" name="Status"
value="Graduate Student">Grad Student</font></td>
<td width="117">
<font face="Arial, Helvetica, sans-serif" size="2"><input type="radio" name="Status"
value="Faculty">Faculty</font></td>
<td width="87">
<font face="Arial, Helvetica, sans-serif" size="2"><input type="radio" name="Status"
value="Staff">Staff</font></td>
<td width="202">
<font face="Arial, Helvetica, sans-serif" size="2"><input type="radio" name="Status"
value="Other">Other</font></td></tr></table>
<br><table width="500" border="0" cellspacing="0" cellpadding="0">
<tr><td width="257">
<b><font face="Arial, Helvetica, sans-serif" size="2">Course title</font></b><br><font face="Arial, Helvetica,
sans-serif" size="3"><input type="text" name="CTitle" size="25"></font></td>
<td width="227">
<b><font face="Arial, Helvetica, sans-serif" size="2">Instructor<br></font></b><font face="Arial, Helvetica,
sans-serif" size="3"><input type="text" name="Instr" size="25"></font></td></tr></table>
<br>
<font face="Arial, Helvetica, sans-serif" size="2"><b>Date due<font size="1"> </font></b><font
face="Arial, Helvetica, sans-serif" size="1">  </font><br><font size="3"><input type="text"
name="NeedBefore" size="15">     </font><font face="Arial, Helvetica, sans-
serif" size="1"><input type="radio" name="TimeIssue" value="Time is not an issue"></font>Anytime is fine
</font>
<p>
<b><font face="Arial, Helvetica, sans-serif" size="2">What type of research are you doing?<br></font>
</b><table width="548" border="0" cellspacing="0" cellpadding="0">
<tr><td width="183">
<font face="Arial, Helvetica, sans-serif" size="2"><input type="radio" name="TypeR" value="Course
assignment">Course assignment</font></td>
<td width="151">
<font face="Arial, Helvetica, sans-serif" size="2"><input type="radio" name="TypeR" value="Undergrad
```

paper">Undergrad paper</font></td>
<td width="214">
<font face="Arial, Helvetica, sans-serif" size="2"><input type="radio" name="TypeR" value="Honors / Grad paper">Honors / Grad paper</font></td></tr>
<tr><td width="183" height="15">
<font face="Arial, Helvetica, sans-serif" size="2"><input type="radio" name="TypeR" value="Grad / Faculty research">Grad / Faculty research</font></td>
<td width="151" height="15">
<font face="Arial, Helvetica, sans-serif" size="2"><input type="radio" name="TypeR" value="Casual research">Casual research</font></td>
<td width="214" height="15">
<font face="Arial, Helvetica, sans-serif" size="2"></font></td></tr>
<tr><td colspan="3">
<font face="Arial, Helvetica, sans-serif"><input type="radio" name="TypeR" value="Other"><font size="2">Other</font> <b><font size="2"> </font></b><font size="1">(please specify) </font></font>
  <input type="text" name="TypeO" size="20"></td></tr></table>
<p>
<font face="Arial, Helvetica, sans-serif" size="2"><b>Topic of your research   </b> <font face="Arial, Helvetica, sans-serif" size="1">(please provide as many details as you can)
<font size="3"><textarea name="Topic" cols="40" rows="10"> </textarea></font></font></font></p>
<p>
<b><font face="Arial, Helvetica, sans-serif" size="2">For sources I must / would like to use </font></b> <font face="Arial, Helvetica, sans-serif" size="2">   <font face="Arial, Helvetica, sans-serif" size="1">(select all that apply)
</font></font>
<table width="548" border="0" cellspacing="0" cellpadding="0">
<tr><td width="183">
<font face="Arial, Helvetica, sans-serif" size="2"><input type="radio" name="B" value="Books">
Books</font></td>
<td width="151">
<font face="Arial, Helvetica, sans-serif" size="2"><input type="radio" name="JA" value="Journal articles">
Journal articles</font></td>
<td width="214">
<font face="Arial, Helvetica, sans-serif" size="2"><input type="radio" name="NA" value="Newspaper articles">Newspaper articles</font></td></tr>
<tr><td width="183" height="15">
<font face="Arial, Helvetica, sans-serif" size="2"><input type="radio" name="OD" value="Online databases">Online databases</font></td>
<td width="151" height="15">
<font face="Arial, Helvetica, sans-serif" size="2"><input type="radio" name="WS" value="Web sites">
Web sites</font></td>
<td width="214" height="15">
<font face="Arial, Helvetica, sans-serif" size="2"><input type="radio" name="CD" value="CD-ROMs">
CD-ROMs</font></td></tr>
<tr><td colspan="3">
<font face="Arial, Helvetica, sans-serif"><input type="radio" name="TypeR" value="Other"><font

size="2">Other</font> <font size="1">(please specify)</font></font>   <input type="text"
name="TypeO2" size="20"></td></tr></table>
<p>
<b><font face="Arial, Helvetica, sans-serif" size="2">Type of help you need</font></b></p>
<dl><dt>
<dd><font face="Arial, Helvetica, sans-serif" size="2"><input type="radio" name="Help" value="I'm not quite
sure how / where to start researching my topic">I'm not quite sure how / where to start researching my topic
</font>
<dd><font face="Arial, Helvetica, sans-serif" size="2"><input type="radio" name="Help" value="I'd like help
locating specific facts / information">I'd like help locating specific facts / information</font>
<dd><font face="Arial, Helvetica, sans-serif" size="2"><input type="radio" name="Help" value="I'd like help
locating relevant books / magazines / Web sites">I'd like help locating relevant books / journal articles/ Web
sites</font>
<dd><font face="Arial, Helvetica, sans-serif" size="2">, etc.</font>
<font face="Arial, Helvetica, sans-serif"
size="2"><input type="radio" name="Help" value="I'd like help organizing the information I find">I'd like help
organizing the information I find</font>
<dd><font face="Arial, Helvetica, sans-serif" size="2"><input type="radio" name="Help" value="I'd like help
citing my sources / creating a bibliography">I'd like help citing my sources / creating a bibliography </font>
<dd><font face="Arial, Helvetica, sans-serif" size="2"><input type="radio" name="Help" value="I'd like to learn
how to do academic research">I'd like to learn how to do academic research</font>
<dd><font face="Arial, Helvetica, sans-serif" size="2"><input type="radio" name="Help" value="Other"> .
Other <font size="1"> (please specify)
<font size="2">   <font
size="3"><textarea name="HelpOther" cols="30" rows="2"></textarea></font></font></font></font></dl>
<p> </p>
<table width="700" border="0" cellspacing="10" cellpadding="1"><tr><td width="240">
<div align="right"><input type="submit" name="send" value="Send Request"></div></td>
<td width="207"> </td><td width="207">
<div align="left"><input type="reset" name="clear" value="Clear Form"></div></td></tr>
<tr colspan=3><td colspan=3>
<table width="500" border="0" height="2" align="center" cellpadding="0" cellspacing="0"
bgcolor="#000000"><tr><td><font size="1" color="#000000">.</font></td></tr></table></td></tr>
<tr><td colspan=3><div align="center">
<font face="Arial, Helvetica, sans-serif" size="1"><b>http://</b></font>
<font size="2">
<font face="Arial, Helvetica, sans-serif" size="1"><b>© 2001</b></font></font>
<font face="Arial, Helvetica, sans-serif" size="2"><a href="**mailto:**">
<b><font size="1">Contact Webmaster</font></b></a></font></div></td></tr>
</table></form>
</body>
</html>

Research Help Request — Perl Script

```perl
#!/usr/local/bin/perl


# ************************************************
# ABOVE is where you MUST specify the path to your
# perl interpreter on your Web server.
# Replace /usr/local/bin/perl with your path.
# ************************************************

if ($ENV{'REQUEST_METHOD'}eq"GET"){$buffer = $ENV{'QUERY_STRING'};}
    elsif($ENV{'REQUEST_METHOD'}eq"POST"){
        read(STDIN,$buffer,$ENV{'CONTENT_LENGTH'});
    }
$bufferb = $buffer;
#separate the name of the input from its value.
@forminputs = split(/&/, $bufferb);

foreach $forminput (@forminputs)
{
    #separate the name of the input from its value
    ($name, $value) = split(/=/, $forminput);

    #Un-Webify plus signs and %-encoding
    $value =~ tr/+/ /;
    $value =~ s/%([a-fA-F0-9][a-fA-F0-9])/pack("C", hex($1))/eg;

    #stick them in the in array
    $in{$name} = $value;
}
print "Content-type: text/html\n\n";

##############################################################
# ABOVE is the required header for a perl script          #
##############################################################


##############################################################
# (Below) Email received by library containing user-entered information #
##############################################################


# ************************************************
# Here's where you MUST specify the path to your
# email program (probably sendmail) ON your Web server.
# Replace /usr/sbin/sendmail with your path.
# ************************************************

open (LMAIL, "|/usr/sbin/sendmail -t");
print LMAIL ("To: $in{LibraryEmail}\n");
print LMAIL ("From: $in{CampusEmail}\n");
print LMAIL ("Subject: $in{Form} - patron submission\n");
```

```
print LMAIL ("------------------\nPatron information\n\n");
print LMAIL ("Name:\n $in{Name}\n\n");
print LMAIL ("Department / Major:\n $in{Department}\n\n");
print LMAIL ("Campus Address:\n $in{CampusAddress}\n\n");
print LMAIL ("Campus Email:\n $in{CampusEmail}\n\n");
print LMAIL ("Campus Phone:\n $in{CampusPhone}\n\n");
print LMAIL ("Other Phone:\n $in{OtherPhone}\n\n");
print LMAIL ("Status:\n $in{Status}\n\n");

print LMAIL ("------------------\nSubmitted information \n\n");

print LMAIL ("Course title:\n $in{CTitle}\n\n");
print LMAIL ("Instructor:\n $in{Instr}\n\n");
print LMAIL ("Date due:\n $in{NeedBefore} $in{TimeIssue}\n\n");
print LMAIL ("The type of research I am doing:\n $in{TypeR}\n\n");
print LMAIL ("Other research type:\n $in{TypeO}\n\n");
print LMAIL ("Topic of my research:\n $in{Topic}\n\n");
print LMAIL ("Sources I must / would like to use:\n $in{B}, $in{JA}, $in{CD}, $in{OD}, $in{WS}, $in{NA}, $in{Oth}\n\n");
print LMAIL ("Other sources:\n $in{TypeO2}\n\n");
print LMAIL ("Type of help I need:\n $in{Help}\n\n");
print LMAIL ("My other type of help:\n $in{HelpOther}\n\n");

print LMAIL ("\n.\n");


###############################################################
# Email received by the user confirming form submission #
###############################################################

# ************************************************
# Here's where you MUST specify the path to your
# email program ON your Web server.
# Replace /usr/sbin/sendmail with your path.
# ************************************************

open (MAIL, "|/usr/sbin/sendmail -t");

# ************************************************
# Here's where you MAY customize the email
# response to the user. You may change any wording
# on the form.
# ************************************************

print MAIL<<toEnd;
To: $in{CampusEmail}
From: $in{LibraryEmail}
Subject: $in{Form}

Thanks for sending us your reference help request.\n\n
A librarian will be sending you an email response in the next couple of days. It will contain suggestions and ideas as
to how you can best proceed with your research.

toEnd
    print MAIL ("\n.\n");
```

```
##########################################################
# Screen response to user after submitting the form  #
##########################################################

print ("<html><head><title>$in{Form}</title></head>");
print ("<body bgcolor=\"ffffff\">");

# ***********************************************
# Here's where you MAY change the screen response
# the user sees after submitting the form. You may
# change any wording between the quotation marks.
# ***********************************************

print ("Thanks for sending us your reference help request.<p>
A librarian will be sending you an email response in the next couple of days. It will contain suggestions and ideas as
to how you can best proceed with your research.");

# ***********************************************
# Here's where you MAY change the name of the link
# back to your main page. You may replace Return
# to our main page with your own wording.
# ***********************************************

print ("<p><center><a href=$in{LibraryURL}>Return to our main page.</a></center>");
print ("</body></html>");
```

Library Use Survey

We'd like to find out how and why you use the library, learn how we can improve our services, staff, building, and equipment, as well as learn how you feel about the services/resources we offer. Please complete this brief survey in order to help us create the best possible library for everyone.

You and the Library

How many times have you used the library in the last 30 days?

If less than 4 times, why don't you visit more often?

Off-campus students - How far is it to the library?
(express in miles / partial miles)

When do you use the library? (select all that apply)
○ Morning ○ Early afternoon ○ Late afternoon ○ Evening

What days do you use the library? (select all that apply)
○ Sun. ○ Mon. ○ Tues. ○ Wed. ○ Thurs. ○ Fri. ○ Sat.

What language(s), other than English, do you speak / read?

How do you find out about what is happening at the library? (select all that apply)
○ Friend / colleague / faculty ○ Library publications ○ Library staff member
○ Campus publications / news ○ Library Web site ○ Other

While using the library's Web site you usually find...
○ More than you expected to find ○ Exactly what you expected to find
○ Some things you expected to find ○ A few things you expected to find
○ Nothing you expected to find

When you need help using the library what do you do?
○ Ask a staff member ○ Ask a friend ○ Refer to printed documentation
○ Use our Web site ○ Leave the library ○ Don't ask for help

The Library

Which library resources / services do you use most often?

What do you like the *most* about the library?

What do you like the *least* about the library?

What difficulties / barriers have you encountered while using the library?

What new library services / resources would you like to see added?

When the library doesn't have what you need, what do you do?

○ Ask a staff member   ○ Search the Internet   ○ Check the online catalog again

○ Fill out an ILL form   ○ Leave the library   ○ Don't ask for help

Grade the Library

(1-poor 2-fair 3-good 4-very good 5-excellent)

	1	2	3	4	5
Organization of information	○	○	○	○	○
Value of information	○	○	○	○	○
Staff availabiliy / courtesy	○	○	○	○	○
Staff response to requests	○	○	○	○	○
Number of hours / days open	○	○	○	○	○
Building space / furniture	○	○	○	○	○
Computers / other equipment	○	○	○	○	○
Library publications / newsletters	○	○	○	○	○
Ability to provide feedback / comments	○	○	○	○	○
Overall rating	○	○	○	○	○

Name (last, first middle)

Department / Major

Campus e-mail

Campus phone

Status

- ○ Freshman
- ○ Sophomore
- ○ Junior
- ○ Senior
- ○ Grad Student
- ○ Faculty
- ○ Staff
- ○ Other

[Send Survey]   [Clear Survey]

Library Use Survey — HTML Form

```
<html>
<head><title>Library Use Survey</title></head>
<body bgcolor="#FFFFFF">
<table width="700" border="0" height="85" bgcolor="#000000">
<tr valign="middle" align="center"><td>
<p>
<font halign=center color="#FFFFFF" face="Arial, Helvetica, sans-serif" size="5">
<b><i><font size="+3">Library Use Survey</font></i></b></font></p>
</td></tr></table>
<form method="post" action="http://www.yourLibrary.edu/cgi-bin/arg3.pl"><p> </p>
<p>
<b><font size="2" face="Arial, Helvetica, sans-serif">We'd like to find out how and why you use the library, learn
how we can improve our services, staff, <br>building, and equipment, as well as learn how you feel about the
services/resources we offer. <br>Please complete this brief survey in order to help us create the best possible
library for everyone. </font></b></p>
<p> </p>
<input type="hidden" name="LibraryEmail" value="you@yourLibrary.edu">
<input type="hidden" name="LibraryURL" value="http://www.yourLibrary.edu">
<input type="hidden" name="Form" value="Library Use Survey"><p></p>
<p>
<b><font face="Arial, Helvetica, sans-serif" size="3">You and the Library</font></b></p>
<p>
<font face="Arial, Helvetica, sans-serif" size="2"><b>How many times have you used the library in the last 30
days?</b><font size="3"><input type="text" name="Visits" size="5"></font></font></p>
<p>
<font face="Arial, Helvetica, sans-serif" size="2"><b>If less than 4 times, why don't you visit more often?
</b><font size="3"><br><textarea name="WhyNotMore" cols="40" rows="2"></textarea></font></font></p>
<p><font face="Arial, Helvetica, sans-serif" size="2"><b>Off-campus students - How far is it to the library?
</b><br><font size="1">(express in miles / partial miles)</font><br><font size="3"><input type="text"
name="Far" size="40" value=""> </font></font></p>
<p>
<font face="Arial, Helvetica, sans-serif" size="2"><b>When do you use the library?</b>
   <font size="1">(select all that apply)</font><br><font face="Arial, Helvetica, sans-serif"
size="2">
<input type="radio" name="M" value="Morning"></font><font face="Arial, Helvetica, sans-serif"
size="2">Morning  
<input type="radio" name="EA" value="Early afternoon">Early afternoon  
<input type="radio" name="LA" value="Late afternoon">Late afternoon   
<input type="radio" name="E" value="Evening">Evening</font></font></p>
<p>
<font face="Arial, Helvetica, sans-serif" size="2"><b>What days do you use the library?</b>
   <font size="1">(select all that apply)</font><br><font face="Arial, Helvetica, sans-serif"
size="2">
```

```
<input type="radio" name="S" value="Sun."></font>Sun.  
<input type="radio" name="MO" value="Mon.">Mon.  
<input type="radio" name="T" value="Tues.">Tues.   
<input type="radio" name="W" value="Wed.">Wed.  
<input type="radio" name="R" value="Thurs.">Thurs.  
<input type="radio" name="F" value="Fri.">Fri.   
<input type="radio" name="SN" value="Sat.">Sat.</font></p>
<p>
<font face="Arial, Helvetica, sans-serif" size="2"><b>What language(s), other than English, do you speak /
read?</b><font size="3"> <br><input type="text" name="OtherLan" size="40" value=""></font></font></p>
<p>
<font face="Arial, Helvetica, sans-serif" size="2"><b>How do you find out about what is happening at the li-
brary?</b>    <font size="1">(select all that apply)</font><br></font><table width="600"
border="0" cellspacing="0" cellpadding="0">
<tr><td width="207">
<font face="Arial, Helvetica, sans-serif" size="2"><input type="radio" name="FCT" value="Friend / colleague /
faculty">Friend / colleague / faculty</font></td>
<td width="190">
<font face="Arial, Helvetica, sans-serif" size="2"><input type="radio" name="LPP" value="Library publications /
posters">Library publications</font></td>
<td width="203">
<font face="Arial, Helvetica, sans-serif" size="2"><input type="radio" name="LSM" value="Library Staff
member">Library staff member</font></td></tr>
<tr><td width="207">
<font face="Arial, Helvetica, sans-serif" size="2"><input type="radio" name="LPN" value="Local publications /
news">Campus publications / news</font></td>
<td width="190">
<font face="Arial, Helvetica, sans-serif" size="2"><input type="radio" name="LWS" value="Library Web
site">Library Web site</font></td>
<td width="203">
<font face="Arial, Helvetica, sans-serif" size="2"><input type="radio" name="O" value="Other">Other</font>
</td></tr></table>
<p>
<font face="Arial, Helvetica, sans-serif" size="2"><b>While using the library's Web site you usually find... </b>
</font><br><table width="600" border="0" cellspacing="0" cellpadding="0">
<tr><td width="256">
<font face="Arial, Helvetica, sans-serif" size="2"><input type="radio" name="IFound" value="More than you
expected to find">More than you expected to find</font></td>
<td width="344">
<font face="Arial, Helvetica, sans-serif" size="2"><input type="radio" name="IFound" value="Exactly what you
expected to find">Exactly what you expected to find</font></td></tr>
<tr><td width="256">
<font face="Arial, Helvetica, sans-serif" size="2"><input type="radio" name="IFound" value="Some things you
expected to find">Some things you expected to find</font></td>
<td width="344">
```

```
<font face="Arial, Helvetica, sans-serif" size="2"><input type="radio" name="IFound" value="A few things you
expected to find">A few things you expected to find</font></td></tr>
<tr><td width="256">
<font face="Arial, Helvetica, sans-serif" size="2"><input type="radio" name="IFound" value="Nothing you
expected to find">Nothing you expected to find</font></td><td width="344"></td></tr></table>
<p>
<font face="Arial, Helvetica, sans-serif" size="2"><b>When you need help using the library what do you
do?<br></b></font><table width="600" border="0" cellspacing="0" cellpadding="0">
<tr><td width="169">
<b><font face="Arial, Helvetica, sans-serif" size="2"><input type="radio" name="Do" value="Ask a staff mem-
ber"></font></b><font face="Arial, Helvetica, sans-serif" size="2">Ask a staff member</font></td>
<td width="154">
<font face="Arial, Helvetica, sans-serif" size="2"><input type="radio" name="Do" value="Ask a friend">
Ask a friend</font></td>
<td width="275"><font face="Arial, Helvetica, sans-serif" size="2"><input type="radio" name="Do" value="Refer
to printed documentation">Refer to printed documentation</font></td></tr>
<tr><td width="169">
<font face="Arial, Helvetica, sans-serif" size="2"><input type="radio" name="Do" value="Use our Web site">Use
our Web site</font></td>
<td width="154">
<font face="Arial, Helvetica, sans-serif" size="2"><input type="radio" name="Do" value="Leave the library">
Leave the library</font></td>
<td width="275">
<font face="Arial, Helvetica, sans-serif" size="2"><input type="radio" name="Do" value="Don't ask for
help">Don't ask for help</font></td></tr></table>
<p> </p>
<p>
<b><font face="Arial, Helvetica, sans-serif" size="3">The Library</font></b></p>
<p>
<font face="Arial, Helvetica, sans-serif" size="2"><b>Which library resources / services do you use most often?
</b><br><font face="Arial, Helvetica, sans-serif" size="3"><textarea name="Often" cols="40" rows="2">
</textarea></font></font></p>
<p>
<font face="Arial, Helvetica, sans-serif" size="2"><b>What do you like the <i>most</i> about the library? <br>
</b><font face="Arial, Helvetica, sans-serif" size="3"> <textarea name="Most" cols="40" rows="2">
</textarea></font></font></p>
<p>
<font face="Arial, Helvetica, sans-serif" size="2"><b>What do you like the <i>least</i> about the library? <br>
</b><font face="Arial, Helvetica, sans-serif" size="3"> <textarea name="Least" cols="40" rows="2">
</textarea></font></font></p>
<p>
<font face="Arial, Helvetica, sans-serif" size="2"><b>What difficulties / barriers have you encountered while using
the library? <br></b><font face="Arial, Helvetica, sans-serif" size="3">
<textarea name="Difficulties" cols="40" rows="2"></textarea></font></font></p>
<p>
```

```
<font face="Arial, Helvetica, sans-serif" size="2"><b>What new library services / resources would you like to see added? <br></b><font face="Arial, Helvetica, sans-serif" size="3"><textarea name="Added" cols="40" rows="2"></textarea></font></font></p>
<p>
<font face="Arial, Helvetica, sans-serif" size="2"><b>When the library doesn't have what you need, what do you do?<br></b></font><table width="600" border="0" cellspacing="0" cellpadding="0">
<tr><td width="162">
<b><font face="Arial, Helvetica, sans-serif" size="2"><input type="radio" name="NeedSomething" value="Ask a staff member"></font></b> <font face="Arial, Helvetica, sans-serif" size="2">Ask a staff member</font></td>
<td width="158">
<font face="Arial, Helvetica, sans-serif" size="2"><input type="radio" name="NeedSomething" value="Search the Internet">Search the Internet</font></td>
<td width="280">
<font face="Arial, Helvetica, sans-serif" size="2"><input type="radio" name="NeedSomething" value="Check the online catalog again">Check the online catalog again</font></td></tr>
<tr><td width="162">
<font face="Arial, Helvetica, sans-serif" size="2"><input type="radio" name="NeedSomething" value="Fill out an ILL form">Fill out an ILL form</font></td>
<td width="158">
<font face="Arial, Helvetica, sans-serif" size="2"><input type="radio" name="NeedSomething" value="Leave the library">Leave the library</font></td>
<td width="280">
<font face="Arial, Helvetica, sans-serif" size="2"><input type="radio" name="NeedSomething" value="Don't ask for help">Don't ask for help</font></td></tr></table><br>
<p>
<b><font face="Arial, Helvetica, sans-serif" size="3">Grade the Library</font><br><br></b>
<font face="Arial, Helvetica, sans-serif" size="1">(1-poor   2-fair   3-good   4-very good   5-excellent)</font><br>
<table width="435" border="0"><tr align="center">
<td> </td>
<td><font face="Arial, Helvetica, sans-serif" size="1"><b>1</b></font></td>
<td><font face="Arial, Helvetica, sans-serif" size="1"><b>2</b></font></td>
<td><font face="Arial, Helvetica, sans-serif" size="1"><b>3</b></font></td>
<td><font face="Arial, Helvetica, sans-serif" size="1"><b>4</b></font></td>
<td><font face="Arial, Helvetica, sans-serif" size="1"><b>5</b></font></td></tr>
<tr>
<td><font face="Arial, Helvetica, sans-serif" size="2">Organization of information</font></td>
<td> <input type="radio" name="Organized" value="poor"></td>
<td><input type="radio" name="Organized" value="fair"></td>
<td><input type="radio" name="Organized" value="good"></td>
<td><input type="radio" name="Organized" value="very good"></td>
<td><input type="radio" name="Organized" value="excellent"></td></tr>
<tr>
<td><font face="Arial, Helvetica, sans-serif" size="2">Value of information</font></td>
<td><input type="radio" name="Collections" value="poor"></td>
```

```
<td><input type="radio" name="Collections" value="fair"></td>
<td><input type="radio" name="Collections" value="good"></td>
<td><input type="radio" name="Collections" value="very good"></td>
<td><input type="radio" name="Collections" value="excellent"></td></tr>
<tr>
<td><font face="Arial, Helvetica, sans-serif" size="2">Staff availabiliy / courtesy</font></td>
<td><input type="radio" name="Hours" value="poor"></td>
<td><input type="radio" name="Hours" value="fair"></td>
<td><input type="radio" name="Hours" value="good"></td>
<td><input type="radio" name="Hours" value="very good"></td>
<td><input type="radio" name="Hours" value="excellent"></td></tr>
<tr>
<td height="4"><font face="Arial, Helvetica, sans-serif" size="2">Staff response to requests </font></td>
<td height="4"><input type="radio" name="Space" value="poor"></td>
<td height="4"><input type="radio" name="Space" value="fair"></td>
<td height="4"><input type="radio" name="Space" value="good"></td>
<td height="4"><input type="radio" name="Space" value="very good"></td>
<td height="4"><input type="radio" name="Space" value="excellent"></td></tr>
<tr>
<td><font face="Arial, Helvetica, sans-serif" size="2">Number of hours / days open</font></td>
<td><input type="radio" name="Staff" value="poor"></td>
<td><input type="radio" name="Staff" value="fair"></td>
<td><input type="radio" name="Staff" value="good"></td>
<td><input type="radio" name="Staff" value="very good"></td>
<td><input type="radio" name="Staff" value="excellent"></td></tr>
<tr>
<td><font face="Arial, Helvetica, sans-serif" size="2">Building space / furniture</font></td>
<td><input type="radio" name="Response" value="poor"></td>
<td><input type="radio" name="Response" value="fair"></td>
<td><input type="radio" name="Response" value="good"></td>
<td><input type="radio" name="Response" value="very good"></td>
<td><input type="radio" name="Response" value="excellent"></td></tr>
<tr>
<td><font face="Arial, Helvetica, sans-serif" size="2">Computers / other equipment</font></td>
<td><input type="radio" name="Computer" value="poor"></td>
<td><input type="radio" name="Computer" value="fair"></td>
<td><input type="radio" name="Computer" value="good"></td>
<td><input type="radio" name="Computer" value="very good"></td>
<td><input type="radio" name="Computer" value="excellent"></td></tr>
<tr>
<td><font face="Arial, Helvetica, sans-serif" size="2">Library publications / newsletters </font></td>
<td><input type="radio" name="LibraryPub" value="poor"></td>
<td><input type="radio" name="LibraryPub" value="fair"></td>
<td><input type="radio" name="LibraryPub" value="good"></td>
<td><input type="radio" name="LibraryPub" value="very good"></td>
```

```
<td><input type="radio" name="LibraryPub" value="excellent"></td></tr>
<tr>
<td><font face="Arial, Helvetica, sans-serif" size="2">Ability to provide feedback / comments</font></td>
<td><input type="radio" name="Feedback" value="poor"></td>
<td><input type="radio" name="Feedback" value="fair"></td>
<td><input type="radio" name="Feedback" value="good"></td>
<td><input type="radio" name="Feedback" value="very good"></td>
<td><input type="radio" name="Feedback" value="excellent"></td></tr>
<tr>
<td><font face="Arial, Helvetica, sans-serif" size="2"><b>Overall rating</b></font></td>
<td><input type="radio" name="Overall" value="poor"></td>
<td><input type="radio" name="Overall" value="fair"></td>
<td><input type="radio" name="Overall" value="good"></td>
<td><input type="radio" name="Overall" value="very good"></td>
<td><input type="radio" name="Overall" value="excellent"></td></tr>
</table><p> </p>
<p></p>
<table width="500" border="0" cellspacing="4" cellpadding="1">
<tr><td width="257">
<b><font face="Arial, Helvetica, sans-serif" size="2">Name </font></b><font face="Arial, Helvetica, sans-
serif" size="2"> <font size="1">(last, first middle)</font></font><br><font face="Arial, Helvetica, sans-serif"
size="2"><input type="text" name="Name" size="25"></font></td>
<td width="227">
<b><font face="Arial, Helvetica, sans-serif" size="2">Department / Major<br></font></b><font face="Arial,
Helvetica, sans-serif" size="2"><input type="text" name="Department" size="25"></font></td></tr>
<tr><td width="257">
<b><font face="Arial, Helvetica, sans-serif" size="2">Campus e-mail<br></font></b><font face="Arial, Helvetica,
sans-serif" size="2"><input type="text" name="CampusEmail" size="25"></font></td>
<td width="227">
<b><font face="Arial, Helvetica, sans-serif" size="2">Campus phone</font></b><b><font face="Arial, Helvetica,
sans-serif" size="2"><br></font></b><font face="Arial, Helvetica, sans-serif" size="2"><input type="text"
name="CampusPhone2" size="25"></font></td></tr></table>
<p>
<b><font face="Arial, Helvetica, sans-serif" size="2">Status</font></b><table width="550" border="0"
cellspacing="0" cellpadding="0">
<tr><td width="126" height="13">
<font face="Arial, Helvetica, sans-serif" size="2"><input type="radio" name="Status" value=
"Freshman">Freshman</font></td>
<td width="117" height="13">
<font face="Arial, Helvetica, sans-serif" size="2"><input type="radio" name="Status" value=
"Sophomore">Sophomore</font></td>
<td width="87" height="13">
<font face="Arial, Helvetica, sans-serif" size="2"><input type="radio" name="Status" value=
"Junior">Junior</font></td>
<td width="202" height="13">
```

```
<font face="Arial, Helvetica, sans-serif" size="2"><input type="radio" name="Status" value=
"Senior">Senior</font></td></tr>
<tr><td width="126" height="9">
<font face="Arial, Helvetica, sans-serif" size="2"><input type="radio" name="Status" value=
"Graduate Student">Grad Student</font></td>
<td width="117" height="9">
<font face="Arial, Helvetica, sans-serif" size="2"><input type="radio" name="Status" value=
"Faculty">Faculty</font></td>
<td width="87" height="9">
<font face="Arial, Helvetica, sans-serif" size="2"><input type="radio" name="Status" value=
"Staff">Staff</font></td>
<td width="202" height="9">
<font face="Arial, Helvetica, sans-serif" size="2"><input type="radio" name="Status" value=
"Other">Other</font></td></tr></table>
<p> </p>
<table width="700" border="0" cellspacing="10" cellpadding="1"><tr><td width="213">
<div align="right"><input type="submit" name="send" value="Send Survey"></div></td>
<td width="225"> </td><td width="216">
<div align="left"><input type="reset" name="clear" value="Clear Survey"></div></td></tr>
<tr colspan=3><td colspan=3>
<table width="500" border="0" height="2" align="center" cellpadding="0" cellspacing="0"
bgcolor="#000000"><tr><td><font size="1" color="#000000">.</font></td></tr></table></td></tr><tr><td
colspan=3><div align="center">
<font face="Arial, Helvetica, sans-serif" size="1"><b>http://</b></font><br> 
<font face="Arial, Helvetica, sans-serif" size="1"><b>&copy; 2001</b></font>
<font face="Arial, Helvetica, sans-serif" size="2"><a href="mailto:">
<b><font size="1">Contact Webmaster</font></b></a></font></div></td></tr>
</table></form>
</body>
</html>
```

Library Use Survey — Perl Script

```perl
#!/usr/local/bin/perl

# ************************************************
# ABOVE is where you MUST specify the path to your
# perl interpreter on your Web server.
# Replace /usr/local/bin/perl with your path.
# ************************************************

if ($ENV{'REQUEST_METHOD'}eq"GET"){$buffer = $ENV{'QUERY_STRING'};}
    elsif($ENV{'REQUEST_METHOD'}eq"POST"){
        read(STDIN,$buffer,$ENV{'CONTENT_LENGTH'});
    }
$bufferb = $buffer;
#separate the name of the input from its value.
@forminputs = split(/&/, $bufferb);

foreach $forminput (@forminputs)
{
    #separate the name of the input from its value
    ($name, $value) = split(/=/, $forminput);

    #Un-Webify plus signs and %-encoding
    $value =~ tr/+/ /;
    $value =~ s/%([a-fA-F0-9][a-fA-F0-9])/pack("C", hex($1))/eg;

    #stick them in the in array
    $in{$name} = $value;
}
print "Content-type: text/html\n\n";

##############################################################
# ABOVE is the required header for a perl script        #
##############################################################

##################################################################
# (Below) Email received by library containing user-entered information #
##################################################################

# ************************************************
# Here's where you MUST specify the path to your
# email program (probably sendmail) ON your Web server.
# Replace /usr/sbin/sendmail with your path.
# ************************************************
```

```
open (LMAIL, "I/usr/sbin/sendmail -t");
print LMAIL ("To: $in{LibraryEmail}\n");
print LMAIL ("From: $in{CampusEmail}\n");
print LMAIL ("Subject: $in{Form} - patron submission\n");

print LMAIL ("------------------\nPatron information\n\n");
print LMAIL ("Name:\n $in{Name}\n\n");
print LMAIL ("Department / Major:\n $in{Department}\n\n");
print LMAIL ("Campus Email:\n $in{CampusEmail}\n\n");
print LMAIL ("Campus Phone:\n $in{CampusPhone}\n\n");
print LMAIL ("Status:\n $in{Status}\n\n");

print LMAIL ("------------------\nSubmitted information \n\n");

print LMAIL ("Visits to the library in the past 30 days:\n $in{Visits}\n\n");
print LMAIL ("Why not more often?\n $in{WhyNotMore}\n\n");
print LMAIL ("How far my home is from the library:\n $in{Far}\n\n");
print LMAIL ("When I visit the library:\n $in{M}, $in{EA}, $in{LA}, $in{E}\n\n");
print LMAIL ("Days I visit:\n $in{S}, $in{MO}, $in{T}, $in{W}, $in{R}, $in{F}, $in{SN}\n\n");
print LMAIL ("Foreign languages I speak:\n $in{OtherLan}\n\n");
print LMAIL ("How I find out what is happening in the library:\n $in{FCT}, $in{LPN}, $in{LPP}, $in{LWS}, $in{LSM},
$in{Oth}\n\n");
print LMAIL ("When using the library I find:\n $in{IFound}\n\n");
print LMAIL ("When I need help I:\n $in{Do}\n\n");
print LMAIL ("Library resources I use most often:\n $in{Often}\n\n");
print LMAIL ("What I like most about the library:\n $in{Most}\n\n");
print LMAIL ("What I like least about the library:\n $in{Least}\n\n");
print LMAIL ("Difficulties I encounter at the library:\n $in{Difficulties}\n\n");
print LMAIL ("Library resources I would like to see added:\n $in{Added}\n\n");
print LMAIL ("When a library doesn't have something I need I:\n $in{NeedSomething}\n\n");

print LMAIL ("Library grades\n\n");
print LMAIL ("Organization of information:\t $in{Organized}\n");
print LMAIL ("Value of information:\t $in{Collections}\n");
print LMAIL ("Staff availabiliy / courtesy:\t $in{Hours}\n");
print LMAIL ("Staff response to requests:\t $in{Space}\n");
print LMAIL ("Number of hours / days open:\t $in{Staff}\n");
print LMAIL ("Building space / furniture:\t $in{Response}\n");
print LMAIL ("Computers / Other equipment:\t $in{Computer}\n");
print LMAIL ("Library publications / newsletters:\t $in{LibraryPub}\n");
print LMAIL ("Ability to provide feedback / comments:\t $in{Feedback}\n");
print LMAIL ("OVERALL RATING:\t $in{Overall}\n");
print LMAIL ("\n.\n");
```

```
#######################################################
# Email received by the user confirming form submission #
#######################################################


# ************************************************
# Here's where you MUST specify the path to your
# email program ON your Web server.
# Replace /usr/sbin/sendmail with your path.
# ************************************************

open (MAIL, "I/usr/sbin/sendmail -t");


# ************************************************
# Here's where you MAY customize the email
# response to the user. You may change any wording
# on the form.
# ************************************************

print MAIL<<toEnd;
To: $in{CampusEmail}
From: $in{LibraryEmail}
Subject: $in{Form}

Thanks for taking the time to fill out our Library Use Survey.\n\n
We will use your input to help improve our library services, collections, building and equipment.

toEnd
    print MAIL ("\n.\n");


#######################################################
# Screen response to user after submitting the form  #
#######################################################

print ("<html><head><title>$in{Form}</title></head>");
print ("<body bgcolor=\"ffffff\">");


# ************************************************
# Here's where you MAY change the screen response
# the user sees after submitting the form. You may
# change any wording between the quotation marks.
# ************************************************

print ("Thanks for taking the time to fill out our Library Use Survey.<p>
We will use your input to help improve our library services, collections, building and equipment.");
```

```
# ************************************************
# Here's where you MAY change the name of the link
# back to your main page. You may replace Return
# to our main page with your own wording.
# ************************************************

print ("<p><center><a href=$in{LibraryURL}>Return to our main page.</a></center>");
print ("</body></html>");
```

Comments, Suggestions

Please take a few minutes to send us your comments about, and suggestions for, improving our library and its resources/services. We'd also like to know what you think of our Web site and Web links.

Name (last, first middle)

Department / Major

Campus address

Campus e-mail

Campus phone

Fax / Other phone

Status

○ Freshman   ○ Sophomore   ○ Junior   ○ Senior
○ Grad Student   ○ Faculty   ○ Staff   ○ Other

Type of message

○ Comment   ○ Suggestion   ○ New idea   ○ Compliment   ○ Complaint

Subject of your message

Your message

Would you like a reply?

○ Yes   ○ No

[Send Message]   [Clear Form]

Comments, Suggestions — HTML Form

```
<html>
<head><title>Comments, Suggestions</title></head>
<body bgcolor="#FFFFFF">
<table width="700" border="0" height="85" bgcolor="#000000">
<tr valign="middle" align="center"><td>
<p>
<font halign=center color="#FFFFFF" face="Arial, Helvetica, sans-serif" size="+3"> <b><i>Comments, Sugges-
tions </i></b></font></p>
</td></tr></table>
<form method="post" action="http://www.yourLibrary.edu/cgi-bin/arg4.pl"><p> </p>
<p>
<font face="Arial, Helvetica, sans-serif" size="2"><b>Please take a few minutes to send us your comments
about, and suggestions for, improving our library <br>and its resources/services. We'd also like to know what you
think of our Web site and Web links.</b></font></p>
<p> </p>
<input type="hidden" name="LibraryEmail" value="you@yourLibrary.edu">
<input type="hidden" name="LibraryURL" value="http://www.yourLibrary.edu">
<input type="hidden" name="Form" value="Comments, Suggestions"><p></p>
<p></p>
<table width="500" border="0" cellspacing="4" cellpadding="1">
<tr><td width="257">
<b><font face="Arial, Helvetica, sans-serif" size="2">Name </font></b><font face="Arial, Helvetica, sans-
serif" size="1"> (last, first middle)</font><br><font face="Arial, Helvetica, sans-serif" size="2"><input
type="text" name="Name" size="25"></font></td>
<td width="227">
<b><font face="Arial, Helvetica, sans-serif" size="2">Department / Major<br><font></b> font face="Arial,
Helvetica, sans-serif" size="2"><input type="text" name="Department" size="25"></font></td></tr>
<tr><td width="257">
<b><font face="Arial, Helvetica, sans-serif" size="2">Campus address<br></font></b><font face="Arial,
Helvetica, sans-serif" size="2"><input type="text" name="CampusAddress" size="25"></font></td>
<td width="227">
<b><font face="Arial, Helvetica, sans-serif" size="2">Campus e-mail<br></font></b><font face="Arial, Helvetica,
sans-serif" size="2"><input type="text" name="CampusEmail" size="25"></font></td></tr>
<tr><td width="257">
<b><font face="Arial, Helvetica, sans-serif" size="2">Campus phone</font></b><br><ont face="Arial, Helvetica,
sans-serif" size="2"><input type="text" name="CampusPhone" size="25"></font></td>
<td width="227">
<b><font face="Arial, Helvetica, sans-serif" size="2">Fax / Other phone<br></font></b><font face="Arial,
Helvetica, sans-serif" size="2"><input type="text" name="OtherPhone" size="25"></font></td></tr> </table>
<p>
<b><font face="Arial, Helvetica, sans-serif" size="2">Status</font></b><table width="550" border="0"
cellspacing="0" cellpadding="0">
<tr><td width="126" height="13">
```

```
<font face="Arial, Helvetica, sans-serif" size="2"><input type="radio" name="Status"
value="Freshman">Freshman</font></td>
<td width="117" height="13">
<font face="Arial, Helvetica, sans-serif" size="2"><input type="radio" name="Status"
value="Sophomore">Sophomore</font></td>
<td width="87" height="13">
<font face="Arial, Helvetica, sans-serif" size="2"><input type="radio" name="Status"
value="Junior">Junior</font></td>
<td width="202" height="13">
<font face="Arial, Helvetica, sans-serif" size="2"><input type="radio" name="Status"
value="Senior">Senior</font></td></tr>
<tr><td width="126" height="9">
<font face="Arial, Helvetica, sans-serif" size="2"><input type="radio" name="Status"
value="Graduate Student">Grad Student</font></td>
<td width="117" height="9">
<font face="Arial, Helvetica, sans-serif" size="2"><input type="radio" name="Status"
value="Faculty">Faculty</font></td>
<td width="87" height="9">
<font face="Arial, Helvetica, sans-serif" size="2"><input type="radio" name="Status"
value="Staff">Staff</font></td>
<td width="202" height="9">
<font face="Arial, Helvetica, sans-serif" size="2"><input type="radio" name="Status"
value="Other">Other</font></td></tr></table>
<p>
<b><font face="Arial, Helvetica, sans-serif" size="2">Type of message<br></font></b>
<font face="Arial, Helvetica, sans-serif" size="2">
<input type="radio" name="Type" value="Comment">Comment    
<input type="radio" name="Type" value="Suggestion">Suggestion    
<input type="radio" name="Type" value="New idea">New idea   
<input type="radio" name="Type" value="Compliment">Compliment   
<input type="radio" name="Type" value="Complaint">Complaint</font>
<p>
<b><font face="Arial, Helvetica, sans-serif" size="2">Subject of your message </font></b>
<br><font face="Arial, Helvetica, sans-serif" size="3"><textarea name="Subject" cols="40" rows="2">
</textarea></font></p>
<p>
<b><font face="Arial, Helvetica, sans-serif" size="2">Your message</font></b><br><font face="Arial, Helvetica,
sans-serif" size="3"><textarea name="Message" cols="40" rows="10"></textarea></font></p>
<p>
<><font face="Arial, Helvetica, sans-serif" size="2">Would you like a reply?<br>
<input type="radio" name="Reply" value="Yes">/font></b><font face="Arial, Helvetica, sans-serif" size="2">Yes
  </font> <font face="Arial, Helvetica, sans-serif" size="2">
<input type="radio" name="Reply" value="No">No</font>
<p> 
<table width="700" border="0" cellspacing="10" cellpadding="1"><tr><td width="255">
```

```
<div align="right"><input type="submit" name="send" value="Send Message"></div></td>
<td width="192"> </td><td width="207"><div align="left">
<input type="reset" name="clear" value="Clear Form"></div></td>
</tr><tr colspan=3><td colspan=3>
<table width="500" border="0" height="2" align="center" cellpadding="0" cellspacing="0"
bgcolor="#000000"><tr><td><font size="1" color="#000000">.</font></td></tr></table>
</td></tr>
<tr><td colspan=3><div align="center">
<font face="Arial, Helvetica, sans-serif" size="1"><b>http://</b></font><br> 
<font face="Arial, Helvetica, sans-serif" size="1"><b>&copy; 2001</b></font>
<font face="Arial, Helvetica, sans-serif" size="2"><a href="mailto:">
<b><font size="1">Contact Webmaster</font></b></a></font></div></td></tr>
</table></form>
</body>
</html>
```

Comments, Suggestions — Perl Script

```perl
#!/usr/local/bin/perl

# **************************************************
# ABOVE is where you MUST specify the path to your
# perl interpreter on your Web server.
# Replace /usr/local/bin/perl with your path.
# **************************************************

if ($ENV{'REQUEST_METHOD'}eq"GET"){$buffer = $ENV{'QUERY_STRING'};}
    elsif($ENV{'REQUEST_METHOD'}eq"POST"){
        read(STDIN,$buffer,$ENV{'CONTENT_LENGTH'});
    }
$bufferb = $buffer;
#separate the name of the input from its value.
@forminputs = split(/&/, $bufferb);

foreach $forminput (@forminputs)
{
        #separate the name of the input from its value
        ($name, $value) = split(/=/, $forminput);

        #Un-Webify plus signs and %-encoding
        $value =~ tr/+/ /;
        $value =~ s/%([a-fA-F0-9][a-fA-F0-9])/pack("C", hex($1))/eg;

        #stick them in the in array
        $in{$name} = $value;
}
print "Content-type: text/html\n\n";

#######################################################################
# ABOVE is the required header for a perl script          #
#######################################################################


#######################################################################
# (Below) Email received by library containing user-entered information #
#######################################################################


# **************************************************
# Here's where you MUST specify the path to your
# email program (probably sendmail) ON your Web server.
# Replace /usr/sbin/sendmail with your path.
# **************************************************

open (LMAIL, "|/usr/sbin/sendmail -t");
print LMAIL ("To: $in{LibraryEmail}\n");
print LMAIL ("From: $in{CampusEmail}\n");
print LMAIL ("Subject: $in{Form} - patron submission\n");
```

```
print LMAIL ("------------------\nPatron information\n\n");
print LMAIL ("Name:\n $in{Name}\n\n");
print LMAIL ("Department / Major:\n $in{Department}\n\n");
print LMAIL ("Campus Address:\n $in{CampusAddress}\n\n");
print LMAIL ("Campus Email:\n $in{CampusEmail}\n\n");
print LMAIL ("Campus Phone:\n $in{CampusPhone}\n\n");
print LMAIL ("Other Phone:\n $in{OtherPhone}\n\n");
print LMAIL ("Status:\n $in{Status}\n\n");

print LMAIL ("------------------\nSubmitted information \n\n");

print LMAIL ("Type of message:\n $in{Type}\n\n");
print LMAIL ("Message subject:\n $in{Subject}\n\n");
print LMAIL ("My message:\n $in{Message}\n\n");
print LMAIL ("Would I like a reply?\n $in{Reply}\n\n");

print LMAIL ("\n.\n");

############################################################
# Email received by the user confirming form submission #
############################################################

# ***********************************************
# Here's where you MUST specify the path to your
# email program ON your Web server.
# Replace /usr/sbin/sendmail with your path.
# ***********************************************

open (MAIL, "|/usr/sbin/sendmail -t");

# ***********************************************
# Here's where you MAY customize the email
# response to the user. You may change any wording
# on the form.
# ***********************************************

print MAIL<<toEnd;
To: $in{CampusEmail}
From: $in{LibraryEmail}
Subject: $in{Form}

Thanks for sending us your comments and suggestions.\n\n
We are always looking for new ideas and ways we can make the library better!

toEnd
   print MAIL ("\n.\n");

############################################################
# Screen response to user after submitting the form  #
############################################################

print ("<html><head><title>$in{Form}</title></head>");
```

```
print ("<body bgcolor=\"ffffff\">");

# ************************************************
# Here's where you MAY change the screen response
# the user sees after submitting the form. You may
# change any wording between the quotation marks.
# ************************************************

print ("Thanks for sending us your comments and suggestions.<p>
We are always looking for new ideas and ways we can make the library better!");

# ************************************************
# Here's where you MAY change the name of the link
# back to your main page. You may replace Return
# to our main page with your own wording.
# ************************************************

print ("<p><center><a href=$in{LibraryURL}>Return to our main page.</a></center>");
print ("</body></html>");
```

Complete Citation Request

If you need a complete citation for a book or journal / newspaper article and are having trouble locating all the required information, fill in the information you already have on the form below. We'll do our best to send you a completed citation with 48 hours. (Weekend requests may take longer.)

Name (last, first middle)

Department / Major

Campus address

Campus e-mail

Campus phone

Fax / Other phone

Status

- ○ Freshman
- ○ Sophomore
- ○ Junior
- ○ Senior
- ○ Grad Student
- ○ Faculty
- ○ Staff
- ○ Other

Fill in the information you already have.

Title

Author / Editor / Artist (last, first)

Edition

ISBN number

Publisher

Date of publication

If a Journal / Newspaper article also include...

Journal / Newspaper title

Issue date

Volume number

Issue number

ISSN number

The above information was cited in / by...

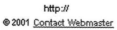

I need it before (specify date)

⊙ Anytime is fine

Send Request

Clear Form

http://

Complete Citation Request — HTML Form

```
<html>
<head><title>Complete Citation Request</title></head>
<body bgcolor="#FFFFFF">
<table width="700" border="0" height="85" bgcolor="#000000">
<tr valign="middle" align="center"><td>
<p>
<font halign=center color="#FFFFFF" face="Arial, Helvetica, sans-serif" size="+3"><b><i>Complete Citation
Request</i></b></font></p>
</td></tr></table>
<form method="post" action="http://www.yourLibrary.edu/cgi-bin/arg6.pl"><p> </p>
<p>
<font face="Arial, Helvetica, sans-serif" size="2"><b>If you need a complete citation for a book or journal /
newspaper article and are having trouble locating <br>all the required information, fill in the information you
already have on the form below. We'll do our best <br>to send you a completed citation with 48 hours. (Weekend
requests may take longer.)</b></font></p>
<p> </p>
<input type="hidden" name="LibraryEmail" value="you@yourLibrary.edu">
<input type="hidden" name="LibraryURL" value="http://www.yourLibrary.edu">
<input type="hidden" name="Form" value="InterLibrary Loan Request">
<p></p>
<table width="500" border="0" cellspacing="4" cellpadding="1">
<tr><td width="257">
<b><font face="Arial, Helvetica, sans-serif" size="2">Name </font></b><font face="Arial, Helvetica, sans-
serif" size="1"> (last, first middle)</font><br><font face="Arial, Helvetica, sans-serif" size="2"><input
type="text" name="Name" size="25"></font></td>
<td width="227">
<b><font face="Arial, Helvetica, sans-serif" size="2">Department / Major<br></font></b><font face="Arial,
Helvetica, sans-serif" size="2"><input type="text" name="Department" size="25"></font> </td></tr>
<tr><td width="257">
<b><font face="Arial, Helvetica, sans-serif" size="2">Campus address<br></font></b><font face="Arial,
Helvetica, sans-serif" size="2"><input type="text" name="CampusAddress" size="25"></font></td>
 <td width="227">
<b><font face="Arial, Helvetica, sans-serif" size="2">Campus e-mail<br></font></b><font face="Arial, Helvetica,
sans-serif" size="2"><input type="text" name="CampusEmail" size="25"></font></td></tr>
<tr><td width="257">
<b><font face="Arial, Helvetica, sans-serif" size="2">Campus phone</font></b><br><font face="Arial, Helvetica,
sans-serif" size="2"><input type="text" name="CampusPhone" size="25"></font></td>
<td width="227">
<b><font face="Arial, Helvetica, sans-serif" size="2">Fax / Other phone<br></font></b><font face="Arial,
Helvetica, sans-serif" size="2"><input type="text" name="OtherPhone" size="25"></font></td></tr>
</table>
<p>
<b><font face="Arial, Helvetica, sans-serif" size="2">Status</font></b><table width="550" border="0"
```

cellspacing="0" cellpadding="0">
<tr><td width="126" height="13">
<font face="Arial, Helvetica, sans-serif" size="2"><input type="radio" name="Status"
value="Freshman">Freshman</font></td>
<td width="117" height="13">
<font face="Arial, Helvetica, sans-serif" size="2"><input type="radio" name="Status"
value="Sophomore">Sophomore</font></td>
<td width="87" height="13">
<font face="Arial, Helvetica, sans-serif" size="2"><input type="radio" name="Status"
value="Junior">Junior</font></td>
<td width="202" height="13">
<font face="Arial, Helvetica, sans-serif" size="2"><input type="radio" name="Status"
value="Senior">Senior</font></td></tr>
<tr><td width="126" height="9">
<font face="Arial, Helvetica, sans-serif" size="2"><input type="radio" name="Status"
value="Graduate Student">Grad Student</font></td>
<td width="117" height="9">
<font face="Arial, Helvetica, sans-serif" size="2"><input type="radio" name="Status"
value="Faculty">Faculty</font></td>
<td width="87" height="9">
<font face="Arial, Helvetica, sans-serif" size="2"><input type="radio" name="Status"
value="Staff">Staff</font></td>
<td width="202" height="9">
<font face="Arial, Helvetica, sans-serif" size="2"><input type="radio" name="Status"
value="Other">Other</font></td></tr></table>

<p>
<font face="Arial, Helvetica, sans-serif" size="3"><b>Fill in the information you already have. </b></font></p>
<p>
<font face="Arial, Helvetica, sans-serif" size="2"><b>Title</b>
<font size="3"><input type="text"
name="Title" size="40"></font></font></p>
<p>
<font face="Arial, Helvetica, sans-serif" size="2"><b>Author / Editor / Artist </b> <font
size="1">(last, first)</font>
<font size="3"><input type="text" name="Author" size="40"></font></font>
</p><table width="209" border="0">
<tr><td width="92">
<font face="Arial, Helvetica, sans-serif" size="2"><b>Edition</b>
<font size="3"><input type="text"
name="Edition" size="10"></font></font></td>
<td width="107">
<font face="Arial, Helvetica, sans-serif" size="2"><b>ISBN number</b>
<font size="3"><input type="text"
name="ISBN" size="10"></font></font></td></tr></table>
<p>
<font face="Arial, Helvetica, sans-serif" size="2"><b>Publisher </b>
<font size="3"><input type="text"
name="Publisher" size="40"></font></font></p>
<p>
<font face="Arial, Helvetica, sans-serif" size="2"><b>Date of publication</b>
<font size="3"><input

type="text" name="PublisherDate" size="40"></font></font></p>
<p> </p>
<p>
<font face="Arial, Helvetica, sans-serif" size="3"><b>If a Journal / Newspaper article also include...
</b></font></p>
<p>
<font face="Arial, Helvetica, sans-serif" size="2"><b>Journal / Newspaper title</b>
<font size="3">
<input type="text" name="MagName" size="40"></font></font></p>
<table width="600" border="0" cellspacing="0" cellpadding="0">
<tr><td width="117" height="11">
<font face="Arial, Helvetica, sans-serif" size="2"><b>Issue date</b>
<font size="3"><input type="text"
name="IssueDate" size="10"></font></font></td>
<td width="120" height="11">
<font face="Arial, Helvetica, sans-serif" size="2"><b>Volume number</b>
<font size="3"><input type="text"
name="VolNum" size="10"></font></font></td>
<td width="102" height="11">
<font face="Arial, Helvetica, sans-serif" size="2"><font face="Arial, Helvetica, sans-serif" size="2"> <b>Issue
number </b>
<font size="3"><input type="text" name="IssueNum" size="10"></font></font></font></td>
<td width="261" height="11">
<font face="Arial, Helvetica, sans-serif" size="2"><b>ISSN number</b>
<font size="3"><input type="text"
name="ISSN" size="10"></font></font></td></tr></table>
<p> </p>
<p>
<font face="Arial, Helvetica, sans-serif" size="2"><b>The above information was cited in / by...
</b><font
face="Arial, Helvetica, sans-serif" size="3"><textarea name= "Cited" cols="40" rows="2"> </textarea></font>
</font>
</p>
<p>
<font face="Arial, Helvetica, sans-serif" size="2"><b>I need it before </b><font face="Arial, Helvetica,
sans-serif" size="1"> (specify date)</font>
<font size="3"><input type="text" name="NeedBefore"
size="15">   </font>
<input type="radio" name="TimeIssue" value="Time is not an issue">Anytime is fine</font></p>
<p> </p>
<table width="700" border="0" cellspacing="10" cellpadding="1"><tr><td width="249">
<div align="right"><input type="submit" name="send" value="Send Request"></div></td>
<td width="198"> </td><td width="207">
<div align="left"><input type="reset" name="clear" value="Clear Form"></div></td></tr>
<tr colspan=3><td colspan=3>
<table width="500" border="0" height="2" align="center" cellpadding="0" cellspacing="0"
bgcolor="#000000"><tr><td><font size="1" color="#000000">.</font></td></tr></table>
</td></tr>
<tr><td colspan=3><div align="center">
<font face="Arial, Helvetica, sans-serif" size="1"><b>http://</b></font>
<font size="2">
<font face="Arial, Helvetica, sans-serif" size="1"><b>© 2001</b></font></font>
<font face="Arial, Helvetica, sans-serif" size="2"><a href="mailto:">
<b><font size="1">Contact Webmaster</font></b></a> </font></div></td></tr>
</table></form>

```
</body>
</html>
```

Complete Citation Request — Perl Script

```perl
#!/usr/local/bin/perl


# ***************************************************
# ABOVE is where you MUST specify the path to your
# perl interpreter on your Web server.
# Replace /usr/local/bin/perl with your path.
# ***************************************************


if ($ENV{'REQUEST_METHOD'}eq"GET"){$buffer = $ENV{'QUERY_STRING'};}
     elsif($ENV{'REQUEST_METHOD'}eq"POST"){
         read(STDIN,$buffer,$ENV{'CONTENT_LENGTH'});
     }
$bufferb = $buffer;
#separate the name of the input from its value.
@forminputs = split(/&/, $bufferb);

foreach $forminput (@forminputs)
{
     #separate the name of the input from its value
     ($name, $value) = split(/=/, $forminput);

     #Un-Webify plus signs and %-encoding
     $value =~ tr/+/ /;
     $value =~ s/%([a-fA-F0-9][a-fA-F0-9])/pack("C", hex($1))/eg;

     #stick them in the in array
     $in{$name} = $value;
}
print "Content-type: text/html\n\n";


###############################################################
# ABOVE is the required header for a perl script          #
###############################################################


###################################################################
# (Below) Email received by library containing user-entered information #
###################################################################


# ***********************************************
# Here's where you MUST specify the path to your
# email program (probably sendmail) ON your Web server.
# Replace /usr/sbin/sendmail with your path.
# ***********************************************
```

```
open (LMAIL, "I/usr/sbin/sendmail -t");
print LMAIL ("To: $in{LibraryEmail}\n");
print LMAIL ("From: $in{CampusEmail}\n");
print LMAIL ("Subject: $in{Form} - patron submission\n");

print LMAIL ("------------------\nPatron information\n\n");
print LMAIL ("Name:\n $in{Name}\n\n");
print LMAIL ("Department / Major:\n $in{Department}\n\n");
print LMAIL ("Campus Address:\n $in{CampusAddress}\n\n");
print LMAIL ("Campus Email:\n $in{CampusEmail}\n\n");
print LMAIL ("Campus Phone:\n $in{CampusPhone}\n\n");
print LMAIL ("Other Phone:\n $in{OtherPhone}\n\n");
print LMAIL ("Status:\n $in{Status}\n\n");

print LMAIL ("------------------\nSubmitted information \n\n");

print LMAIL ("Title:\n $in{Title}\n\n");
print LMAIL ("Author / Editor / Artist:\n $in{Author}\n\n");
print LMAIL ("Edition:\n $in{Edition}\n\n");
print LMAIL ("ISBN number:\n $in{ISBN}\n\n");
print LMAIL ("Publisher:\n $in{Publisher}\n\n");
print LMAIL ("Date of publication:\n $in{PublisherDate}\n\n");

print LMAIL ("Journal / Newspaper\n");
print LMAIL ("Journal / Newspaper title:\n $in{MagName}\n\n");
print LMAIL ("Issue date:\n $in{IssueDate}\n\n");
print LMAIL ("Volume number:\n $in{VolNum}\n\n");
print LMAIL ("Issue number:\n $in{IssueNum}\n\n");
print LMAIL ("ISSN number:\n $in{ISSN}\n\n");
print LMAIL ("The above information was cited in:\n $in{Cited}\n\n");
print LMAIL ("I need it before:\n $in{NeedBefore} $in{TimeIssue}\n\n");
print LMAIL ("\n.\n");

##################################################
# Email received by the user confirming form submission #
##################################################

# ***********************************************
# Here's where you MUST specify the path to your
# email program ON your Web server.
# Replace /usr/sbin/sendmail with your path.
# ***********************************************
```

```
open (MAIL, "|/usr/sbin/sendmail -t");


# ***********************************************
# Here's where you MAY customize the email
# response to the user. You may change any wording
# on the form.
# ***********************************************


print MAIL<<toEnd;
To: $in{CampusEmail}
From: $in{LibraryEmail}
Subject: $in{Form}

Thanks for sending us your complete citation request.\n\n
We'll do our best to send you a completed citation within 48 hours.
toEnd
    print MAIL ("\n.\n");


####################################################
# Screen response to user after submitting the form  #
####################################################


print ("<html><head><title>$in{Form}</title></head>");
print ("<body bgcolor=\"ffffff\">");


# ***********************************************
# Here's where you MAY change the screen response
# the user sees after submitting the form. You may
# change any wording between the quotation marks.
# ***********************************************


print ("Thanks for sending us your complete citation request.<p>
We'll do our best to send you a completed citation within 48 hours.");


# ***********************************************
# Here's where you MAY change the name of the link
# back to your main page. You may replace Return
# to our main page with your own wording.
# ***********************************************


print ("<p><center><a href=$in{LibraryURL}>Return to our main page.</a></center>");
print ("</body></html>");
```

Group 2 — Library Instruction Forms / Surveys

In this section you'll find two Web-based forms. One lets faculty and staff request a face-to-face meeting with library staff in order to get help with research projects and/or class assignments. The other lets faculty members and teaching assistants e-mail requests to library staff regarding class-related library instruction sessions. The survey will enable patrons to give your staff feedback on the current library instruction sessions and programs you offer and input on new instruction sessions and programs that patrons want and need.

Meet With a Librarian

Do students need help with class assignments? Do faculty members and grad students need help with research projects? Patrons can use this form to arrange, via e-mail or phone, to meet with you or another librarian at a mutually agreeable time. Make sure to place a link to this form on you Web site's reference page.

Library Instruction / Program Survey

Encourage students, faculty, and staff to fill out this brief survey to help you get an idea of how effective your current library instruction sessions and programs are. You'll also be able to find out any new programs and sessions that patrons would like you to develop and when they'd like them offered. Finally, you can find out how patrons learn about currently offered programs/classes as well as how you can notify them of such opportunities in the future. Place a link to this survey periodically on your Web site's library instruction and programs pages.

Library Instruction Request form

Make it easy for faculty and teaching assistants to ask library staff members to speak to their classes, present subject-related research instruction, or provide any other type of library instruction. Post this form on your library's homepage so that faculty can simply e-mail you a request.

Meet With a Librarian

Do you need help with course assignments, papers, and research projects? We'll arrange, via e-mail or phone, to meet with you at a mutually agreeable time.

Name (last, first middle)

Department / Major

Campus address

Campus e-mail

Campus phone

Fax / Other phone

Status

- ○ Freshman
- ○ Sophomore
- ○ Junior
- ○ Senior
- ○ Grad Student
- ○ Faculty
- ○ Staff
- ○ Other

Date / Time (list 3 date / time options)

Date	Time	to
Date	Time	to
Date	Time	to

We need to meet before (specify date)

○ Any time is fine

Reason for the meeting (please provide as many details as you can)

What library resources have you already checked / used? (select all that apply)

- ○ Online catalog
- ○ Reference materials
- ○ Books
- ○ Journal articles
- ○ Newspaper articles
- ○ Online databases
- ○ CD-ROMs
- ○ Web sites
- ○ Other (please specify)

Send Request

Clear Form

http://

Meet With a Librarian — HTML Form

```
<html>
<head><title>Meet With a Librarian</title></head>
<body bgcolor="#FFFFFF">
<table width="700" border="0" height="85" bgcolor="#000000"><tr valign="middle" align="center"> <td>
<p>
<font halign=center color="#FFFFFF" face="Arial, Helvetica, sans-serif" size="+3">
<b><i>Meet With a Librarian</i></b></font></p>
</td></tr></table>
<form method="post" action="http://www.yourLibrary.edu/cgi-bin/ali1.pl"><p> </p>
<p>
<font face="Arial, Helvetica, sans-serif" size="2"><b>Do you need help with course assignments, papers, and
research projects? We'll arrange, via</b></font><font face="Arial, Helvetica, sans-serif" size="2"><b>
e-mail <br>or phone, to meet with you at a mutually agreeable time.</b></font></p>
<p> </p>
<input type="hidden" name="LibraryEmail" value="you@yourLibrary.edu">
<input type="hidden" name="LibraryURL" value="http://www.yourLibrary.edu">
<input type="hidden" name="Form" value="Meet With a Librarian"><p></p>
<p></p>
<table width="500" border="0" cellspacing="4" cellpadding="1">
<tr><td width="257">
<b><font face="Arial, Helvetica, sans-serif" size="2">Name </font></b><font face="Arial, Helvetica, sans-
serif" size="1"> (last, first middle)</font><br><font face="Arial, Helvetica, sans-serif" size="2"><input
type="text" name="Name" size="25"></font></td>
<td width="227">
<b><font face="Arial, Helvetica, sans-serif" size="2">Department / Major<br></font></b><font face="Arial,
Helvetica, sans-serif" size="2"><input type="text" name="Department" size="25"></font> </td></tr>
<tr><td width="257">
<b><font face="Arial, Helvetica, sans-serif" size="2">Campus address<br></font></b><font face="Arial,
Helvetica, sans-serif" size="2"><input type="text" name="CampusAddress" size="25"></font></td>
<td width="227">
<b><font face="Arial, Helvetica, sans-serif" size="2">Campus e-mail<br></font></b><font face="Arial, Helvetica,
sans-serif" size="2"><input type="text" name="CampusEmail" size="25"></font></td></tr>
<tr><td width="257">
<b><font face="Arial, Helvetica, sans-serif" size="2">Campus phone</font></b><br><font face="Arial, Helvetica,
sans-serif" size="2"><input type="text" name="CampusPhone" size="25"></font></td>
<td width="227">
<b><font face="Arial, Helvetica, sans-serif" size="2">Fax / Other phone<br></font></b><font face="Arial,
Helvetica, sans-serif" size="2"><input type="text" name="OtherPhone" size="25"></font></td></tr>
</table>
<p>
<b><font face="Arial, Helvetica, sans-serif" size="2">Status</font></b><table width="550" border="0"
cellspacing="0" cellpadding="0">
<tr><td width="126" height="13">
```

```
<font face="Arial, Helvetica, sans-serif" size="2"><input type="radio" name="Status"
 value="Freshman">Freshman</font></td>
<td width="117" height="13">
<font face="Arial, Helvetica, sans-serif" size="2"><input type="radio" name="Status"
value="Sophomore">Sophomore</font></td>
<td width="87" height="13">
<font face="Arial, Helvetica, sans-serif" size="2"><input type="radio" name="Status"
value="Junior">Junior</font></td>
<td width="202" height="13">
<font face="Arial, Helvetica, sans-serif" size="2"><input type="radio" name="Status"
value="Senior">Senior</font></td></tr>
<tr><td width="126" height="9">
<font face="Arial, Helvetica, sans-serif" size="2"><input type="radio" name="Status"
value="Graduate Student">Grad Student</font></td>
<td width="117" height="9">
<font face="Arial, Helvetica, sans-serif" size="2"><input type="radio" name="Status"
value="Faculty">Faculty</font></td>
<td width="87" height="9">
<font face="Arial, Helvetica, sans-serif" size="2"><input type="radio" name="Status"
value="Staff">Staff</font></td>
<td width="202" height="9">
<font face="Arial, Helvetica, sans-serif" size="2"><input type="radio" name="Status"
value="Other">Other</font></td></tr></table>
<p>
<b><font face="Arial, Helvetica, sans-serif" size="2">Date / Time </font></b><font face="Arial, Helvetica,
sans-serif" size="1"> (list 3 date / time options)</font><br>
<font face="Arial, Helvetica, sans-serif" size="2">Date</font><font size="3"><font face="Arial, Helvetica, sans-
serif"><input type="text" name="Date1" size="15"></font>     
<font face="Arial, Helvetica, sans-serif" size="2">Time</font><font face="Arial, Helvetica, sans-serif"><input
type="text" name="TimeBegin1" size="10"><font size="2">to</font><input type="text" name="TimeEnd1"
size="10"><br>
<font face="Arial, Helvetica, sans-serif" size="2">Date</font><font size="3"><font face="Arial, Helvetica, sans-
serif"><input type="text" name="Date2" size="15"></font>       <font face="Arial,
Helvetica, sans-serif" size="2">Time</font><font face="Arial, Helvetica, sans-serif"><input type="text"
name="TimeBegin2" size="10"><font size="2">to</font><input type="text" name="TimeEnd2" size="10"
</font></font><br></font>
<font face="Arial, Helvetica, sans-serif" size="2">Date</font><font size="3"><font face="Arial, Helvetica, sans-
serif"><input type="text" name="Date3" size="15"></font>     
<font face="Arial, Helvetica, sans-serif" size="2">Time</font><font face="Arial, Helvetica, sans-serif">
<input type="text" name="TimeBegin3" size="10"><font size="2">to</font><input type="text"
name="TimeEnd3" size="10"></font></font></font></p>
<p>
<font face="Arial, Helvetica, sans-serif" size="2"> <b>We need to meet before<font size="1">  </font></b>
<font face="Arial, Helvetica, sans-serif" size="1"> (specify date)</font><br><font size="3" face="Arial,
Helvetica, sans-serif"><input type="text" name="MeetBefore" size="15"></font>
```

     <font face="Arial, Helvetica, sans-serif" size="2"><input type="radio" name="TimeIssue" value="Time is not an issue">Any time is fine</font></font></p><font face="Arial, Helvetica, sans-serif" size="2">
<p>
<b><font face="Arial, Helvetica, sans-serif" size="2">Reason for the meeting </font></b><font face="Arial, Helvetica, sans-serif" size="1"> (please provide as many details as you can)</font>
<font face="Arial, Helvetica, sans-serif" size="3"><textarea name="Reason4Meeting" cols="40" rows="10"></textarea></font>
</p>
<p>
<b><font face="Arial, Helvetica, sans-serif" size="2">What library resources have you already checked / used? </font></b><font face="Arial, Helvetica, sans-serif" size="1"> (select all that apply)</font>
</font><table width="550" border="0" cellspacing="0" cellpadding="0">
<tr><td width="154">
<font face="Arial, Helvetica, sans-serif" size="2"><input type="radio" name="OC" value="Online catalog">
Online catalog</font></td>
<td width="157">
<font face="Arial, Helvetica, sans-serif" size="2"><input type="radio" name="RM" value="Reference materials">Reference materials</font></td>
<td width="102">
<font face="Arial, Helvetica, sans-serif" size="2"><input type="radio" name="B" value="Books">
Books</font></td>
<td width="137">
<font face="Arial, Helvetica, sans-serif" size="2"><input type="radio" name="MNA" value="Journal atricles">Journal articles</font></td></tr>
<tr><td width="154">
<font face="Arial, Helvetica, sans-serif" size="2"><input type="radio" name="MNA" value="Newspaper atricles">Newspaper articles</font></td>
<td width="157">
<font face="Arial, Helvetica, sans-serif" size="2"><input type="radio" name="OID" value="Online indexes / databases">Online databases</font></td>
<td width="102">
<font face="Arial, Helvetica, sans-serif" size="2"><input type="radio" name="CD" value="CDROMs">
CD-ROMs</font></td>
<td width="137">
<font face="Arial, Helvetica, sans-serif" size="2"><input type="radio" name="WS" value="WebSites">
Web sites</font></td></tr>
<tr><td colspan="3">
<font face="Arial, Helvetica, sans-serif" size="2"><input type="radio" name="O" value="Other">
Other   <font face="Arial, Helvetica, sans-serif" size="1">(please specify)</font>   <font size="3"><input type="text" name="OtherMatUsed" size="10"></font></font></td>
<td width="137"> </td></tr></table>
<p> </p>
<font face="Arial, Helvetica, sans-serif" size="2"><table width="700" border="0" cellspacing="10" cellpadding="1"><tr><td width="242">
<div align="right"><input type="submit" name="send" value="Send Request"></div></td>

```
<td width="205"> </td><td width="207">
<div align="left"><input type="reset" name="clear" value="Clear Form"></div></td></tr>
<tr colspan=3><td colspan=3>
<table width="500" border="0" height="2" align="center" cellpadding="0" cellspacing="0"
bgcolor="#000000"><tr><td><font size="1" color="#000000">.</font></td></tr></table>
</td></tr>
<tr><td colspan=3><div align="center">
<font face="Arial, Helvetica, sans-serif" size="1"><b>http://</b></font><br><font size="2"> 
<font face="Arial, Helvetica, sans-serif" size="1"><b>&copy; 2001</b></font></font>
<font face="Arial, Helvetica, sans-serif" size="2"><a href="mailto:">
<b><font size="1">Contact Webmaster</font></b></a></font></div></td></tr>
</table></font></form>
</body>
</html>
```

Meet With a Librarian — Perl Script

```perl
#!/usr/local/bin/perl

# *************************************************
# ABOVE is where you MUST specify the path to your
# perl interpreter on your Web server.
# Replace /usr/local/bin/perl with your path.
# *************************************************

if ($ENV{'REQUEST_METHOD'}eq"GET"){$buffer = $ENV{'QUERY_STRING'};}
     elsif($ENV{'REQUEST_METHOD'}eq"POST"){
         read(STDIN,$buffer,$ENV{'CONTENT_LENGTH'});
     }
$bufferb = $buffer;
#separate the name of the input from its value.
@forminputs = split(/&/, $bufferb);

foreach $forminput (@forminputs)
{
     #separate the name of the input from its value
     ($name, $value) = split(/=/, $forminput);

     #Un-Webify plus signs and %-encoding
     $value =~ tr/+/ /;
     $value =~ s/%([a-fA-F0-9][a-fA-F0-9])/pack("C", hex($1))/eg;

     #stick them in the in array
     $in{$name} = $value;
}
print "Content-type: text/html\n\n";

#############################################################
# ABOVE is the required header for a perl script         #
#############################################################


################################################################
# (Below) Email received by library containing user-entered information #
################################################################


# *************************************************
# Here's where you MUST specify the path to your
# email program (probably sendmail) ON your Web server.
# Replace /usr/sbin/sendmail with your path.
# *************************************************
```

```
open (LMAIL, "I/usr/sbin/sendmail -t");
print LMAIL ("To: $in{LibraryEmail}\n");

print LMAIL ("From: $in{CampusEmail}\n");
print LMAIL ("Subject: $in{Form} - patron submission\n");

print LMAIL ("------------------\nPatron information\n\n");
print LMAIL ("Name:\n $in{Name}\n\n");
print LMAIL ("Department / Major:\n $in{Department}\n\n");
print LMAIL ("Campus Address:\n $in{CampusAddress}\n\n");
print LMAIL ("Campus Email:\n $in{CampusEmail}\n\n");
print LMAIL ("Campus Phone:\n $in{CampusPhone}\n\n");
print LMAIL ("Other Phone:\n $in{OtherPhone}\n\n");
print LMAIL ("Status:\n $in{Status}\n\n");

print LMAIL ("------------------\nSubmitted information \n\n");

print LMAIL ("First date / time to meet:\n $in{Date1}\n $in{TimeBegin1} to $in{TimeEnd1}\n\n");
print LMAIL ("Second date / time to meet:\n $in{Date2}\n $in{TimeBegin2} to $in{TimeEnd2}\n\n");
print LMAIL ("Third date / time to meet:\n $in{Date3}\n $in{TimeBegin3} to $in{TimeEnd3}\n\n");
print LMAIL ("I need to meet before:\n $in{MeetBefore} $in{TimeIssue}\n\n");
print LMAIL ("Reason for meeting:\n $in{Reason4Meet}\n\n");
print LMAIL ("Sources I have already checked:\n ");
print LMAIL ("$in{OC}, $in{RM}, $in{B}, $in{JA}, $in{NA}, $in{OD}, $in{CD}, $in{WS}, $in{O},
${OtherMatUsed}\n\n");

print LMAIL ("\n.\n");


##########################################################
# Email received by the user confirming form submission #
##########################################################


# ************************************************
# Here's where you MUST specify the path to your
# email program ON your Web server.
# Replace /usr/sbin/sendmail with your path.
# ************************************************

open (MAIL, "I/usr/sbin/sendmail -t");

# ************************************************
# Here's where you MAY customize the email
# response to the user. You may change any wording
# on the form.
# ************************************************
```

```
print MAIL<<toEnd;
To: $in{CampusEmail}
From: $in{LibraryEmail}
Subject: $in{Form}

Thanks for wanting to set up a meeting with one of our librarians.\n\n
A librarian will contact you in the next couple of days to set up an appointment.

toEnd
    print MAIL ("\n.\n");


######################################################
# Screen response to user after submitting the form  #
######################################################


print ("<html><head><title>$in{Form}</title></head>");
print ("<body bgcolor=\"ffffff\">");


# ************************************************
# Here's where you MAY change the screen response
# the user sees after submitting the form. You may
# change any wording between the quotation marks.
# ************************************************


print ("Thanks for wanting to set up a meeting with one of our librarians.<p>
A librarian will contact you in the next couple of days to set up an appointment.");


# ************************************************
# Here's where you MAY change the name of the link
# back to your main page. You may replace Return
# to our main page with your own wording.
# ************************************************


print ("<p><center><a href=$in{LibraryURL}>Return to our main page.</a></center>");
print ("</body></html>");
```

Library Instruction / Program Survey

Please complete this brief survey to help us get an idea how effective our library instruction sessions and programs are. Please tell us about any new instruction sessions or programs and training sessions you'd like us to develop and when you'd like us to offer them. Finally, we'd like to know how you learn about currently offered instruction sessions / programs and how we should notify you about them in the future.

Library Instruction Sessions

Have you attended any library instruction sessions? ○ Yes ○ No

    If yes, how many have you attended? [____]

Which one session was the *most* useful / interesting / effective?

[_____]

What new / additional library instruction sessions would you like to see us offer?

[_____]

What is the most convenient day / time for instruction sessions?

[_____]

What types of training do you prefer? (select all that apply)

○ Instructor-led classes   ○ One-on-one sessions   ○ Web-based tutorials

○ Printed help sheets / manuals   ○ Audio / video-based lessons   ○ Other

Instruction Session / Program Awareness

How do you *currently* find out about library instruction sessions / programs?

○ Library newsletter   ○ Library bulletin boards   ○ Community posters   ○ Library Web site

○ Other (specify) [_____]

How would you like to find out about *future* library instruction sessions / programs?

○ Email message   ○ Electronic bulletin board   ○ Community Web sites   ○ Library Web site

○ Other (specify) [_____]

Programs

Have you attended any programs presented by the library? ○ Yes ○ No

    If yes, how many have you attended? [____]

Which one program was the most useful / interesting / effective?

[   ]

What new / additional programs would you like to see us offer?

[   ]

What is the most convenient day / time for library programs?

[   ]

Name (last, first middle)

[   ]

Department / Major

[   ]

Campus e-mail

[   ]

Campus phone

[   ]

Status

○ Freshman   ○ Sophomore   ○ Junior   ○ Senior

○ Grad Student   ○ Faculty   ○ Staff   ○ Other

[Send Survey]   [Clear Survey]

Library Instruction / Program Survey — HTML Form

```
<html>
<head><title>Library Instruction / Program Survey</title></head>
<body bgcolor="#FFFFFF">
<table width="700" border="0" height="85" bgcolor="#000000">
<tr valign="middle" align="center"><td>
<p>
<font halign=center color="#FFFFFF" face="Arial, Helvetica, sans-serif" size="+3"><b><i>Library Instruction /
Program Survey</i></b></font></p>
</td></tr></table>
<form method="post" action="http://www.yourLibrary.edu/cgi-bin/ali3.pl"><p> </p>
<p>
<font face="Arial, Helvetica, sans-serif" size="2"><b>Please complete this brief survey to help us get an idea how
effective our library instruction sessions <br>and programs are. Please tell us about any new instruction sessions
or programs and training sessions <br>you'd like us to develop and when you'd like us to offer them. Finally, we'd
like to know how you learn about <br>currently offered instruction sessions / programs and how we should notify
you about them in the future.</b></font></p>
<p> </p>
<input type="hidden" name="LibraryEmail" value="you@yourLibrary.edu">
<input type="hidden" name="LibraryURL" value="http://www.yourLibrary.edu">
<input type="hidden" name="Form" value="Program / Training Survey">
<p>
<b><font face="Arial, Helvetica, sans-serif" size="3">Library Instruction Sessions</font></b></p>
<p>
<font face="Arial, Helvetica, sans-serif" size="2"><b>Have you attended any library instruction sessions?
</b> 
<input type="radio" name="TrainingAttend" value="Yes">Yes  
<input type="radio" name="TrainingAttend" value="No">No<br>      </font>
<font face="Arial, Helvetica, sans-serif" size="2"><b>If yes, how many have you attended?  </b> <font
size="3"><input type="text" name="HowManyTrain" size="5"></font></font></p>
<p>
<b><font face="Arial, Helvetica, sans-serif" size="2">Which one session was the <i>most</i> useful / interesting
/ effective?   <br></font></b><font face="Arial, Helvetica, sans-serif" size="3"> <input type="text"
name="UsefulTrain" size="40"></font></p>
<p>
<b><font face="Arial, Helvetica, sans-serif" size="2">What new / additional library instruction sessions would you
like to see us offer?<br></font></b><font face="Arial, Helvetica, sans-serif" size="3"><textarea
name="AdditionalTrain" cols="40" rows="2"></textarea></font></p>
<p>
<b><font face="Arial, Helvetica, sans-serif" size="2">What is the most convenient day / time for instruction
sessions?   <br></font></b><font face="Arial, Helvetica, sans-serif" size="3">
<input type="text" name="TrainDayTime" size="40"></font></p>
<p>
<font face="Arial, Helvetica, sans-serif" size="2"><b>What types of training do you prefer?
```

```
</b>   <font size="1">(select all that apply)</font><br></font>
<table width="600" border="0" cellspacing="0" cellpadding="0"><tr><td width="216" height="3">
<font face="Arial, Helvetica, sans-serif" size="2"><input type="radio" name="ILC" value="Instructor-led
classes">Instructor-led classes</font></td>
<td width="199" height="3">
<font face="Arial, Helvetica, sans-serif" size="2"><input type="radio" name="OOOS" value="One-on-one
sessions">One-on-one sessions</font></td>
<td width="185" height="3">
<font face="Arial, Helvetica, sans-serif" size="2"><input type="radio" name="WBT" value="Web-based
tutorials">Web-based tutorials</font></td></tr>
<tr><td width="216">
<font face="Arial, Helvetica, sans-serif" size="2"><input type="radio" name="PHSM" value="Printed help sheets
/ manuals">Printed help sheets / manuals</font></td>
<td width="199">
<font face="Arial, Helvetica, sans-serif" size="2"><input type="radio" name="AVBL" value="Audio / video-based
lessons">Audio / video-based lessons</font></td>
<td width="185">
<font face="Arial, Helvetica, sans-serif" size="2"><input type="radio" name="O" value="Other">
Other</font></td></tr></table>
<p> </p>
<p>
<b><font face="Arial, Helvetica, sans-serif" size="3">Instruction Session / Program Awareness</font> </b></p>
<p>
<font face="Arial, Helvetica, sans-serif" size="2"><b>How do you <i>currently</i> find out about library instruc-
tion sessions / programs?</b> <br>
<input type="radio" name="Currently" value="Library newsletter">Library newsletter   
<input type="radio" name="Currently" value="Library bulletin boards">Library bulletin boards   
<input type="radio" name="Currently" value="Community posters">Community posters   
<input type="radio" name="Currently" value="Library Web site">Library Web site<br>
<input type="radio" name="Currently" value="Other">Other   <font size="1">
(specify )</font><font size="3">   <input type="text" name="CurrentlyOther" size="10"></font> </font>
</p>
<p>
<font face="Arial, Helvetica, sans-serif" size="2"><b>How would you like to find out about <i>future</i> library
instruction sessions / programs?<br>
<input type="radio" name="Future" value="Email message"></b>Email message  
<input type="radio" name="Future" value="Electronic bulletin board">Electronic bulletin board   
<input type="radio" name="Future" value="Community Web sites">Community Web sites   
<input type="radio" name="Future" value="Library Web site">Library Web site<br>
<input type="radio" name="Future" value="Other">Other   <font size="1">(specify)
</font><font size="3">  <input type="text" name="FutureOther" size="10"></font></font></p>
<p> </p>
<p>
<b><font face="Arial, Helvetica, sans-serif" size="3">Programs</font></b></p>
<p>
```

```
<font face="Arial, Helvetica, sans-serif" size="2"><b>Have you attended any programs presented by the
library? 
<input type="radio" name="Attended" value="Yes"></b>Yes<b>  
<input type="radio" name="Attended" value="No"></b>No<br>      </font> <font
face="Arial, Helvetica, sans-serif" size="2"><b>If yes, how many have you attended?  </b> <font
size="3"><input type="text" name="HowMany2" size="5"></font></font></p>
<p>
<b><font face="Arial, Helvetica, sans-serif" size="2">Which one program was the most useful / interesting /
effective?   <br></font></b><font face="Arial, Helvetica, sans-serif" size="3"><input type="text"
name="MostUseful2" size="40"></font></p>
<p>
<b><font face="Arial, Helvetica, sans-serif" size="2">What new / additional programs would you like to see us
offer?<br></font></b><font face="Arial, Helvetica, sans-serif" size="3"><textarea name="textarea" cols="40"
rows="2"></textarea></font></p>
<p>
<b><font face="Arial, Helvetica, sans-serif" size="2">What is the most convenient day / time for library pro-
grams?   <br></font></b><font face="Arial, Helvetica, sans-serif" size="3"><input type="text"
name="ProgramDayTime2" size="40"></font></p>
<p> </p>
<p></p>
<table width="500" border="0" cellspacing="4" cellpadding="1"><tr>
<td width="257">
<b><font face="Arial, Helvetica, sans-serif" size="2">Name </font></b><font face="Arial, Helvetica, sans-
serif" size="2"> <font size="1">(last, first middle)</font></font><br><font face="Arial, Helvetica, sans-serif"
size="2"><input type="text" name="Name" size="25"></font></td>
<td width="227">
<b><font face="Arial, Helvetica, sans-serif" size="2">Department / Major<br></font></b><font face="Arial,
Helvetica, sans-serif" size="2"><input type="text" name="Department" size="25"></font> </td></tr>
<tr><td width="257">
<b><font face="Arial, Helvetica, sans-serif" size="2">Campus e-mail<br></font></b><font face="Arial, Helvetica,
sans-serif" size="2"><input type="text" name="CampusEmail" size="25"></font></td>
<td width="227">
<b><font face="Arial, Helvetica, sans-serif" size="2">Campus phone</font></b><br><font face="Arial, Helvetica,
sans-serif" size="2"><input type="text" name="CampusPhone2" size="25"></font></td></tr> </table>
<p>
<b><font face="Arial, Helvetica, sans-serif" size="2">Status</font></b><table width="550" border="0"
cellspacing="0" cellpadding="0">
<tr><td width="126" height="13">
<font face="Arial, Helvetica, sans-serif" size="2"><input type="radio" name="Status"
value="Freshman">Freshman</font></td>
<td width="117" height="13">
<font face="Arial, Helvetica, sans-serif" size="2"><input type="radio" name="Status"
value="Sophomore">Sophomore</font></td>
<td width="87" height="13">
<font face="Arial, Helvetica, sans-serif" size="2"><input type="radio" name="Status"
```

```
value="Junior">Junior</font></td>
<td width="202" height="13">
<font face="Arial, Helvetica, sans-serif" size="2"><input type="radio" name="Status"
value="Senior">Senior</font></td></tr>
<tr><td width="126" height="9">
<font face="Arial, Helvetica, sans-serif" size="2"><input type="radio" name="Status"
value="Graduate Student">Grad Student</font></td>
<td width="117" height="9">
<font face="Arial, Helvetica, sans-serif" size="2"><input type="radio" name="Status"
value="Faculty">Faculty</font></td>
<td width="87" height="9">
<font face="Arial, Helvetica, sans-serif" size="2"><input type="radio" name="Status"
value="Staff">Staff</font></td>
<td width="202" height="9">
<font face="Arial, Helvetica, sans-serif" size="2"><input type="radio" name="Status"
value="Other">Other</font></td></tr><table>
<p> </p>
<table width="700" border="0" cellspacing="10" cellpadding="1"><tr><td width="213">
<div align="right"><input type="submit" name="send" value="Send Survey"></div></td>
<td width="225"> </td>
<td width="216">
<div align="left"><input type="reset" name="clear" value="Clear Survey"></div></td></tr>
<tr colspan=3><td colspan=3><table width="500" border="0" height="2" align="center" cellpadding="0"
cellspacing="0" bgcolor="#000000"><tr><td><font size="1" color="#000000">.</font></td></tr>
</table></td></tr>
<tr><td colspan=3><div align="center">
<font face="Arial, Helvetica, sans-serif" size="1"><b>http://</b></font><br> 
<font face="Arial, Helvetica, sans-serif" size="1"><b>&copy; 2001</b></font>
<font face="Arial, Helvetica, sans-serif" size="2"><a href="mailto:">
<b><font size="1">Contact Webmaster</font></b></a></font></div></td></tr>
<table></form>
</body>
</html>
```

Library Instruction / Program Survey — Perl Script

```perl
#!/usr/local/bin/perl


# ************************************************
# ABOVE is where you MUST specify the path to your
# perl interpreter on your Web server.
# Replace /usr/local/bin/perl with your path.
# ************************************************


if ($ENV{'REQUEST_METHOD'}eq"GET"){$buffer = $ENV{'QUERY_STRING'};}
     elsif($ENV{'REQUEST_METHOD'}eq"POST"){
         read(STDIN,$buffer,$ENV{'CONTENT_LENGTH'});
     }
$bufferb = $buffer;
#separate the name of the input from its value.
@forminputs = split(/&/, $bufferb);

foreach $forminput (@forminputs)
{
     #separate the name of the input from its value
     ($name, $value) = split(/=/, $forminput);

     #Un-Webify plus signs and %-encoding
     $value =~ tr/+/ /;
     $value =~ s/%([a-fA-F0-9][a-fA-F0-9])/pack("C", hex($1))/eg;

     #stick them in the in array
     $in{$name} = $value;
}
print "Content-type: text/html\n\n";


############################################################
# ABOVE is the required header for a perl script           #
############################################################


##############################################################
# (Below) Email received by library containing user-entered information #
##############################################################


# ********************************************
# Here's where you MUST specify the path to your
# email program (probably sendmail) ON your Web server.
# Replace /usr/sbin/sendmail with your path.
# ********************************************
```

```
open (LMAIL, "I/usr/sbin/sendmail -t");
print LMAIL ("To: $in{LibraryEmail}\n");

print LMAIL ("From: $in{CampusEmail}\n");
print LMAIL ("Subject: $in{Form} - patron submission\n");

print LMAIL ("------------------\nPatron information\n\n");
print LMAIL ("Name:\n $in{Name}\n\n");
print LMAIL ("Department / Major:\n $in{Department}\n\n");
print LMAIL ("Campus Address:\n $in{CampusAddress}\n\n");
print LMAIL ("Campus Email:\n $in{CampusEmail}\n\n");
print LMAIL ("Campus Phone:\n $in{CampusPhone}\n\n");
print LMAIL ("Other Phone:\n $in{OtherPhone}\n\n");
print LMAIL ("Status:\n $in{Status}\n\n");

print LMAIL ("------------------\nSubmitted information \n\n");

print LMAIL ("Have I attended any library programs?\n $in{TrainingAttend}\n\n");
print LMAIL ("If yes, how many?\n $in{HowManyTrain}\n\n");
print LMAIL ("The one session that was the most useful:\n $in{UsefulTrain}\n\n");
print LMAIL ("Additional instruction sessions that I would like to see offered:\n $in{AdditionalTrain}\n\n");
print LMAIL ("My most convenient day / time for instruction sessions:\n $in{TrainDayTime}\n\n");
print LMAIL ("Preferred training types:\n $in{ILC}, $in{OOOS}, $in{PHSM}, $in{WBT}, $in{AVBL}, $in{O}\n\n");
print LMAIL ("I currently find out about instruction sessions / programs using:\n $in{Currently}\n\n");
print LMAIL ("Other method I find out:\n $in{CurrentlyOther}\n\n");
print LMAIL ("I would like to find out about future instruction sessions / programs using:\n $in{Future}\n\n");
print LMAIL ("Other method I would like to find out:\n $in{FutureOther}\n\n");
print LMAIL ("Have I attended any programs presented at the library?\n $in{Attended}\n\n");
print LMAIL ("If yes, how many?\n $in{HowMany2}\n\n");
print LMAIL ("The program I found most useful / interesting / effective:\n $in{MostUseful2}\n\n");
print LMAIL ("New / Additional programs I would like to see offered:\n $in{AdditionalP}\n\n");
print LMAIL ("My most convenient day / time for programs:\n $in{ProgramDayTime2}\n\n");
print LMAIL ("\n.\n");

######################################################
# Email received by the user confirming form submission #
######################################################


# ************************************************
# Here's where you MUST specify the path to your
# email program ON your Web server.
# Replace /usr/sbin/sendmail with your path.
# ************************************************

open (MAIL, "I/usr/sbin/sendmail -t");
```

```
# ************************************************
# Here's where you MAY customize the email
# response to the user. You may change any wording
# on the form.
# ************************************************

print MAIL<<toEnd;
To: $in{CampusEmail}
From: $in{LibraryEmail}
Subject: $in{Form}

Thanks for taking the time to fill out our Program/Training Survey.\n\n
We will use your input to improve the types of programs and training sessions we offer.

toEnd
    print MAIL ("\n.\n");

###################################################
# Screen response to user after submitting the form  #
###################################################

print ("<html><head><title>$in{Form}</title></head>");
print ("<body bgcolor=\"ffffff\">");

# ************************************************
# Here's where you MAY change the screen response
# the user sees after submitting the form. You may
# change any wording between the quotation marks.
# ************************************************

print ("Thanks for taking the time to fill out our Program/Training Survey.<p>
We will use your input to improve the types of programs and training sessions we offer.");

# ************************************************
# Here's where you MAY change the name of the link
# back to your main page. You may replace Return
# to our main page with your own wording.
# ************************************************

print ("<p><center><a href=$in{LibraryURL}>Return to our main page.</a></center>");
print ("</body></html>");
```

Library Instruction Request

Faculty only

Do you want to have a librarian teach your students how to do library-based research, write a paper or cite their sources correctly, or provide your students an overview of the most important subject resources in your discipline, etc? Fill out this form to let us know what you want us to teach and some convenient times for one of our librarians to meet with you and your students. We'll contact you as soon as possible to make the arrangements.

Name (last, first middle)

Department / Major

Campus address

Campus e-mail

Campus phone

Fax / Other phone

Course title

Course number

Section number

Number of students

Type of class assignment / instruction you wish us to provide
(please provide as many details as you can)

Date / Time (list 3 date / time options)

Date   Time   to

Date   Time   to

Date   Time   to

Equipment needed / Other information

Send Request   Clear Form

Library Instruction Request — HTML Form

```
<html>
<head><title>Library Instruction Request</title></head>
<body bgcolor="#FFFFFF">
<table width="700" border="0" height="85" bgcolor="#000000">
<tr valign="middle" align="center"><d>
<p>
<font halign=center color="#FFFFFF" face="Arial, Helvetica, sans-serif" size="+3"><b><i>Library
 Instruction Request</i></b></font></p>
</td></tr></table>
<form method="post" action="http://www.yourLibrary.edu/cgi-bin/ali4.pl"><p> </p>
<p>
<font face="Arial, Helvetica, sans-serif" size="2"><font size="4"><b><font size="3"> <i>Faculty only</i></
font></b></font></font></p>
<p>
<font face="Arial, Helvetica, sans-serif" size="2"><b>Do you want to have a librarian teach your students how to
do library-based research, write a paper <br>or cite their sources correctly, or provide your students an overview
of the most important subject <br>resources in your discipline, etc? Fill out this form to let us know what you
want us to teach and <br>some convenient times for one of our librarians to meet with you and your students.
We'll contact you <br>as soon as possible to make the arrangements.</b></font></p>
<p> </p>
<input type="hidden" name="LibraryEmail" value="you@yourLibrary.edu">
<input type="hidden" name="LibraryURL" value="http://www.yourLibrary.edu">
<input type="hidden" name="Form" value="Reserve a Library Computer"><p></p>
<p></p>
<table width="500" border="0" cellspacing="4" cellpadding="1">
<tr><td width="257">
<b><font face="Arial, Helvetica, sans-serif" size="2">Name </font></b><font face="Arial, Helvetica, sans-
serif" size="2"> <font size="1">(last, first middle)</font></font><br><font face="Arial, Helvetica, sans-serif"
size="2"><input type="text" name="Name" size="25"></font></td>
<td width="227">
<b><font face="Arial, Helvetica, sans-serif" size="2">Department / Major<br></font></b><font face="Arial,
Helvetica, sans-serif" size="2"><input type="text" name="Department" size="25">
</font></td></tr><tr><td width="257">
<b><font face="Arial, Helvetica, sans-serif" size="2">Campus address<br></font></b><font face="Arial,
Helvetica, sans-serif" size="2"><input type="text" name="CampusAddress" size="25"></font></td>
<td width="227">
<b><font face="Arial, Helvetica, sans-serif" size="2">Campus e-mail<br></font></b><font face="Arial, Helvetica,
sans-serif" size="2"><input type="text" name="CampusEmail" size="25"></font></td></tr>
<tr><td width="257">
<b><font face="Arial, Helvetica, sans-serif" size="2">Campus phone</font></b><br><font face="Arial, Helvetica,
sans-serif" size="2"><input type="text" name="CampusPhone" size="25"></font></td>
<td width="227">
<b><font face="Arial, Helvetica, sans-serif" size="2">Fax / Other phone<br></font></b><font face="Arial,
```

Helvetica, sans-serif" size="2"><input type="text" name="OtherPhone" size="25">
</font></td></tr></table>
<p>
<table width="500" border="0" cellspacing="0" cellpadding="0">
<tr><td width="257">
<b><font face="Arial, Helvetica, sans-serif" size="2">Course title</font></b>
<font face="Arial, Helvetica, sans-serif" size="3"><input type="text" name="CTitle" size="25"></font></td>
<td width="227">
<b><font face="Arial, Helvetica, sans-serif" size="2">Course number
</font></b><font face="Arial, Helvetica, sans-serif" size="3"><input type="text" name="CNum" size="25"></font></td></tr>
<tr><td width="257">
<b><font face="Arial, Helvetica, sans-serif" size="2">Section number
</font></b><font face="Arial, Helvetica, sans-serif" size="3"><input type="text" name="SNum" size="25"></font></td>
<td width="227">
<b><font face="Arial, Helvetica, sans-serif" size="2">Number of students
</font></b><font face="Arial, Helvetica, sans-serif" size="3"><input type="text" name="NumOfS" size="25">
</font></td></tr></table>
<p>
<b><font face="Arial, Helvetica, sans-serif" size="2">Type of class assignment / instruction you wish us to provide
</font></b><font face="Arial, Helvetica, sans-serif" size="1">(please provide as many details as you can)</font>
<font face="Arial, Helvetica, sans-serif" size="3"><textarea name="textarea" cols="40" rows="2"></textarea></font></p>
<p>
<b><font face="Arial, Helvetica, sans-serif" size="2">Date / Time </font></b><font face="Arial, Helvetica, sans-serif" size="1"> (list 3 date / time options)</font>
<font face="Arial, Helvetica, sans-serif" size="2">Date</font><font size="3">
<font face="Arial, Helvetica, sans-serif"><input type="text" name="Date1" size="15"></font>   <font size="3">
<font face="Arial, Helvetica, sans-serif">   </font></font><font face="Arial, Helvetica, sans-serif" size="2">Time</font>
<font face="Arial, Helvetica, sans-serif"><input type="text" name="TimeBegin1" size="10">
<font size="2">to</font><input type="text" name="TimeEnd1" size="10">
<font face="Arial, Helvetica, sans-serif" size="2">Date</font><font size="3"><font face="Arial, Helvetica, sans-serif"><input type="text" name="Date2" size="15"> </font>
<font face="Arial, Helvetica, sans-serif" size="2">Time</font><font face="Arial, Helvetica, sans-serif"><input type="text" name="TimeBegin2" size="10"><font size="2">to</font><input type="text" name="TimeEnd2" size="10"></font></font>
</font><font face="Arial, Helvetica, sans-serif" size="2">Date</font><font size="3"><font face="Arial, Helvetica, sans-serif"><input type="text" name="Date3" size="15">
</font>   <font face="Arial, Helvetica, sans-serif" size="2">Time </font><font face="Arial, Helvetica, sans-serif"><input type="text" name="TimeBegin3" size="10"><font size="2">to
</font><input type="text" name="TimeEnd3" size="10"></font></font></font></p>
<p>
<b><font face="Arial, Helvetica, sans-serif" size="2">Equipment needed / Other information
</font><font face="Arial, Helvetica, sans-serif" size="3"><textarea name="Equipment" cols="40" rows="2">
</textarea>

```
</font></b></p>
<p> </p>
<table width="700" border="0" cellspacing="10" cellpadding="1"><tr><td width="244">
<div align="right"><input type="submit" name="send" value="Send Request"></div></td>
<td width="203"> </td><td width="207">
<div align="left"><input type="reset" name="clear" value="Clear Form"></div></td></tr>
<tr colspan=3><td colspan=3>
<table width="500" border="0" height="2" align="center" cellpadding="0" cellspacing="0"
bgcolor="#000000"><tr><td><font size="1" color="#000000">.</font></td></tr></table>
</td></tr>
<tr><td colspan=3><div align="center">
<font face="Arial, Helvetica, sans-serif" size="1"><b>http://</b></font><br><font size="2"> 
<font face="Arial, Helvetica, sans-serif" size="1"><b>&copy; 2001</b></font></font>
<font face="Arial, Helvetica, sans-serif" size="2"><a href="mailto:">
<b><font size="1">Contact Webmaster</font></b></a></font></div></td></tr>
</table></form>
</body>
</html>
```

Library Instruction Request — Perl Script

```perl
#!/usr/local/bin/perl

# ************************************************
# ABOVE is where you MUST specify the path to your
# perl interpreter on your Web server.
# Replace /usr/local/bin/perl with your path.
# ************************************************

if ($ENV{'REQUEST_METHOD'}eq"GET"){$buffer = $ENV{'QUERY_STRING'};}
    elsif($ENV{'REQUEST_METHOD'}eq"POST"){
        read(STDIN,$buffer,$ENV{'CONTENT_LENGTH'});
    }
$bufferb = $buffer;
#separate the name of the input from its value.
@forminputs = split(/&/, $bufferb);

foreach $forminput (@forminputs)
{
        #separate the name of the input from its value
        ($name, $value) = split(/=/, $forminput);

        #Un-Webify plus signs and %-encoding
        $value =~ tr/+/ /;
        $value =~ s/%([a-fA-F0-9][a-fA-F0-9])/pack("C", hex($1))/eg;

        #stick them in the in array
        $in{$name} = $value;
}
print "Content-type: text/html\n\n";

####################################################################
# ABOVE is the required header for a perl script            #
####################################################################


########################################################################
# (Below) Email received by library containing user-entered information #
########################################################################


# ************************************************
# Here's where you MUST specify the path to your
# email program (probably sendmail) ON your Web server.
# Replace /usr/sbin/sendmail with your path.
# ************************************************
```

```
open (LMAIL, "l/usr/sbin/sendmail -t");
print LMAIL ("To: $in{LibraryEmail}\n");

print LMAIL ("From: $in{CampusEmail}\n");
print LMAIL ("Subject: $in{Form} - patron submission\n");

print LMAIL ("------------------\nPatron information\n\n");
print LMAIL ("Name:\n $in{Name}\n\n");
print LMAIL ("Department / Major:\n $in{Department}\n\n");
print LMAIL ("Campus Address:\n $in{CampusAddress}\n\n");
print LMAIL ("Campus Email:\n $in{CampusEmail}\n\n");
print LMAIL ("Campus Phone:\n $in{CampusPhone}\n\n");
print LMAIL ("Other Phone:\n $in{OtherPhone}\n\n");

print LMAIL ("------------------\nSubmitted information \n\n");

print LMAIL ("Course title:\n $in{CTitle}\n\n");
print LMAIL ("Course number:\n $in{CNum} \n\n");
print LMAIL ("Section number:\n $in{SNum}\n\n");
print LMAIL ("Number of students:\n $in{NumOfS}\n\n");

print LMAIL ("Type of class assignment / instruction you wish us to provide:\n $in{TypeAssign}\n\n");
print LMAIL ("First date / time:\n $in{Date1}\n $in{TimeBegin1} to $in{TimeEnd1}\n\n");
print LMAIL ("Second date / time:\n $in{Date2}\n $in{TimeBegin2} to $in{TimeEnd2}\n\n");
print LMAIL ("Third date / time:\n $in{Date3}\n $in{TimeBegin3} to $in{TimeEnd3}\n\n");
print LMAIL ("Equipment / Other information:\n $in{Equipment}\n\n");
print LMAIL ("\n.\n");


########################################################
# Email received by the user confirming form submission #
########################################################


# ***********************************************
# Here's where you MUST specify the path to your
# email program ON your Web server.
# Replace /usr/sbin/sendmail with your path.
# ***********************************************


open (MAIL, "l/usr/sbin/sendmail -t");

# ***********************************************
# Here's where you MAY customize the email
# response to the user. You may change any wording
# on the form.
# ***********************************************
```

```
print MAIL<<toEnd;
To: $in{CampusEmail}
From: $in{LibraryEmail}
Subject: $in{Form}

Thanks for taking the time to fill out our Library Instruction Request.\n\n
We will use your input to improve the types of programs and training sessions we offer.

toEnd
    print MAIL ("\n.\n");


##################################################
# Screen response to user after submitting the form  #
##################################################

print ("<html><head><title>$in{Form}</title></head>");
print ("<body bgcolor=\"ffffff\">");


# ************************************************
# Here's where you MAY change the screen response
# the user sees after submitting the form. You may
# change any wording between the quotation marks.
# ************************************************

print ("Thanks for taking the time to fill out our Library Instruction Request.<p>
We will use your input to improve the types of programs and training sessions we offer.");


# ************************************************
# Here's where you MAY change the name of the link
# back to your main page. You may replace Return
# to our main page with your own wording.
# ************************************************

print ("<p><center><a href=$in{LibraryURL}>Return to our main page.</a></center>");
print ("</body></html>");
```

Group 3 — Library Computers Forms / Surveys

In this section you'll find a Web-based form that will enable students and faculty to reserve one of your library's computers on a day and at a time convenient to them. Here you'll also find two surveys that will enable both your on-campus and off-campus students and faculty to give your staff input on their level of computer knowledge, information about where and how they use the Internet, and how they feel about your library's Web site.

Reserve a Library Computer

Do students and faculty hate to wait in line to use one of your library's computers? Provide them with this form so that they can request a reservation for a computer on a specific date and at a specific time. Put a link to this form on any of your Web site's Internet/Web search or technology pages.

Library Web User Survey

If you have on-campus students who use your library's computers to access the Internet and you'd like to know more about them so that you can help them better use your computers, the Internet, and your library's Web site, make sure you place a link to this survey periodically on any/all of your Web site's search and technology pages.

Off-Campus Web User Survey

If off-campus students, faculty, and staff use an Internet-connected computer, have them complete this brief survey so that you can learn how they use the Internet and your library's Web site when they're not in your library. Put a link to this survey periodically on your library's homepage.

Library Classroom I Lab Request form

If your library has classrooms, conference rooms, or computer labs that faculty and teaching assistants can reserve on an "as needed" basis, place a link to this online form on your Web site to make it simple for them to request a room, time, and date via e-mail.

Reserve a Library Computer

Do you hate to wait in line to use one of the library's computers? Fill out this form to reserve a computer on a specific date and at a specific time. All reservations must be made at least 48 hours in advance. Dates/times are assigned on a first-come-first-serve basis. We'll contact you by e-mail to let you know if a computer is available.

Name (last, first middle)

Department / Major

Campus address

Campus e-mail

Campus phone

Fax / Other phone

Status

- ○ Freshman
- ○ Sophomore
- ○ Junior
- ○ Senior
- ○ Grad Student
- ○ Faculty
- ○ Staff
- ○ Other

Date / Time (list 3 date / time options)

Date _____ Time _____ to _____

Date _____ Time _____ to _____

Date _____ Time _____ to _____

Comments / Additional information

[Send Request]   [Clear Form]

Reserve a Library Computer — HTML Form

```
<html>
<head><title>Reserve a Library Computer</title></head>
<body bgcolor="#FFFFFF">
<table width="700" border="0" height="85" bgcolor="#000000">
<tr valign="middle" align="center"><td>
<p>
<font halign=center color="#FFFFFF" face="Arial, Helvetica, sans-serif" size="+3"><b><i>Reserve a Library
Computer</i></b></font></p>
</td></tr></table>
<form method="post" action="http://www.yourLibrary.edu/cgi-bin/alc1.pl"><p> </p>
<p>
<font face="Arial, Helvetica, sans-serif" size="2"><b>Do you hate to wait in line to use one of the library's com-
puters? Fill out this form to reserve<br> a computer on a specific date and at a specific time. All reservations
must be made at least <br> 48 hours in advance. Dates/times are assigned on a first-come-first-serve basis. We'll
contact<br> you by e-mail to let you know if a computer is available.</b> </font></p>
<p> </p>
<input type="hidden" name="LibraryEmail" value="you@yourLibrary.edu">
<input type="hidden" name="LibraryURL" value="http://www.yourLibrary.edu">
<input type="hidden" name="Form" value="Reserve a Library Computer"><p></p>
<p></p>
<table width="500" border="0" cellspacing="4" cellpadding="1">
<tr><td width="257">
<b><font face="Arial, Helvetica, sans-serif" size="2">Name </font></b><font face="Arial, Helvetica, sans-
serif" size="1"> (last, first middle)</font><br><font face="Arial, Helvetica, sans-serif" size="2"><input
type="text" name="Name" size="25"></font></td>
<td width="227">
<b><font face="Arial, Helvetica, sans-serif" size="2">Department / Major<br></font></b><font face="Arial,
Helvetica, sans-serif" size="2"><input type="text" name="Department" size="25"></font> </td></tr>
<tr><td width="257">
<b><font face="Arial, Helvetica, sans-serif" size="2">Campus address<br></font></b><font face="Arial,
Helvetica, sans-serif" size="2"><input type="text" name="CampusAddress" size="25"></font></td>
<td width="227">
<b><font face="Arial, Helvetica, sans-serif" size="2">Campus e-mail<br></font></b><font face="Arial, Helvetica,
sans-serif" size="2"><input type="text" name="CampusEmail" size="25"></font></td></tr>
<tr><td width="257">
<b><font face="Arial, Helvetica, sans-serif" size="2">Campus phone</font></b><br><font face="Arial, Helvetica,
sans-serif" size="2"><input type="text" name="CampusPhone" size="25"></font></td>
<td width="227">
<b><font face="Arial, Helvetica, sans-serif" size="2">Fax / Other phone<br></font></b><font face="Arial,
Helvetica, sans-serif" size="2"><input type="text" name="OtherPhone" size="25"></font></td></tr>
</table>
<p>
<b><font face="Arial, Helvetica, sans-serif" size="2">Status</font></b><table width="550" border="0"
```

```
cellspacing="0" cellpadding="0">
<tr><td width="126" height="13">
<font face="Arial, Helvetica, sans-serif" size="2"><input type="radio" name="Status"
value="Freshman">Freshman</font></td>
<td width="117" height="13">
<font face="Arial, Helvetica, sans-serif" size="2"><input type="radio" name="Status"
value="Sophomore">Sophomore</font></td>
<td width="87" height="13">
<font face="Arial, Helvetica, sans-serif" size="2"><input type="radio" name="Status" value="Junior">Junior
</font></td>
<td width="202" height="13">
<font face="Arial, Helvetica, sans-serif" size="2"><input type="radio" name="Status"
value="Senior">Senior</font></td></tr>
<tr><td width="126" height="9">
<font face="Arial, Helvetica, sans-serif" size="2"><input type="radio" name="Status"
 value="Graduate Student">Grad Student</font></td>
<td width="117" height="9">
<font face="Arial, Helvetica, sans-serif" size="2"><input type="radio" name="Status"
value="Faculty">Faculty</font></td>
<td width="87" height="9">
<font face="Arial, Helvetica, sans-serif" size="2"><input type="radio" name="Status"
value="Staff">Staff</font></td>
<td width="202" height="9">
<font face="Arial, Helvetica, sans-serif" size="2"><input type="radio" name="Status"
value="Other">Other</font></td></tr></table>
<p>
<b><font face="Arial, Helvetica, sans-serif" size="2">Date / Time </font></b><font face="Arial, Helvetica,
sans-serif" size="1"> (list 3 date / time options)</font><br><font face="Arial, Helvetica, sans-serif"
size="2">Date</font><font size="3" face="Arial, Helvetica, sans-serif"><input type="text" name="Date1"
size="15">      
<font face="Arial, Helvetica, sans-serif" size="2">Time</font>
<input type="text" name="TimeBegin1" size="10"><font size="2">to</font>
<input type="text" name="TimeEnd1" size="10"></font><br>
<font face="Arial, Helvetica, sans-serif" size="2">Date</font><font size="3"><font face="Arial, Helvetica, sans-
serif"><input type="text" name="Date2" size="15"></font>      
<font face="Arial, Helvetica, sans-serif" size="2">Time</font><font face="Arial, Helvetica, sans-serif">
<input type="text" name="TimeBegin2" size="10"><font size="2">to</font>
<input type="text" name="TimeEnd2" size="10"></font></font><br></font>
<font face="Arial, Helvetica, sans-serif" size="2">Date</font><font size="3"><font face="Arial, Helvetica, sans-
serif"><input type="text" name="Date3" size="15"></font><font face="Arial, Helvetica, sans-
serif">   </font><font size="3"><font face="Arial, Helvetica, sans-serif">  
</font></font><font face="Arial, Helvetica, sans-serif" size="2">Time</font><font face="Arial, Helvetica, sans-
serif"><input type="text" name="TimeBegin3" size="10"><font size="2">to</font><input type="text"
name="TimeEnd3" size="10"></font></font></font></p>
<p>
```

```
<b><font face="Arial, Helvetica, sans-serif" size="2">Comments / Additional information<br>    </font></b><font
face="Arial, Helvetica, sans-serif" size="3"><textarea name="Comments" cols="40" rows="2"></textarea>
</font></p>
<p> </p>
<table width="700" border="0" cellspacing="10" cellpadding="1"><tr><td width="244">
<div align="right"><input type="submit" name="send" value="Send Request"></div></td>
<td width="203"> </td><td width="207">
<div align="left"><input type="reset" name="clear" value="Clear Form"></div></td></tr>
<tr colspan=3><td colspan=3>
<table width="500" border="0" height="2" align="center" cellpadding="0" cellspacing="0"
bgcolor="#000000"><tr><td><font size="1" color="#000000">.</font></td></tr></table>
</td></tr>
<tr><td colspan=3><div align="center">
<font face="Arial, Helvetica, sans-serif" size="1"><b>http://</b></font><br><font size="2"> 
<font face="Arial, Helvetica, sans-serif" size="1"><b>&copy; 2001</b></font></font>
<font face="Arial, Helvetica, sans-serif" size="2"><a href="mailto:">
<b><font size="1">Contact Webmaster</font></b></a></font></div></td></tr>
</table></form>
</body>
</html>
```

Reserve a Library Computer — Perl Script

```perl
#!/usr/local/bin/perl

# ***************************************************
# ABOVE is where you MUST specify the path to your
# perl interpreter on your Web server.
# Replace /usr/local/bin/perl with your path.
# ***************************************************

if ($ENV{'REQUEST_METHOD'}eq"GET"){$buffer = $ENV{'QUERY_STRING'};}
    elsif($ENV{'REQUEST_METHOD'}eq"POST"){
        read(STDIN,$buffer,$ENV{'CONTENT_LENGTH'});
    }
$bufferb = $buffer;
#separate the name of the input from its value.
@forminputs = split(/&/, $bufferb);

foreach $forminput (@forminputs)
{
        #separate the name of the input from its value
        ($name, $value) = split(/=/, $forminput);

        #Un-Webify plus signs and %-encoding
        $value =~ tr/+/ /;
        $value =~ s/%([a-fA-F0-9][a-fA-F0-9])/pack("C", hex($1))/eg;

        #stick them in the in array
        $in{$name} = $value;
}
print "Content-type: text/html\n\n";

###############################################################
# ABOVE is the required header for a perl script           #
###############################################################


###################################################################
# (Below) Email received by library containing user-entered information #
###################################################################


# ***************************************************
# Here's where you MUST specify the path to your
# email program (probably sendmail) ON your Web server.
# Replace /usr/sbin/sendmail with your path.
# ***************************************************
```

```
open (LMAIL, "|/usr/sbin/sendmail -t");
print LMAIL ("To: $in{LibraryEmail}\n");

print LMAIL ("From: $in{CampusEmail}\n");
print LMAIL ("Subject: $in{Form} - patron submission\n");

print LMAIL ("------------------\nPatron information\n\n");
print LMAIL ("Name:\n $in{Name}\n\n");
print LMAIL ("Department / Major:\n $in{Department}\n\n");
print LMAIL ("Campus Address:\n $in{CampusAddress}\n\n");
print LMAIL ("Campus Email:\n $in{CampusEmail}\n\n");
print LMAIL ("Campus Phone:\n $in{CampusPhone}\n\n");
print LMAIL ("Other Phone:\n $in{OtherPhone}\n\n");
print LMAIL ("Status:\n $in{Status}\n\n");
print LMAIL ("------------------\nSubmitted information \n\n");
print LMAIL ("First date / time:\n $in{Date1}\n $in{TimeBegin1} to $in{TimeEnd1}\n\n");
print LMAIL ("Second date / time:\n $in{Date2}\n $in{TimeBegin2} to $in{TimeEnd2}\n\n");
print LMAIL ("Third date / time:\n $in{Date3}\n $in{TimeBegin3} to $in{TimeEnd3}\n\n");
print LMAIL ("Comments:\n $in{Comments}\n\n");

print LMAIL ("\n.\n");

############################################################
# Email received by the user confirming form submission #
############################################################

# ***********************************************
# Here's where you MUST specify the path to your
# email program ON your Web server.
# Replace /usr/sbin/sendmail with your path.
# ***********************************************

open (MAIL, "|/usr/sbin/sendmail -t");

# ***********************************************
# Here's where you MAY customize the email
# response to the user. You may change any wording
# on the form.
# ***********************************************

print MAIL<<toEnd;
To: $in{CampusEmail}
From: $in{LibraryEmail}
Subject: $in{Form}

Thanks for sending us a library computer reservation.\n\n
```

A librarian will contact you in the next couple of days to let you know if a computer is available on the day and at the time you requested.

```
toEnd
   print MAIL ("\n.\n");


#####################################################
# Screen response to user after submitting the form  #
#####################################################

print ("<html><head><title>$in{Form}</title></head>");
print ("<body bgcolor=\"ffffff\">");


# ************************************************
# Here's where you MAY change the screen response
# the user sees after submitting the form. You may
# change any wording between the quotation marks.
# ************************************************

print ("Thanks for sending us a library computer reservation.<p>
A librarian will contact you in the next couple of days to let you know if a computer is available on the day and at
the time you requested.");


# ************************************************
# Here's where you MAY change the name of the link
# back to your main page. You may replace Return
# to our main page with your own wording.
# ************************************************

print ("<p><center><a href=$in{LibraryURL}>Return to our main page.</a></center>");
print ("</body></html>");
```

Library Web User Survey

Please complete this brief survey to let us know how you use the Internet while in the library.

Your Computer Experience

What is your level of computer expertise?
O Beginner   O Some experience   O Expert

Where do you have access to a computer when not in the library? (select all that apply)
O Dorm / Home   O Campus office   O Off-campus office   O Other library   O No access
O Other (please specify) [   ]

How do you use your computer ? (select all that apply)
O Word processing   O E-mail   O Web browsing   O Research   O Recreation
O Other (please specify) [   ]

Library Computers

How often do you use the library's computers?
O More than once a day   O Once a day   O Every other day
O Couple times a week   O Once a week   O Couple times a month

How do you use the library's computers? (select all that apply)
O On-line catalog   O Library databases   O Web browsing   O Research   O Email
O Other (please specify) [   ]

How many pages do you print from library computers per visit?
O None   O 1-4 pages   O 5-10 pages   O 11-15 pages   O 16-20 pages   O Over 20 pages

Your Internet Use

How often do you use the Internet at the library?
O More than once a day   O Once a day   O Every other day
O Couple times a week   O Once a week   O Couple times a month

How long have you used the Internet?
O Less than a month   O One month to six months   O More than six months
O Less than a year   O One to two years   O More than two years

When do you use the Internet at the library? (select all that apply)

○ Morning ○ Early afternoon ○ Late afternoon ○ Early evening ○ Night ○ Late night

What would make using the Internet at the library easier?

[text area]

The Library's Web Site

How many times have you used the library's Web site in the last 30 days? [ ]

How often do you visit the library's Web site?

○ More than once a day ○ Once a day ○ Every other day
○ Couple times a week ○ Once a week ○ Couple times a month

When you need help using the library's Web site, what do you do?

○ Use on-line help ○ E-mail library staff ○ Phone library staff
○ Read printed documentation ○ Ask a friend ○ Do not need help

Which sections / features / pages of the library's Web site do you use most often?

[text area]

Name (last, first middle)

[ ]

Department / Major

[ ]

Campus e-mail

[ ]

Campus phone

[ ]

Status

○ Freshman ○ Sophomore ○ Junior ○ Senior
○ Grad Student ○ Faculty ○ Staff ○ Other

[Send Survey]   [Clear Survey]

Library Web User Survey — HTML Form

```
<html>
<head><title>Library Web User Survey</title></head>
<body bgcolor="#FFFFFF">
<table width="700" border="0" height="85" bgcolor="#000000">
<tr valign="middle" align="center"><td>
<p>
<font halign=center color="#FFFFFF" face="Arial, Helvetica, sans-serif" size="5">
<b><i><font size="+3">Library Web User Survey</font></i></b></font></p>
</td></tr></table>
<form method="post" action="http://www.yourLibrary.edu/cgi-bin/alc2.pl"><p> </p>
<p>
<font face="Arial, Helvetica, sans-serif" size="2"><b>Please complete this brief survey to let us know how you
use the Internet while in the library.</b></font><br></p>
<p>
<input type="hidden" name="LibraryEmail" value="you@yourLibrary.edu">
<input type="hidden" name="LibraryURL" value="http://www.yourLibrary.edu">
<input type="hidden" name="Form" value="Library Web User Survey"></p>
<p> </p>
<b><font face="Arial, Helvetica, sans-serif" size="3">Your Computer Experience</font></b>
<p></p><p>
<font face="Arial, Helvetica, sans-serif" size="2"><b>What is your level of computer expertise? </b><br>
<input type="radio" name="Expertise" value="Beginner">Beginner    
<input type="radio" name="Expertise" value="Some experience">Some experience    
<input type="radio" name="Expertise" value="Expert">Expert<br></font></p>
<p>
<b><font face="Arial, Helvetica, sans-serif" size="2">Where do you have access to a computer when not in the
library?   </font></b><font face="Arial, Helvetica, sans-serif" size="1">(select all that apply)
</font><font face="Arial, Helvetica, sans-serif" size="2"><br>
<input type="radio" name="H" value="Dorm / Home">Dorm / Home   
<input type="radio" name="CO" value="Campus office">Campus office   
<input type="radio" name="OCO" value="Off-campus office">Off-campus office   
<input type="radio" name="OL" value="Other library">Other library   
<input type="radio" name="NA" value="No access">No access<br>
<input type="radio" name="OP" value="Other programs">Other<b><font face="Arial, Helvetica, sans-serif"
size="2">  </font></b><font face="Arial, Helvetica, sans-serif" size="1">(please specify) </
font><font face="Arial, Helvetica, sans-serif" size="3"> <input type="text" name="OtherHow" size="20">
</font></font></p>
<p>
<b><font face="Arial, Helvetica, sans-serif" size="2">How do you use your computer ?   </font>
</b><font face="Arial, Helvetica, sans-serif" size="1">(select all that apply) </font><font face="Arial, Helvetica,
sans-serif" size="2"><br>
<input type="radio" name="WP" value="Word processing">Word processing   
<input type="radio" name="E" value="E-mail">E-mail   
<input type="radio" name="WB" value="Web browsing">Web browsing   
```

```
<input type="radio" name="R" value="Research">Research   
<input type="radio" name="RR" value="Recreation">Recreation    <br>
<input type="radio" name="OP2" value="Other programs">Other  <font face="Arial, Helvetica, sans-
serif" size="1">(please specify) </font><font face="Arial, Helvetica, sans-serif" size="3"> <input type="text"
name="OtherHow2" size="20"></font></font></p>
<p> </p>
<p>
<b><font face="Arial, Helvetica, sans-serif" size="3">Library Computers</font></b></p>
<p>
<b><font face="Arial, Helvetica, sans-serif" size="2">How often do you use the library's computers?<br>
</font></b>
<table width="550" border="0" cellspacing="0" cellpadding="0">
<tr><td width="164">
 <input type="radio" name="OftenUse" value="More than once a day"><font face="Arial, Helvetica, sans-serif"
size="2">More than once a day</font></td>
<td width="123">
<font face="Arial, Helvetica, sans-serif" size="2"><input type="radio" name="OftenUse" value="Once a
day">Once a day</font></td>
<td width="263">
<font face="Arial, Helvetica, sans-serif" size="2"><input type="radio" name="OftenUse" value="Every other
day">Every other day</font></td></tr>
<tr><td width="164">
<font face="Arial, Helvetica, sans-serif" size="2"><input type="radio" name="OftenUse" value="Couple times a
week">Couple times a week</font></td>
<td width="123">
<font face="Arial, Helvetica, sans-serif" size="2"><input type="radio" name="OftenUse" value="Once a
week">Once a week</font></td>
<td width="263">
<font face="Arial, Helvetica, sans-serif" size="2"><input type="radio" name="OftenUse" value="Couple times a
month">Couple times a month</font></td></tr></table>
<p>
<font face="Arial, Helvetica, sans-serif" size="2"><b>How do you use the library's computers? </b>
</font>  <font face="Arial, Helvetica, sans-serif" size="1">(select all that apply) </font><br>
<input type="radio" name="OC" value="On-line catalog"><font face="Arial, Helvetica, sans-serif" size="2">On-
line catalog   
<input type="radio" name="LD" value="Library databases">Library databases   
<input type="radio" name="WB" value="Web browsing">Web browsing   
<input type="radio" name="R" value="Research">Research   
<input type="radio" name="E" value="Email">Email    <br>
<input type="radio" name="OU" value="Other uses">Other <b><font face="Arial, Helvetica, sans-serif"
size="2">  </font></b><font face="Arial, Helvetica, sans-serif" size="1">(please specify)
</font><font face="Arial, Helvetica, sans-serif" size="3"> <input type="text" name="OtherHow3"
size="20"></font><br></font></p>
<p>
<font face="Arial, Helvetica, sans-serif" size="2"><b>How many pages do you print from library computers per
visit?</b><br>
```

```
<input type="radio" name="Pages" value="None">
<font face="Arial, Helvetica, sans-serif" size="2">None   
<input type="radio" name="Pages" value="1-4 pages">1-4 pages   
<input type="radio" name="Pages" value="5-10 pages">5-10 pages   
<input type="radio" name="Pages" value="11-15 pages">11-15 pages   
<input type="radio" name="Pages" value="16-20 pages">16-20 pages   
<input type="radio" name="Pages" value="Over 20 pages">Over 20 pages</font></font></p>
<font face="Arial, Helvetica, sans-serif" size="2">
<p> </p>
<p>
<b><font face="Arial, Helvetica, sans-serif" size="3">Your Internet Use</font></b></p>
<p>
<font face="Arial, Helvetica, sans-serif" size="2"><b>How often do you use the Internet at the library?</b>
<br></font></font>
<table width="550" border="0" cellspacing="0" cellpadding="0">
<tr><td width="164"><font face="Arial, Helvetica, sans-serif" size="2"><input type="radio"
 name="InternetUse" value="More than once a day">More than once a day</font></td>
<td width="123">
<font face="Arial, Helvetica, sans-serif" size="2"><input type="radio" name="InternetUse" value="Once a
day">Once a day</font></td>
<td width="263">
<font face="Arial, Helvetica, sans-serif" size="2"><input type="radio" name="InternetUse" value="Every other
day">Every other day</font></td></tr>
<tr><td width="164">
<font face="Arial, Helvetica, sans-serif" size="2"><input type="radio" name="InternetUse" value="Couple times a
week">Couple times a week</font></td>
<td width="123">
<font face="Arial, Helvetica, sans-serif" size="2"><input type="radio" name="InternetUse" value="Once a
week">Once a week</font></td>
<td width="263">
<font face="Arial, Helvetica, sans-serif" size="2"><input type="radio" name="InternetUse" value="Couple times a
month">Couple times a month</font></td></tr></table><br>
<p>
<font face="Arial, Helvetica, sans-serif" size="2"><b>How long have you used the Internet? </b><br>
</font>
<table width="550" border="0" cellspacing="0" cellpadding="0">
<tr><td width="151">
<font face="Arial, Helvetica, sans-serif" size="2"><input type="radio" name="LongUsedInternet" value="Less
than a month">Less than a month</font></td>
<td width="184">
<font face="Arial, Helvetica, sans-serif" size="2"><input type="radio" name="LongUsedInternet" value="One
month to six months">One month to six months</font></td>
<td width="215">
<font face="Arial, Helvetica, sans-serif" size="2"><input type="radio" name="LongUsedInternet" value="More
than six months">More than six months</font></td></tr>
<tr><td width="151">
```

```
<font face="Arial, Helvetica, sans-serif" size="2"><input type="radio" name="LongUsedInternet" value="Less
than a year">Less than a year</font></td>
<td width="184">
<font face="Arial, Helvetica, sans-serif" size="2"><input type="radio" name="LongUsedInternet" value="One to
two years">One to two years</font></td>
<td width="215">
<font face="Arial, Helvetica, sans-serif" size="2"><input type="radio" name="LongUsedInternet" value="More
than two years">More than two years</font></td></tr></table>
<font face="Arial, Helvetica, sans-serif" size="2">
<p><br>
<font face="Arial, Helvetica, sans-serif" size="2"><b>When do you use the Internet at the library?
</b>  <font face="Arial, Helvetica, sans-serif" size="1">(select all that apply)
</font><br>
<input type="radio" name="M" value="Morning">Morning   
<input type="radio" name="EA" value="Early afternoon">Early afternoon  
<input type="radio" name="LA" value="Late aftenoon">Late aftenoon  
<input type="radio" name="EE" value="Early evening">Early evening  
<input type="radio" name="N" value="Night">Night  
<input type="radio" name="LN" value="Late night">Late night</font></p>
<p>
<font face="Arial, Helvetica, sans-serif" size="2"><b>What would make using the Internet at the library
easier?<br></b><font size="3"><textarea name="Easier" cols="40" rows="2"></textarea>
</font></font></p>
<p> </p>
<p> <b><font face="Arial, Helvetica, sans-serif" size="3">The Library's Web Site</font></b></p>
<p>
<font face="Arial, Helvetica, sans-serif" size="2"><b>How many times have you used the library's Web site in the
last 30 days? </b><font size="3">  <input type="text" name="Times" size="5">
</font><br></font></p>
<p>
<font face="Arial, Helvetica, sans-serif" size="2"><b>How often do you visit the library's Web site?
</b><br></font></font>
<table width="550" border="0" cellspacing="0" cellpadding="0">
<tr><td width="230">
<font face="Arial, Helvetica, sans-serif" size="2"><input type="radio" name="OftenVisit" value="More than once
a day">More than once a day</font></td>
<td width="155">
<font face="Arial, Helvetica, sans-serif" size="2"><input type="radio" name="OftenVisit" value="Once a
day">Once a day</font></td>
<td width="165">
<font face="Arial, Helvetica, sans-serif" size="2"><input type="radio" name="OftenVisit" value="Every other
day">Every other day</font></td></tr>
<tr><td width="230">
<font face="Arial, Helvetica, sans-serif" size="2"><input type="radio" name="OftenVisit" value="Couple times a
week">Couple times a week</font></td>
<td width="155">
```

<font face="Arial, Helvetica, sans-serif" size="2"><input type="radio" name="OftenVisit" value="Once a week">Once a week</font></td>
<td width="165">
<font face="Arial, Helvetica, sans-serif" size="2"><input type="radio" name="OftenVisit" value="Couple times a month">Couple times a month</font></td></tr></table>

<font face="Arial, Helvetica, sans-serif" size="2"><p><font face="Arial, Helvetica, sans-serif" size="2"> <b>When you need help using the library's Web site, what do you do?</b>
</font></font>
<table width="550" border="0" cellspacing="0" cellpadding="0">
<tr><td width="230">
<font face="Arial, Helvetica, sans-serif" size="2"><input type="radio" name="WebHelp" value="Use on-line help">Use on-line help</font></td>
<td width="155">
<font face="Arial, Helvetica, sans-serif" size="2"><input type="radio" name="WebHelp" value="E-mail library staff">E-mail library staff</font></td>
<td width="165">
<font face="Arial, Helvetica, sans-serif" size="2"><input type="radio" name="WebHelp" value="Phone library staff">Phone library staff</font></td></tr>
<tr><td width="230">
<font face="Arial, Helvetica, sans-serif" size="2"><input type="radio" name="WebHelp" value="Read printed documentation">Read printed documentation</font></td>
<td width="155"><font face="Arial, Helvetica, sans-serif" size="2"><input type="radio" name="WebHelp" value="Ask a friend">Ask a friend</font></td>
<td width="165">
<font face="Arial, Helvetica, sans-serif" size="2"><input type="radio" name="WebHelp" value="Do not need help">Do not need help</font></td></tr></table>
<table width="550" border="0" cellspacing="0" cellpadding="0"></table>
<font face="Arial, Helvetica, sans-serif" size="2"> <p> <font face="Arial, Helvetica, sans-serif" size="2"><b>Which sections / features / pages of the library's Web site do you use most often?
   </b><font face="Arial, Helvetica, sans-serif" size="3"><textarea name="Features" cols="40" rows="2"></textarea></font></font></p>
<p> </p></font>
<table width="500" border="0" cellspacing="4" cellpadding="1">
<tr><td width="257">
<b><font face="Arial, Helvetica, sans-serif" size="2">Name </font></b><font face="Arial, Helvetica, sans-serif" size="2"> <font size="1">(last, first middle)</font></font>
<font face="Arial, Helvetica, sans-serif" size="2"><input type="text" name="Name" size="25"></font></td>
<td width="227">
<b><font face="Arial, Helvetica, sans-serif" size="2">Department / Major
</font></b><font face="Arial, Helvetica, sans-serif" size="2"><input type="text" name="Department" size="25"></font> </td></tr>
<tr><td width="257">
<b><font face="Arial, Helvetica, sans-serif" size="2">Campus e-mail
</font></b><font face="Arial, Helvetica, sans-serif" size="2"><input type="text" name="CampusEmail" size="25"></font></td>
<td width="227">
<b><font face="Arial, Helvetica, sans-serif" size="2">Campus phone</font></b>
font face="Arial, Helvetica, sans-serif" size="2"><input type="text" name="CampusPhone2" size="25"></font></td></tr>

```
</table><p>
<b><font face="Arial, Helvetica, sans-serif" size="2">Status</font></b><table width="550" border="0"
cellspacing="0" cellpadding="0">
<tr><td width="126" height="13">
<font face="Arial, Helvetica, sans-serif" size="2"><input type="radio" name="Status"
value="Freshman">Freshman</font></td>
<td width="117" height="13">
<font face="Arial, Helvetica, sans-serif" size="2"><input type="radio" name="Status"
value="Sophomore">Sophomore</font></td>
<td width="87" height="13">
<font face="Arial, Helvetica, sans-serif" size="2"><input type="radio" name="Status"
value="Junior">Junior</font></td>
 <td width="202" height="13">
<font face="Arial, Helvetica, sans-serif" size="2"><input type="radio" name="Status"
value="Senior">Senior</font></td></tr>
<tr><td width="126" height="9">
<font face="Arial, Helvetica, sans-serif" size="2"><input type="radio" name="Status"
value="Graduate Student">Grad Student</font></td>
<td width="117" height="9">
<font face="Arial, Helvetica, sans-serif" size="2"><input type="radio" name="Status"
value="Faculty">Faculty</font></td>
 <td width="87" height="9">
<font face="Arial, Helvetica, sans-serif" size="2"><input type="radio" name="Status"
value="Staff">Staff</font></td>
<td width="202" height="9">
<font face="Arial, Helvetica, sans-serif" size="2"><input type="radio" name="Status"
value="Other">Other</font></td></tr></table><font face="Arial, Helvetica, sans-serif" size="2">
<p>  </p>
<table width="700" border="0" cellspacing="10" cellpadding="1">
<tr><td width="226">
<div align="right"><input type="submit" name="send" value="Send Survey"></div></td><td
width="207"> </td>
<td width="221">
<div align="left"><input type="reset" name="clear" value="Clear Survey"></div></td></tr>
<tr colspan=3><td colspan=3>
<table width="500" border="0" height="2" align="center" cellpadding="0" cellspacing="0"
bgcolor="#000000"><tr><td><font size="1" color="#000000">.</font></td></tr></table>
</td></tr><tr>
<td colspan=3><div align="center">
<font face="Arial, Helvetica, sans-serif" size="1"><b>http://</b></font><br> 
<font face="Arial, Helvetica, sans-serif" size="1"><b>&copy; 2001</b></font>
<font face="Arial, Helvetica, sans-serif" size="2"><a href="mailto:">
<b><font size="1">Contact Webmaster</font></b></a></font></div></td></tr>
</table></font></form>
</body>
</html>
```

Library Web User Survey — Perl Script

```perl
#!/usr/local/bin/perl

# ************************************************
# ABOVE is where you MUST specify the path to your
# perl interpreter on your Web server.
# Replace /usr/local/bin/perl with your path.
# ************************************************

if ($ENV{'REQUEST_METHOD'}eq"GET"){$buffer = $ENV{'QUERY_STRING'};}
    elsif($ENV{'REQUEST_METHOD'}eq"POST"){
        read(STDIN,$buffer,$ENV{'CONTENT_LENGTH'});
    }
$bufferb = $buffer;
#separate the name of the input from its value.
@forminputs = split(/&/, $bufferb);

foreach $forminput (@forminputs)
{
    #separate the name of the input from its value
    ($name, $value) = split(/=/, $forminput);

    #Un-Webify plus signs and %-encoding
    $value =~ tr/+/ /;
    $value =~ s/%([a-fA-F0-9][a-fA-F0-9])/pack("C", hex($1))/eg;

    #stick them in the in array
    $in{$name} = $value;
}
print "Content-type: text/html\n\n";

################################################################
# ABOVE is the required header for a perl script         #
################################################################


####################################################################
# (Below) Email received by library containing user-entered information #
####################################################################


# ************************************************
# Here's where you MUST specify the path to your
# email program (probably sendmail) ON your Web server.
# Replace /usr/sbin/sendmail with your path.
# ************************************************
```

```
open (LMAIL, "I/usr/sbin/sendmail -t");
print LMAIL ("To: $in{LibraryEmail}\n");

print LMAIL ("From: $in{CampusEmail}\n");
print LMAIL ("Subject: $in{Form} - patron submission\n");

print LMAIL ("------------------\nPatron information\n\n");
print LMAIL ("Name:\n $in{Name}\n\n");
print LMAIL ("Department / Major:\n $in{Department}\n\n");
print LMAIL ("Campus Email:\n $in{CampusEmail}\n\n");
print LMAIL ("Campus Phone:\n $in{CampusPhone}\n\n");
print LMAIL ("Status:\n $in{Status}\n\n");

print LMAIL ("------------------\nSubmitted information \n\n");

print LMAIL ("My level of computer expertise:\n $in{Expertise}\n\n");
print LMAIL ("Where I have access to a computer:\n $in{H}, $in{OCO}, $in{OL}, $in{CO}, $in{OP}, $in{NA},
$in{OtherHow}\n\n");
print LMAIL ("How I use my computer:\n $in{WP}, $in{E}, $in{WB}, $in{R}, $in{RR}, $in{OP2},
$in{OtherHow2}\n\n");
print LMAIL ("How often I use library computers:\n $in{OftenUse}\n\n");
print LMAIL ("How I use library computers:\n $in{OC2} $in{LD}, $in{WB2}, $in{R2}, $in{E2}, $in{OU},
$in{OtherHow3}\n\n");
print LMAIL ("How many pages I print per visit:\n $in{Pages}\n\n");
print LMAIL ("How often I use the Internet at the library:\n $in{InternetUse}\n\n");
print LMAIL ("How long I have used the Internet:\n $in{LongUsedInternet}\n\n");
print LMAIL ("When I use the Internet at the library:\n $in{M}, $in{EA}, $in{LA}, $in{EE}, $in{N}, $in{LN}\n\n");
print LMAIL ("What would make using the Internet at the library easier:\n $in{Easier}\n\n");
print LMAIL ("How many times I have visited the library's Web site in the last 30 days:\n $in{Times}\n\n");
print LMAIL ("How often I visit the library's Web site:\n $in{OftenVisit}\n\n");
print LMAIL ("When I need help using the library's Web site I:\n $in{WebHelp}\n\n");
print LMAIL ("Sections / features / pages I use most often:\n $in{Features}\n\n");

print LMAIL ("\n.\n");

############################################################
# Email received by the user confirming form submission #
############################################################

# ************************************************
# Here's where you MUST specify the path to your
# email program ON your Web server.
# Replace /usr/sbin/sendmail with your path.
# ************************************************
```

```
open (MAIL, "l/usr/sbin/sendmail -t");

# **************************************************
# Here's where you MAY customize the email
# response to the user. You may change any wording
# on the form.
# **************************************************

print MAIL<<toEnd;
To: $in{CampusEmail}
From: $in{LibraryEmail}
Subject: $in{Form}

Thanks for taking the time to fill out our Web User Survey.\n\n
We will use your input to help us improve our Web site and our library's Internet-connected computers.

toEnd
    print MAIL ("\n.\n");

#####################################################
# Screen response to user after submitting the form  #
#####################################################

print ("<html><head><title>$in{Form}</title></head>");
print ("<body bgcolor=\"ffffff\">");

# **************************************************
# Here's where you MAY change the screen response
# the user sees after submitting the form. You may
# change any wording between the quotation marks.
# **************************************************

print ("Thanks for taking the time to fill out our Web User Survey.<p>
We will use your input to help us improve our Web site and our library's Internet-connected computers.");

# **************************************************
# Here's where you MAY change the name of the link
# back to your main page. You may replace Return
# to our main page with your own wording.
# **************************************************

print ("<p><center><a href=$in{LibraryURL}>Return to our main page.</a></center>");
print ("</body></html>");
```

Off-Campus Web User Survey

Please complete this brief survey to let us know how you use the Internet and our Library's Web site, when you're not in the library.

Your Computer

What is your level of computer expertise?
○ Beginner   ○ Some experience   ○ Expert

How do you use your computer? (select all that apply)
○ Word processing   ○ E-mail   ○ Web browsing   ○ Research   ○ Recreation
○ Other (please specify) [   ]

What kind of computer do you use off-campus?
○ Windows (PC)   ○ Macintosh   ○ UNIX   ○ Don't know

How often do you use the *library's* computers when on campus?
○ Often   ○ Occasionally   ○ Rarely   ○ Never

The Internet and Your Computer

Who is your off-campus Internet provider? [   ]   ○ Don't know

How fast is your off-campus Internet connection?
○ Less than 56K   ○ 56K   ○ ISDN   ○ DSL   ○ T1/T3   ○ Don't know

Which Web browser(s) do you use? (select all that apply)
○ Internet Explorer   ○ Netscape   ○ AOL   ○ CompuServe   ○ Other   ○ Don't know

Your Internet Use

How often do you use the Internet?
○ More than once a day   ○ Once a day   ○ Every other day
○ Couple times a week   ○ Once a week   ○ Couple times a month

How long have you used the Internet?
○ Less than a month   ○ One month to six months   ○ More than six months
○ Less than a year   ○ One to two years   ○ More than two years

When do you use the Internet? (select all that apply)

○ Morning ○ Early afternoon ○ Late afternoon ○ Early evening ○ Night ○ Late night

The Library's Web Site

How many times have you used the library's Web site in the last 30 days? [____]

How often do you use the library's Web site?

○ More than once a day   ○ Once a day   ○ Every other day
○ Couple times a week   ○ Once a week   ○ Couple times a month

When you need help using the library's Web site, what do you do?

○ Use on-line help   ○ E-mail library staff   ○ Phone library staff
○ Read printed documentation   ○ Ask a friend   ○ Do not need help

Which sections / pages of the library's Web site do you use most often?

[_____]

Name (last, first middle)

[_____]

Campus e-mail

[_____]

Department / Major

[_____]

Campus phone

[_____]

Status

○ Freshman   ○ Sophomore   ○ Junior   ○ Senior
○ Grad Student   ○ Faculty   ○ Staff   ○ Other

[Send Survey]   [Clear Survey]

Off-Campus Web User Survey — HTML Form

```
<html>
<head><title>Off-Campus Web User Survey</title></head>
<body bgcolor="#FFFFFF">
<table width="700" border="0" height="85" bgcolor="#000000">
<tr valign="middle" align="center"><td>
<p><font halign=center color="#FFFFFF" face="Arial, Helvetica, sans-serif" size="5">
<b><i><font size="+3">Off-Campus Web User Survey</font></i></b></font></p>
</td></tr></table>
<form method="post" action="http://www.yourLibrary.edu/cgi-bin/alc3.pl"><p> </p>
<p><b><font size="2" face="Arial, Helvetica, sans-serif">Please complete this brief survey to let us know how
you use the Internet and our Library's<br> Web site, when you're not in the library. </font></b></p>
<p>
<input type="hidden" name="LibraryEmail" value="you@yourLibrary.edu">
<input type="hidden" name="LibraryURL" value="http://www.yourLibrary.edu">
<input type="hidden" name="Form" value="Remote Web User Survey"></p>
<p> </p>
<b><font face="Arial, Helvetica, sans-serif" size="3">Your Computer</font></b><p></p>
<p>
<font face="Arial, Helvetica, sans-serif" size="2"><b>What is your level of computer expertise?</b><br>
<input type="radio" name="Expertise" value="Beginner">Beginner   
<input type="radio" name="Expertise" value="Some experience">Some experience nbsp;  
<input type="radio" name="Expertise" value="Expert">Expert<br></font></p>
<p>
<b><font face="Arial, Helvetica, sans-serif" size="2">How do you use your computer ?   </font>
</b><font face="Arial, Helvetica, sans-serif" size="1">(select all that apply) </font><font face="Arial, Helvetica,
sans-serif" size="2"><br>
<input type="radio" name="WP" value="Word processing">Word processing   
<input type="radio" name="E" value="E-mail">E-mail   
<input type="radio" name="WB" value="Web browsing">Web browsing   
<input type="radio" name="R" value="Research">Research   
<input type="radio" name="RR" value="Recreation">Recreation    <br>
<input type="radio" name="OP" value="Other programs">Other<b><font face="Arial, Helvetica, sans-serif"
size="2">  </font></b><font face="Arial, Helvetica, sans-serif" size="1">(please specify)
</font><font face="Arial, Helvetica, sans-serif" size="3"> <input type="text" name="OtherHow"
size="20"></font></font></p>
<p>
<b><font face="Arial, Helvetica, sans-serif" size="2">What kind of computer do you use off-campus?<br>
</font></b><font face="Arial, Helvetica, sans-serif" size="2">
<input type="radio" name="Computer" value="Windows (PC)">Windows (PC)  
<input type="radio" name="Computer" value="Macintosh">Macintosh  
<input type="radio" name="Computer" value="UNIX">UNIX   
<input type="radio" name="Computer" value="Don't know">Don't know</font></p>
<p>
```

```
<b><font face="Arial, Helvetica, sans-serif" size="2">How often do you use the <i>library's</i> computers when
on campus?<br></font></b><font face="Arial, Helvetica, sans-serif" size="2">
<input type="radio" name="LibraryComputers" value="Often">Often  
<input type="radio" name="LibraryComputers" value="Occasionally">Occasionally  
<input type="radio" name="LibraryComputers" value="Rarely">Rarely   
<input type="radio" name="LibraryComputers" value="Never">Never </font></p>
<p> </p><p>
<b><font face="Arial, Helvetica, sans-serif" size="3">The Internet and Your Computer </font></b></p>
<p>
<font face="Arial, Helvetica, sans-serif" size="2"><b>Who is your off-campus Internet provider? </b></font><font
face="Arial, Helvetica, sans-serif" size="3"> <input type="text" name="ISP"
size="10">   <input type="radio" name="ISPDoNotKnow" value="Don't know"><font
size="2">Don't know</font> </font></p>
<p>
<b><font face="Arial, Helvetica, sans-serif" size="2">How fast is your off-campus Internet connection? </font>
</b><font face="Arial, Helvetica, sans-serif" size="2"><br>
<input type="radio" name="Fast" value="Less than 56K">Less than 56K   
<input type="radio" name="Fast" value="56K">56K   
<input type="radio" name="Fast" value="ISDN">ISDN   
<input type="radio" name="Fast" value="DSL">DSL   
<input type="radio" name="Fast" value="T1/T3">T1/T3   
<input type="radio" name="Fast" value="Don't know">Don't know</font><br></p>
<p>
<b><font face="Arial, Helvetica, sans-serif" size="2">Which Web browser(s) do you use?   </font>
</b><font face="Arial, Helvetica, sans-serif" size="1">(select all that apply) </font><font face="Arial, Helvetica,
sans-serif" size="2"><br>
<input type="radio" name="IE" value="Internet explorer">Internet Explorer   
<input type="radio" name="NET" value="Netscape">Netscape   
<input type="radio" name="AOL" value="AOL">AOL   
<input type="radio" name="CS" value="CompuServe">CompuServe   
<input type="radio" name="O" value="Other">Other   
<input type="radio" name="DK" value="Don't know">Don't know</font></p>
<p> </p><p>
<b><font face="Arial, Helvetica, sans-serif" size="3">Your Internet Use</font></b></p>
<p>
<font face="Arial, Helvetica, sans-serif" size="2"><b>How often do you use the Internet?<br> </b></font>
<table width="550" border="0" cellspacing="0" cellpadding="0">
 <tr><td width="187">
<font face="Arial, Helvetica, sans-serif" size="2"><input type="radio" name="InternetUse" value="More than
once a day">More than once a day</font></td>
<td width="127">
<font face="Arial, Helvetica, sans-serif" size="2"><input type="radio" name="InternetUse" value="Once a
day">Once a day</font></td>
<td width="236">
<font face="Arial, Helvetica, sans-serif" size="2"><input type="radio" name="InternetUse" value="Every other
```

day">Every other day</font></td></tr>
<tr><td width="187">
<font face="Arial, Helvetica, sans-serif" size="2"><input type="radio" name="InternetUse" value="Couple times a week">Couple times a week</font></td>
<td width="127"><font face="Arial, Helvetica, sans-serif" size="2"><input type="radio" name="Internet Use" value="Once a week">Once a week</font></td>
<td width="236">
<font face="Arial, Helvetica, sans-serif" size="2"><input type="radio" name="InternetUse" value="Couple times a month">Couple times a month</font></td></tr></table>
<p>
<font face="Arial, Helvetica, sans-serif" size="2"><b>How long have you used the Internet? </b>
</font>
<font face="Arial, Helvetica, sans-serif" size="2"></font>
<table width="550" border="0" cellspacing="0" cellpadding="0">
<tr><td width="161">
<font face="Arial, Helvetica, sans-serif" size="2"><input type="radio" name="LongUsedInternet" value="Less than a month">Less than a month</font></td>
<td width="192">
<font face="Arial, Helvetica, sans-serif" size="2"><input type="radio" name="LongUsedInternet" value="One month to six months">One month to six months</font></td>
<td width="197">
<font face="Arial, Helvetica, sans-serif" size="2"><input type="radio" name="LongUsedInternet" value="More than six months">More than six months</font></td></tr>
<tr><td width="161">
<font face="Arial, Helvetica, sans-serif" size="2"><input type="radio" name="LongUsedInternet" value="Less than a year">Less than a year</font></td>
<td width="192">
<font face="Arial, Helvetica, sans-serif" size="2"><input type="radio" name="LongUsedInternet" value="One to two years">One to two years</font></td>
<td width="197">
<font face="Arial, Helvetica, sans-serif" size="2"><input type="radio" name="LongUsedInternet" value="More than two years">More than two years</font></td></tr></table>
<font face="Arial, Helvetica, sans-serif" size="2">
<p>
<font face="Arial, Helvetica, sans-serif" size="2"><b>When do you use the Internet?</b>
</font><font face="Arial, Helvetica, sans-serif" size="1">(select all that apply) </font>
<font face="Arial, Helvetica, sans-serif" size="2">
<input type="radio" name="M" value="Morning">Morning
<input type="radio" name="EA" value="Early afternoon">Early afternoon
<input type="radio" name="LA" value="Late afternoon">Late afternoon
<input type="radio" name="EE" value="Early evening">Early evening
<input type="radio" name="N" value="Night">Night
<input type="radio" name="LN" value="Late night">Late night</font></p>
<p> </p>
<p><b><font face="Arial, Helvetica, sans-serif" size="3">The Library's Web Site</font></b></p>
<p>

<font face="Arial, Helvetica, sans-serif" size="2"><b>How many times have you used the library's Web site in the last 30 days? </b><font size="3"><input type="text" name="Visits" size="5"> </font>
</font></p>
<p>
<font face="Arial, Helvetica, sans-serif" size="2"><b>How often do you use the library's Web site? </b>
</font>
</font>
<table width="550" border="0" cellspacing="0" cellpadding="0">
 <tr><td width="230">
 <font face="Arial, Helvetica, sans-serif" size="2"><input type="radio" name="OftenVisitSite" value="More than once a day">More than once a day</font></td>
<td width="155">
<font face="Arial, Helvetica, sans-serif" size="2"><input type="radio" name="OftenVisitSite" value="Once a day">Once a day</font></td>
<td width="165">
<font face="Arial, Helvetica, sans-serif" size="2"><input type="radio" name="OftenVisitSite" value="Every other day">Every other day</font></td></tr>
<tr><td width="230">
<font face="Arial, Helvetica, sans-serif" size="2"><input type="radio" name="OftenVisitSite" value=" Couple times a week">Couple times a week</font></td>
<td width="155">
<font face="Arial, Helvetica, sans-serif" size="2"><input type="radio" name="OftenVisitSite" value="Once a week">Once a week</font></td>
<td width="165">
 <font face="Arial, Helvetica, sans-serif" size="2"><input type="radio" name="OftenVisitSite" value="Couple times a month">Couple times a month</font></td></tr></table><font face="Arial, Helvetica, sans-serif" size="2">
<p>
<font face="Arial, Helvetica, sans-serif" size="2"><b>When you need help using the library's Web site, what do you do? </b>
</font></font><table width="550" border="0" cellspacing="0" cellpadding="0">
<tr><td width="230">
<font face="Arial, Helvetica, sans-serif" size="2"><input type="radio" name="WebHelp" value="Use on-line help">Use on-line help</font></td>
<td width="155">
<font face="Arial, Helvetica, sans-serif" size="2"><input type="radio" name="WebHelp" value="E-mail library staff">E-mail library staff</font></td>
<td width="165">
<font face="Arial, Helvetica, sans-serif" size="2"><input type="radio" name="WebHelp" value="Phone library staff">Phone library staff</font></td></tr>
<tr><td width="230">
<font face="Arial, Helvetica, sans-serif" size="2"><input type="radio" name="WebHelp" value="Read printed documentation">Read printed documentation</font></td>
<td width="155">
<font face="Arial, Helvetica, sans-serif" size="2"><input type="radio" name="WebHelp" value="Ask a friend">Ask a friend</font></td>
<td width="165">
<font face="Arial, Helvetica, sans-serif" size="2"><input type="radio" name="WebHelp" value="Do not need

help">Do not need help</font></td></tr></table>

<p>

<font face="Arial, Helvetica, sans-serif" size="2"><b>Which sections / pages of the library's Web site do you use most often? </b>
<font face="Arial, Helvetica, sans-serif" size="3"><textarea name="Features" cols="40" rows="2"></textarea></font></font></p>

<p> </p>

<table width="500" border="0" cellspacing="4" cellpadding="1">

<tr><td width="257">

<b><font face="Arial, Helvetica, sans-serif" size="2">Name </font></b><font face="Arial, Helvetica, sans-serif" size="1"> (last, first middle)</font>
<font face="Arial, Helvetica, sans-serif" size="2"><input type="text" name="Name" size="25"></font></td>

<td width="227">

<b><font face="Arial, Helvetica, sans-serif" size="2">Department / Major
</font></b><font face="Arial, Helvetica, sans-serif" size="2"><input type="text" name="Department" size="25">

</font></td></tr>

<tr><td width="257">

<b><font face="Arial, Helvetica, sans-serif" size="2">Campus e-mail
</font></b><font face="Arial, Helvetica, sans-serif" size="2"><input type="text" name="CampusEmail" size="25"></font></td>

<td width="227">

<b><font face="Arial, Helvetica, sans-serif" size="2">Campus phone</font></b>
<font face="Arial, Helvetica, sans-serif" size="2"><input type="text" name="CampusPhone2" size="25"></font> </td></tr></table>

<p>

<b><font face="Arial, Helvetica, sans-serif" size="2">Status</font></b><table width="550" border="0" cellspacing="0" cellpadding="0">

<tr><td width="126" height="13">

<font face="Arial, Helvetica, sans-serif" size="2"><input type="radio" name="Status" value="Freshman">Freshman</font></td>

<td width="117" height="13">

<font face="Arial, Helvetica, sans-serif" size="2"><input type="radio" name="Status" value="Sophomore">Sophomore</font></td>

<td width="87" height="13">

<font face="Arial, Helvetica, sans-serif" size="2"><input type="radio" name="Status" value="Junior">Junior </font></td>

<td width="202" height="13">

<font face="Arial, Helvetica, sans-serif" size="2"><input type="radio" name="Status" value="Senior">Senior </font></td></tr>

<tr><td width="126" height="9">

<font face="Arial, Helvetica, sans-serif" size="2"><input type="radio" name="Status" value="Graduate Student">Grad Student</font></td>

<td width="117" height="9">

<font face="Arial, Helvetica, sans-serif" size="2"><input type="radio" name="Status" value="Faculty">Faculty </font></td>

<td width="87" height="9">

<font face="Arial, Helvetica, sans-serif" size="2"><input type="radio" name="Status" value="Staff">Staff </font></td>

```
<td width="202" height="9">
<font face="Arial, Helvetica, sans-serif" size="2"><input type="radio" name="Status" value="Other">Other
</font></td></tr></table>
<font face="Arial, Helvetica, sans-serif" size="2"><font face="Arial, Helvetica, sans-serif" size="2"> <p> 
</p>
<table width="700" border="0" cellspacing="10" cellpadding="1"><tr><td width="226">
<div align="right"><input type="submit" name="send" value="Send Survey"></div></td>
<td width="207"> </td><td width="221">
<div align="left"><input type="reset" name="clear" value="Clear Survey"></div></td></tr>
<tr colspan=3><td colspan=3>
<table width="500" border="0" height="2" align="center" cellpadding="0" cellspacing="0"
bgcolor="#000000"><tr><td><font size="1" color="#000000">.</font></td></tr></table></td> </tr>
<tr><td colspan=3><div align="center">
<font face="Arial, Helvetica, sans-serif" size="1"><b>http://</b></font><br><font size="2"> 
<font face="Arial, Helvetica, sans-serif" size="1"><b>&copy; 2001</b></font></font>
<font face="Arial, Helvetica, sans-serif" size="2"><a href="mailto:">
<b><font size="1">Contact Webmaster</font></b></a></font></div></td></tr>
</table></font></font></form>
</body>
</html>
```

Off-Campus Web User Survey — Perl Script

```perl
#!/usr/local/bin/perl

# ************************************************
# ABOVE is where you MUST specify the path to your
# perl interpreter on your Web server.
# Replace /usr/local/bin/perl with your path.
# ************************************************

if ($ENV{'REQUEST_METHOD'}eq"GET"){$buffer = $ENV{'QUERY_STRING'};}
    elsif($ENV{'REQUEST_METHOD'}eq"POST"){
        read(STDIN,$buffer,$ENV{'CONTENT_LENGTH'});
    }
$bufferb = $buffer;
#separate the name of the input from its value.
@forminputs = split(/&/, $bufferb);

foreach $forminput (@forminputs)
{
        #separate the name of the input from its value
        ($name, $value) = split(/=/, $forminput);

        #Un-Webify plus signs and %-encoding
        $value =~ tr/+/ /;
        $value =~ s/%([a-fA-F0-9][a-fA-F0-9])/pack("C", hex($1))/eg;

        #stick them in the in array
        $in{$name} = $value;
}
print "Content-type: text/html\n\n";


################################################################
# ABOVE is the required header for a perl script          #
################################################################


##################################################################
# (Below) Email received by library containing user-entered information #
##################################################################


# ************************************************
# Here's where you MUST specify the path to your
# email program (probably sendmail) ON your Web server.
# Replace /usr/sbin/sendmail with your path.
# ************************************************
```

```
open (LMAIL, "I/usr/sbin/sendmail -t");
print LMAIL ("To: $in{LibraryEmail}\n");

print LMAIL ("From: $in{Email}\n");
print LMAIL ("Subject: $in{Form} - patron submission\n");

print LMAIL ("------------------\nPatron information\n\n");
print LMAIL ("Name:\n $in{Name}\n\n");
print LMAIL ("Department / Major:\n $in{Department}\n\n");
print LMAIL ("Campus Email:\n $in{CampusEmail}\n\n");
print LMAIL ("Campus Phone:\n $in{CampusPhone}\n\n");
print LMAIL ("Status:\n $in{Status}\n\n");

print LMAIL ("------------------\nSubmitted information \n\n");

print LMAIL ("My level of computer expertise:\n $in{Expertise}\n\n");
print LMAIL ("Why I use my computer:\n $in{WP}, $in{E}, $in{WB}, $in{R}, $in{RR}, $in{OP}, $in{OtherHow} \n\n");
print LMAIL ("Kind of computer that I use off-campus:\n $in{Computer}\n\n");
print LMAIL ("How often I use library computers:\n $in{LibraryComputers}\n\n");

print LMAIL ("My internet provider:\n $in{ISP} $in{ISPDoNotKnow}\n\n");
print LMAIL ("Speed of my Internet connection:\n $in{Fast}\n\n");
print LMAIL ("My web browser(s):\n  $in{IE}, $in{NET}, $in{AOL}, $in{CS}, $in{O}, $in{DK}\n\n");
print LMAIL ("How often I use the Internet:\n $in{InternetUse}\n\n");
print LMAIL ("How long I have used the Internet:\n $in{LongUsedInternet}\n\n");
print LMAIL ("When I use the Internet:\n $in{M}, $in{EA}, $in{LA}, $in{EE}, $in{N}, $in{LN}\n\n");
print LMAIL ("How many times I have visited the library's Web site in the past 30 days:\n $in{Visits}\n\n");
print LMAIL ("How often I visit the library's Web site:\n $in{OftenVisitSite}\n\n");
print LMAIL ("When I need help using the library's Web site, I:\n $in{WebHelp}\n\n");
print LMAIL ("Sections / Features / Pages I use most often:\n $in{Features}\n\n");

print LMAIL ("\n.\n");

#####################################################
# Email received by the user confirming form submission #
#####################################################

# ***********************************************
# Here's where you MUST specify the path to your
# email program ON your Web server.
# Replace /usr/sbin/sendmail with your path.
# ***********************************************

open (MAIL, "I/usr/sbin/sendmail -t");

# ***********************************************
```

```
# Here's where you MAY customize the email
# response to the user. You may change any wording
# on the form.
# **************************************************

print MAIL<<toEnd;
To: $in{CampusEmail}
From: $in{LibraryEmail}
Subject: $in{Form}

Thanks for taking the time to fill out our Remote Web User Survey.\n\n
We will use your input to help us improve our Web site and its content.

toEnd
    print MAIL ("\n.\n");


#####################################################
# Screen response to user after submitting the form  #
#####################################################

print ("<html><head><title>$in{Form}</title></head>");
print ("<body bgcolor=\"ffffff\">");


# **************************************************
# Here's where you MAY change the screen response
# the user sees after submitting the form. You may
# change any wording between the quotation marks.
# **************************************************

print ("Thanks for taking the time to fill out our Remote Web User Survey.<p>
We will use your input to help us improve our Web site and its content.");


# **************************************************
# Here's where you MAY change the name of the link
# back to your main page. You may replace Return
# to our main page with your own wording.
# **************************************************

print ("<p><center><a href=$in{LibraryURL}>Return to our main page.</a></center>");
print ("</body></html>");
```

Library Classroom / Lab Request

Faculty only

If you would like to reserve one of the library's classrooms or computer labs for any of your classes, please fill out the form below. If you prefer a specific room, please indicate its floor and room number. Please provide us with three date/time options, as our classrooms and labs are often reserved or busy.

Name (last, first middle)
[   ]

Department / Major
[   ]

Campus address
[   ]

Campus e-mail
[   ]

Campus phone
[   ]

Fax / Other phone
[   ]

Course title
[   ]

Course number
[   ]

Section number
[   ]

Number of students
[   ]

Type of room
○ Classroom   ○ Meeting / Seminar room   ○ Computer lab

Please indicate location, floor, room number
[   ]

Date / Time (list 3 date / time options)

Date [   ]   Time [   ] to [   ]

Date [   ]   Time [   ] to [   ]

Date [   ]   Time [   ] to [   ]

Comments / Special requests
[   ]

[Send Request]   [Clear Form]

Library Classroom / Lab Request — HTML Form

```
<html>
<head><title>Library Classroom / Lab Request</title></head>
<body bgcolor="#FFFFFF">
<table width="700" border="0" height="85" bgcolor="#000000">
<tr valign="middle" align="center"><td>
<p>
<font halign=center color="#FFFFFF" face="Arial, Helvetica, sans-serif" size="+3"><b><i>Library Classroom /
Lab Request</i></b></font></p>
</td></tr></table>
<form method="post" action="http://www.yourLibrary.edu/cgi-bin/alc4.pl"><p> </p>
<p>
<font face="Arial, Helvetica, sans-serif" size="2"><font size="4"><b><font size="3"><i>Faculty only</i>
</font></b></font></font></p>
<p>
<font face="Arial, Helvetica, sans-serif" size="2"><b>If you would like to reserve one of the library's classrooms
or computer labs for any of your classes, <br>please fill out the form below. If you prefer a specific room, please
indicate its floor and room number. <br>Please provide us with three date/time options, as our classrooms and
labs are often reserved or busy.</b></font></p>
<p> </p>
<input type="hidden" name="LibraryEmail" value="you@yourLibrary.edu">
<input type="hidden" name="LibraryURL" value="http://www.yourLibrary.edu">
<input type="hidden" name="Form" value="Reserve a Library Computer"><p></p>
<p></p>
<table width="500" border="0" cellspacing="4" cellpadding="1">
 <tr><td width="257">
<b><font face="Arial, Helvetica, sans-serif" size="2">Name </font></b><font face="Arial, Helvetica, sans-
serif" size="1"> (last, first middle)</font><br><font face="Arial, Helvetica, sans-serif" size="2"><input
type="text" name="Name" size="25"></font></td>
<td width="227">
<b><font face="Arial, Helvetica, sans-serif" size="2">Department / Major<br></font></b><font face="Arial,
Helvetica, sans-serif" size="2"><input type="text" name="Department" size="25"></font> </td></tr>
<tr><td width="257">
<b><font face="Arial, Helvetica, sans-serif" size="2">Campus address<br></font></b><font face="Arial,
Helvetica, sans-serif" size="2"><input type="text" name="CampusAddress" size="25"></font></td>
<td width="227">
<b><font face="Arial, Helvetica, sans-serif" size="2">Campus e-mail<br></font></b><font face="Arial, Helvetica,
sans-serif" size="2"><input type="text" name="CampusEmail" size="25">/font></td></tr>
<tr><td width="257">
<b><font face="Arial, Helvetica, sans-serif" size="2">Campus phone</font></b><br><font face="Arial, Helvetica,
sans-serif" size="2"><input type="text" name="CampusPhone" size="25"></font></td>
<td width="227">
<b><font face="Arial, Helvetica, sans-serif" size="2">Fax / Other phone<br></font></b><font face="Arial,
Helvetica, sans-serif" size="2"><input type="text" name="OtherPhone" size="25"></font></td></tr>
```

```
</table>
<p> 
<table width="500" border="0" cellspacing="0" cellpadding="0">
 <tr><td width="257">
<b><font face="Arial, Helvetica, sans-serif" size="2">Course title</font></b><br><font face="Arial, Helvetica,
sans-serif" size="3"><input type="text" name="CTitle" size="25"></font></td>
<td width="227">
<b><font face="Arial, Helvetica, sans-serif" size="2">Course number <br></font></b><font face="Arial,
Helvetica, sans-serif" size="3"><input type="text" name="CNum" size="25"></font></td></tr>
<tr><td width="257">
<b><font face="Arial, Helvetica, sans-serif" size="2">Section number <br></font></b><font face="Arial,
Helvetica, sans-serif" size="3"><input type="text" name="SNum" size="25"></font></td>
<td width="227">
<b><font face="Arial, Helvetica, sans-serif" size="2">Number of students<br></font></b><font face="Arial,
Helvetica, sans-serif" size="3"><input type="text" name="NumOfS" size="25"></font></td>
</tr></table>
<p>
<b><font face="Arial, Helvetica, sans-serif" size="2">Type of room<br></font></b><font face="Arial, Helvetica,
sans-serif" size="2">
<input type="radio" name="Type" value="Classroom">Classroom    
<input type="radio" name="Type" value="Meeting / Seminar room">Meeting / Seminar room
   
<input type="radio" name="Type" value="Computer lab">Computer lab</font></p>
<p>
<b><font face="Arial, Helvetica, sans-serif" size="2">Please indicate location, floor, room number<br>
</font><font face="Arial, Helvetica, sans-serif" size="3"><input type="text" name="Floor" size="40" value="">
</font></b></p>
<p><b><font face="Arial, Helvetica, sans-serif" size="2">Date / Time </font></b><font face="Arial,
Helvetica, sans-serif" size="1"> (list 3 date / time options)</font><br><font face="Arial, Helvetica, sans-
serif" size="2">Date</font><font size="3"><font face="Arial, Helvetica, sans-serif"><input type="text"
name="Date1" size="15"></font><font face="Arial, Helvetica, sans-serif">   </font><font
size="3"><font face="Arial, Helvetica, sans-serif">    </font></font><font face="Arial,
Helvetica, sans-serif" size="2">Time    </font><font face="Arial, Helvetica, sans-serif">
<input type="text" name="TimeBegin1" size="10"><font size="2">to</font><input type="text"
name="TimeEnd1" size="10"><br><font face="Arial, Helvetica, sans-serif" size="2">Date</font><font
size="3"><font face="Arial, Helvetica, sans-serif"><input type="text" name="Date2" size="15"> </
font>      <font face="Arial, Helvetica, sans-serif" size="2">Time</font>
<font face="Arial, Helvetica, sans-serif"><input type="text" name="TimeBegin2" size="10"><font size="2">to</
font> <input type="text" name="TimeEnd2" size="10"></font></font><br></font>
<font face="Arial, Helvetica, sans-serif" size="2">Date</font><font size="3"><font face="Arial, Helvetica, sans-
serif"><input type="text" name="Date3" size="15"></font>      
<font face="Arial, Helvetica, sans-serif" size="2">Time<input type="text" name="TimeBegin3" size="10"><font
size="2">to</font><input type="text" name="TimeEnd3" size="10"></font></font></font></p>
<p>
<b><font face="Arial, Helvetica, sans-serif" size="2">Comments / Special requests<br></font><font face="Arial,
```

Helvetica, sans-serif" size="3"><textarea name="Comments" cols="40" rows="2"></textarea>
</font></b></p>
<p> </p>
<table width="700" border="0" cellspacing="10" cellpadding="1"><tr><td width="244">
<div align="right"><input type="submit" name="send" value="Send Request"></div></td>
<td width="203"> </td><td width="207">
<div align="left"><input type="reset" name="clear" value="Clear Form"></div></td></tr>
<tr colspan=3><td colspan=3><table width="500" border="0" height="2" align="center" cellpadding="0"
cellspacing="0" bgcolor="#000000"><tr><td><font size="1" color="#000000">.</font></td></tr></table>
</td></tr>
<tr><td colspan=3><div align="center">
<font face="Arial, Helvetica, sans-serif" size="1"><b>http://</b></font><font>
<font size="2">
<font face="Arial, Helvetica, sans-serif" size="1"><b>© 2001</b></font></font>
<font face="Arial, Helvetica, sans-serif" size="2"><a href="mailto:">
<b><font size="1">Contact Webmaster</font></b></a></font></div></td></tr>
</table></form>
</body>
</html>

Library Classroom / Lab Request — Perl Script

```perl
#!/usr/local/bin/perl

# **************************************************
# ABOVE is where you MUST specify the path to your
# perl interpreter on your Web server.
# Replace /usr/local/bin/perl with your path.
# **************************************************

if ($ENV{'REQUEST_METHOD'}eq"GET"){$buffer = $ENV{'QUERY_STRING'};}
    elsif($ENV{'REQUEST_METHOD'}eq"POST"){
        read(STDIN,$buffer,$ENV{'CONTENT_LENGTH'});
    }
$bufferb = $buffer;
#separate the name of the input from its value.
@forminputs = split(/&/, $bufferb);

foreach $forminput (@forminputs)
{
        #separate the name of the input from its value
        ($name, $value) = split(/=/, $forminput);

        #Un-Webify plus signs and %-encoding
        $value =~ tr/+/ /;
        $value =~ s/%([a-fA-F0-9][a-fA-F0-9])/pack("C", hex($1))/eg;

        #stick them in the in array
        $in{$name} = $value;
}
print "Content-type: text/html\n\n";

##############################################################
# ABOVE is the required header for a perl script        #
##############################################################


####################################################################
# (Below) Email received by library containing user-entered information #
####################################################################


# **************************************************
# Here's where you MUST specify the path to your
# email program (probably sendmail) ON your Web server.
# Replace /usr/sbin/sendmail with your path.
# **************************************************
```

```
open (LMAIL, "I/usr/sbin/sendmail -t");
print LMAIL ("To: $in{LibraryEmail}\n");

print LMAIL ("From: $in{Email}\n");
print LMAIL ("Subject: $in{Form} - patron submission\n");

print LMAIL ("------------------\nPatron information\n\n");
print LMAIL ("Name:\n $in{Name}\n\n");
print LMAIL ("Department / Major:\n $in{Department}\n\n");
print LMAIL ("Campus Address:\n $in{CampusAddress}\n\n");
print LMAIL ("Campus Email:\n $in{CampusEmail}\n\n");
print LMAIL ("Campus Phone:\n $in{CampusPhone}\n\n");
print LMAIL ("Other Phone:\n $in{OtherPhone}\n\n");

print LMAIL ("------------------\nSubmitted information \n\n");

print LMAIL ("Course title:\n $in{CTitle}\n\n");
print LMAIL ("Course number:\n $in{CNum} \n\n");
print LMAIL ("Section number:\n $in{SNum}\n\n");
print LMAIL ("Number of students:\n $in{NumOfS}\n\n");

print LMAIL ("Type of room:\n $in{Type}\n\n");
print LMAIL ("Location, floor, room number:\n $in{Floor}\n\n");
print LMAIL ("First date / time:\n $in{Date1}\n $in{TimeBegin1} to $in{TimeEnd1}\n\n");
print LMAIL ("Second date / time:\n $in{Date2}\n $in{TimeBegin2} to $in{TimeEnd2}\n\n");
print LMAIL ("Third date / time:\n $in{Date3}\n $in{TimeBegin3} to $in{TimeEnd3}\n\n");
print LMAIL ("Comments / Special requests:\n $in{Comments}\n\n");

print LMAIL ("\n.\n");


#########################################################
# Email received by the user confirming form submission #
#########################################################


# ************************************************
# Here's where you MUST specify the path to your
# email program ON your Web server.
# Replace /usr/sbin/sendmail with your path.
# ************************************************

open (MAIL, "I/usr/sbin/sendmail -t");

# ************************************************
# Here's where you MAY customize the email
# response to the user. You may change any wording
```

```
# on the form.
# **********************************************

print MAIL<<toEnd;
To: $in{CampusEmail}
From: $in{LibraryEmail}
Subject: $in{Form}

Thanks for taking the time to fill out our Library Classroom / Lab Request.\n\n
A librarian will be in contact with you shortly.

toEnd
    print MAIL ("\n.\n");


####################################################
# Screen response to user after submitting the form  #
####################################################

print ("<html><head><title>$in{Form}</title></head>");
print ("<body bgcolor=\"ffffff\">");


# **********************************************
# Here's where you MAY change the screen response
# the user sees after submitting the form. You may
# change any wording between the quotation marks.
# **********************************************

print ("Thanks for taking the time to fill out our Library Classroom / Lab Request.<p>
A librarian will be in contact with you shortly.");


# **********************************************
# Here's where you MAY change the name of the link
# back to your main page. You may replace Return
# to our main page with your own wording.
# **********************************************

print ("<p><center><a href=$in{LibraryURL}>Return to our main page.</a></center>");
print ("</body></html>");
```

Group 4 — Library Web Site Forms / Surveys

In this section you'll find two Web-based forms that will enable students, faculty, or staff either to suggest a new link or to report a broken link on, or other probem with, your Web site. Here you'll also find a survey that will enable patrons to give your staff their opinions about the content and arrangement of information on your Web site.

Suggest a New Web Link

Encourage faculty, staff, and students to take a few minutes to recommend a new Web link they've found. Patrons can provide you with the site's URL, why they think you should add it your Web site, and even where on your site they think it should be located. Place a link to this form on any/all of your Web site's pages.

Report a Broken Link or Problem

It's a time-consuming job keeping all of your Web site links current. Faculty, students, and staff can help by reporting any changed or broken links they run into while using your Web site, any graphics/images that don't load properly, or any plug-ins that you need to acquire and/or update. Patrons can also let you know if they notice any typos, grammatical errors, or any other problems with your site. Put a link to this form on any/all of your Web site's pages.

Library Web Site Survey

If you'd like to know what on-campus students, faculty, and staff, as well as long-distance Web visitors, think of your library's Web site, have them complete this brief survey. Place a link to this survey periodically on your library's homepage.

Suggest a New Web Link

Help enrich our Web site by taking a few minutes to recommend a link you've found. Fill out the form below with the site's URL, why you think we should add it to our Web site, and where on our site you think it should be located. We'll send you an e-mail message letting you know if and when your suggestion will debut on our site.

Name (last, first middle)

Department / Major

Campus address

Campus e-mail

Campus phone

Fax / Other phone

Status

○ Freshman   ○ Sophomore   ○ Junior   ○ Senior
○ Grad Student   ○ Faculty   ○ Staff   ○ Other

The Web site URL

http://

Describe the Web site

Reason(s) for suggesting this site

Where on *our* Web site would you place it?

Send Suggestion   Clear Form

Suggest a New Web Link — HTML Form

```
<html>
<head><title>Suggest a New Web Link</title></head>
<body bgcolor="#FFFFFF">
<table width="700" border="0" height="85" bgcolor="#000000">
<tr valign="middle" align="center">
<td>
<p>
<font halign=center color="#FFFFFF" face="Arial, Helvetica, sans-serif" size="+3"> <b><i>Suggest a New Web
Link</i></b></font></p>
</td></tr></table>
<form method="post" action="http://www.yourLibrary.edu/cgi-bin/alw1.pl"><p> </p>
<p>
<font face="Arial, Helvetica, sans-serif" size="2"><b>Help enrich our Web site by taking a few minutes to recom-
mend a link you've found. Fill out<br>the form below with the site's URL, why you think we should add it to our
Web site, and where <br>on our site you think it should be located. We'll send you an e-mail message letting you
know<br>if and when your suggestion will debut on our site.</b></font>
</p><p> </p>
<input type="hidden" name="LibraryEmail" value="you@yourLibrary.edu">
<input type="hidden" name="LibraryURL" value="http://www.yourLibrary.edu">
<input type="hidden" name="Form" value="Suggest a New Web Link"><p></p>
<p></p>
<table width="500" border="0" cellspacing="4" cellpadding="1">
<tr><td width="257">
<b><font face="Arial, Helvetica, sans-serif" size="2">Name </font></b><font face="Arial, Helvetica, sans-
serif" size="1"> (last, first middle)</font><br><font face="Arial, Helvetica, sans-serif" size="2"><input
type="text" name="Name" size="25"></font></td>
<td width="227">
<b><font face="Arial, Helvetica, sans-serif" size="2">Department / Major<br></font></b><font face="Arial,
Helvetica, sans-serif" size="2"><input type="text" name="Department" size="25"></font>
</td></tr>
<tr><td width="257">
<b><font face="Arial, Helvetica, sans-serif" size="2">Campus address<br></font></b><font face="Arial,
Helvetica, sans-serif" size="2"><input type="text" name="CampusAddress" size="25"></font></td>
<td width="227">
<b><font face="Arial, Helvetica, sans-serif" size="2">Campus  e-mail<br></font></b><font face="Arial,
Helvetica, sans-serif" size="2"><input type="text" name="CampusEmail" size="25"></font></td></tr>
<tr><td width="257">
<b><font face="Arial, Helvetica, sans-serif" size="2">Campus phone</font></b><br><font face="Arial, Helvetica,
sans-serif" size="2"><input type="text" name="CampusPhone" size="25"></font></td>
<td width="227">
<b><font face="Arial, Helvetica, sans-serif" size="2">Fax / Other phone<br></font></b><font face="Arial,
Helvetica, sans-serif" size="2"><input type="text" name="OtherPhone" size="25"></font></td></tr>
</table>
```

```
<p>
<b><font face="Arial, Helvetica, sans-serif" size="2">Status</font></b><table width="550" border="0"
cellspacing="0" cellpadding="0">
<tr><td width="126" height="13">
<font face="Arial, Helvetica, sans-serif" size="2"><input type="radio" name="Status"
value="Freshman">Freshman</font></td>
<td width="117" height="13">
<font face="Arial, Helvetica, sans-serif" size="2"><input type="radio" name="Status"
value="Sophomore">Sophomore</font></td>
<td width="87" height="13">
<font face="Arial, Helvetica, sans-serif" size="2"><input type="radio" name="Status"
value="Junior">Junior</font></td>
<td width="202" height="13">
<font face="Arial, Helvetica, sans-serif" size="2"><input type="radio" name="Status"
value="Senior">Senior</font></td></tr>
<tr><td width="126" height="9">
<font face="Arial, Helvetica, sans-serif" size="2"><input type="radio" name="Status"
value="Graduate Student">Grad Student</font></td>
<td width="117" height="9">
<font face="Arial, Helvetica, sans-serif" size="2"><input type="radio" name="Status"
value="Faculty">Faculty</font></td>
<td width="87" height="9">
<font face="Arial, Helvetica, sans-serif" size="2"><input type="radio" name="Status"
value="Staff">Staff</font></td>
<td width="202" height="9">
<font face="Arial, Helvetica, sans-serif" size="2"><input type="radio" name="Status"
value="Other">Other</font></td></tr></table>
<p>
<b><font face="Arial, Helvetica, sans-serif" size="2">The Web site URL</font></b><br><font face="Arial,
Helvetica, sans-serif" size="3"><input type="text" name="URL" size="40" value="http://"></font>
<p>
<b><font face="Arial, Helvetica, sans-serif" size="2">Describe the Web site</font></b><br><font face="Arial,
Helvetica, sans-serif" size="3"><textarea name="Description" cols="40" rows="2">
</textarea></font></p>
<p>
<b><font face="Arial, Helvetica, sans-serif" size="2">Reason(s) for suggesting this site</font></b><br>
<font face="Arial, Helvetica, sans-serif" size="3"><textarea name="Reason" cols="40" rows="2">
</textarea></font></p>
<p>
<b><font face="Arial, Helvetica, sans-serif" size="2">Where on <i>our </i>Web site would you place it?</font>
</b><br><font face="Arial, Helvetica, sans-serif" size="3"><textarea name="Placement" cols="40" rows="2">
</textarea></font></p>
<p>  </p>
<table width="700" border="0" cellspacing="10" cellpadding="1"><tr> <td width="270">
<div align="right"><input type="submit" name="send" value="Send Suggestion"></div></td>
```

```
<td width="177"> </td><td width="207">
<div align="left"><input type="reset" name="clear" value="Clear Form"></div></td></tr>
<tr colspan=3><td colspan=3>
<table width="500" border="0" height="2" align="center" cellpadding="0" cellspacing="0"
bgcolor="#000000"><tr><td><font size="1" color="#000000">.</font></td></tr></table>
</td></tr>
<tr><td colspan=3><div align="center">
<font face="Arial, Helvetica, sans-serif" size="1"><b>http://</b></font><br><font size="2"> 
<font face="Arial, Helvetica, sans-serif" size="1"><b>&copy; 2001</b></font></font>
<font face="Arial, Helvetica, sans-serif" size="2"><a href="mailto:">
<b><font size="1">Contact Webmaster</font></b></a></font></div></td></tr>
</table></form>
</body>
</html>
```

Suggest a New Web Link — Perl Script

```perl
#!/usr/local/bin/perl


# **************************************************
# ABOVE is where you MUST specify the path to your
# perl interpreter on your Web server.
# Replace /usr/local/bin/perl with your path.
# **************************************************

if ($ENV{'REQUEST_METHOD'}eq"GET"){$buffer = $ENV{'QUERY_STRING'};}
    elsif($ENV{'REQUEST_METHOD'}eq"POST"){
        read(STDIN,$buffer,$ENV{'CONTENT_LENGTH'});
    }
$bufferb = $buffer;
#separate the name of the input from its value.
@forminputs = split(/&/, $bufferb);

foreach $forminput (@forminputs)
{
    #separate the name of the input from its value
    ($name, $value) = split(/=/, $forminput);

    #Un-Webify plus signs and %-encoding
    $value =~ tr/+/ /;
    $value =~ s/%([a-fA-F0-9][a-fA-F0-9])/pack("C", hex($1))/eg;

    #stick them in the in array
    $in{$name} = $value;
}
print "Content-type: text/html\n\n";


#############################################################
# ABOVE is the required header for a perl script        #
#############################################################


###################################################################
# (Below) Email received by library containing user-entered information #
###################################################################


# **************************************************
# Here's where you MUST specify the path to your
# email program (probably sendmail) ON your Web server.
# Replace /usr/sbin/sendmail with your path.
# **************************************************
```

```perl
open (LMAIL, "l/usr/sbin/sendmail -t");
print LMAIL ("To: $in{LibraryEmail}\n");

print LMAIL ("From: $in{CampusEmail}\n");
print LMAIL ("Subject: $in{Form} - patron submission\n");

print LMAIL ("------------------\nPatron information\n\n");
print LMAIL ("Name:\n $in{Name}\n\n");
print LMAIL ("Department / Major:\n $in{Department}\n\n");
print LMAIL ("Campus Address:\n $in{CampusAddress}\n\n");
print LMAIL ("Campus Email:\n $in{CampusEmail}\n\n");
print LMAIL ("Campus Phone:\n $in{CampusPhone}\n\n");
print LMAIL ("Other Phone:\n $in{OtherPhone}\n\n");
print LMAIL ("Status:\n $in{Status}\n\n");

print LMAIL ("------------------\nSubmitted information \n\n");

print LMAIL ("Web site URL:\n $in{URL}\n\n");
print LMAIL ("Description of the Web site:\n $in{Description}\n\n");
print LMAIL ("Reason for the new link:\n $in{Reason}\n\n");
print LMAIL ("Where on the library Web site I would place it:\n $in{Placement}\n\n");

print LMAIL ("\n.\n");

#####################################################
# Email received by the user confirming form submission #
#####################################################

# ***********************************************
# Here's where you MUST specify the path to your
# email program ON your Web server.
# Replace /usr/sbin/sendmail with your path.
# ***********************************************

open (MAIL, "l/usr/sbin/sendmail -t");

# ***********************************************
# Here's where you MAY customize the email
# response to the user. You may change any wording
# on the form.
# ***********************************************

print MAIL<<toEnd;
To: $in{CampusEmail}
From: $in{LibraryEmail}
```

```
Subject: $in{Form}
Thanks for sending us your suggestion for a new Web link.\n\n
We are always looking for new online resources to enrich our Web site.


toEnd
    print MAIL ("\n.\n");


######################################################
# Screen response to user after submitting the form  #
######################################################

print ("<html><head><title>$in{Form}</title></head>");
print ("<body bgcolor=\"ffffff\">");


# ************************************************
# Here's where you MAY change the screen response
# the user sees after submitting the form. You may
# change any wording between the quotation marks.
# ************************************************

print ("Thanks for sending us your suggestion for a new Web link.<p>
We are always looking for new online resources to enrich our Web site.");


# ************************************************
# Here's where you MAY change the name of the link
# back to your main page. You may replace Return
# to our main page with your own wording.
# ************************************************

print ("<p><center><a href=$in{LibraryURL}>Return to our main page.</a></center>");
print ("</body></html>");
```

Report a Broken Link or Problem

Please report any broken links you find while using our Web site, any graphics/images that don't load properly, or any plug-ins that we need to acquire and/or update. Also, let us know if you notice any typos, grammatical errors, or other problems with our site. We'll send you an e-mail message informing you when we've fixed the problem(s).

Name (last, first middle)

Department / Major

Campus address

Campus e-mail

Campus phone

Fax / Other phone

Status

○ Freshman   ○ Sophomore   ○ Junior   ○ Senior
○ Grad Student   ○ Faculty   ○ Staff   ○ Other

Title of the Web page where you found the problem (eg. Web Resources)

Type of problem

○ Link doesn't work   ○ Image / plug-in doesn't load   ○ Typo / grammatical error

Describe the problem (please provide as many details as you can)

If a broken link, what is the *current* URL?

http://

If a broken link, what is the *new* URL?

http://

[Send Report]   [Clear Form]

Report a Broken Link or Problem — HTML Form

```
<html>
<head><title>Report a Broken Link or Problem</title></head>
<body bgcolor="#FFFFFF">
<table width="700" border="0" height="85" bgcolor="#000000"><tr valign="middle" align="center"><td><p>
<font halign=center color="#FFFFFF" face="Arial, Helvetica, sans-serif" size="+3">
<b><i>Report a Broken Link or Problem</i></b></font></p>
</td></tr></table>
<form method="post" action="http://www.yourLibrary.edu/cgi-bin/alw2.pl"><p> </p>
<p>
<font face="Arial, Helvetica, sans-serif" size="2"><b>Please report any broken links you find while using our Web
site, any graphics/images that <br>don't load properly, or any plug-ins that we need to acquire and/or update.
Also, let us know<br> if you notice any typos, grammatical errors, or other problems with our site. We'll send you
an<br> e-mail message informing you when we've fixed the problem(s).</b> </font></p>
<p> </p>
<input type="hidden" name="LibraryEmail" value="you@yourLibrary.edu">
<input type="hidden" name="LibraryURL" value="http://www.yourLibrary.edu">
<input type="hidden" name="Form" value="Report a Broken Link or Problem"><p></p>
<p></p>
<table width="500" border="0" cellspacing="4" cellpadding="1">
<tr><td width="257">
<b><font face="Arial, Helvetica, sans-serif" size="2">Name </font></b><font face="Arial, Helvetica, sans-serif" size="1"> (last, first middle)</font><br><font face="Arial, Helvetica, sans-serif" size="2"><input type="text" name="Name" size="25"></font></td>
<td width="227">
<b><font face="Arial, Helvetica, sans-serif" size="2">Department / Major<br></font></b><font face="Arial, Helvetica, sans-serif" size="2"><input type="text" name="Department" size="25"></font> </td></tr>
<tr><td width="257">
<b><font face="Arial, Helvetica, sans-serif" size="2">Campus address<br></font></b><font face="Arial, Helvetica, sans-serif" size="2"><input type="text" name="CampusAddress" size="25"></font></td>
<td width="227">
<b><font face="Arial, Helvetica, sans-serif" size="2">Campus e-mail<br></font></b><font face="Arial, Helvetica, sans-serif" size="2"><input type="text" name="CampusEmail" size="25"></font></td></tr>   <tr><td width="257">
<b><font face="Arial, Helvetica, sans-serif" size="2">Campus phone</font></b><br><font face="Arial, Helvetica, sans-serif" size="2"><input type="text" name="CampusPhone" size="25"></font></td>
<td width="227">
 <b><font face="Arial, Helvetica, sans-serif" size="2">Fax / Other phone<br></font></b><font face="Arial, Helvetica, sans-serif" size="2"><input type="text" name="OtherPhone" size="25"></font></td></tr> </table>
<p>
<b><font face="Arial, Helvetica, sans-serif" size="2">Status</font></b>
<table width="550" border="0" cellspacing="0" cellpadding="0">
<tr><td width="126" height="13">
<font face="Arial, Helvetica, sans-serif" size="2"><input type="radio" name="Status"
```

value="Freshman">Freshman</font></td>
<td width="117" height="13">
<font face="Arial, Helvetica, sans-serif" size="2"><input type="radio" name="Status"
value="Sophomore">Sophomore</font></td>
<td width="87" height="13">
<font face="Arial, Helvetica, sans-serif" size="2"><input type="radio" name="Status"
value="Junior">Junior</font></td>
<td width="202" height="13">
<font face="Arial, Helvetica, sans-serif" size="2"><input type="radio" name="Status"
value="Senior">Senior</font></td></tr>
<tr><td width="126" height="9">
<font face="Arial, Helvetica, sans-serif" size="2"><input type="radio" name="Status"
value="Graduate Student">Grad Student</font></td>
<td width="117" height="9">
<font face="Arial, Helvetica, sans-serif" size="2"><input type="radio" name="Status"
value="Faculty">Faculty</font></td>
<td width="87" height="9">
<font face="Arial, Helvetica, sans-serif" size="2"><input type="radio" name="Status"
value="Staff">Staff</font></td>
<td width="202" height="9">
<font face="Arial, Helvetica, sans-serif" size="2"><input type="radio" name="Status"
value="Other">Other</font></td></tr></table>
<p>
<b><font face="Arial, Helvetica, sans-serif" size="2">Title of the Web page where you found the problem
</font></b><font face="Arial, Helvetica, sans-serif" size="1">   (eg. Web Resources)
</font>
<font face="Arial, Helvetica, sans-serif" size="3"><input type="text" name="SpecificPage"
size="40"></font>
<p>
<b><font face="Arial, Helvetica, sans-serif" size="2">Type of problem
</font></b></p>
<table width="544" border="0" cellspacing="0" cellpadding="0">
<tr><td width="139">
<font face="Arial, Helvetica, sans-serif" size="2"><input type="radio" name="TypeOfProblem" value="Link
doesn't work">Link doesn't work</font></td>
<td width="192">
<font face="Arial, Helvetica, sans-serif" size="2"><input type="radio" name="TypeOfProblem" value="Image/
plug-in doesn't load">Image / plug-in doesn't load</font></td>
<td width="169">
<font face="Arial, Helvetica, sans-serif" size="2"><input type="radio" name="TypeOfProblem" value="Typo/
grammar error">Typo / grammatical error</font></td></tr></table>
<p>
<b><font face="Arial, Helvetica, sans-serif" size="2">Describe the problem </font></b><font face="Arial,
Helvetica, sans-serif" size="1"> (please provide as many details as you can) </font>
<font
face="Arial, Helvetica, sans-serif" size="3"><textarea name="Description" cols="40" rows="2"></textarea>
</font></p>
<p>

```
<b><font face="Arial, Helvetica, sans-serif" size="2">If a broken link, what is the <i>current</i> URL?</font></
b><br><font face="Arial, Helvetica, sans-serif" size="3"><input type="text" name="BrokenURL" size="40"
value="http://"></font></p>
<p>
<b><font face="Arial, Helvetica, sans-serif" size="2">If a broken link, what is the <i>new</i> URL?</font></
b><br><font face="Arial, Helvetica, sans-serif" size="3"><input type="text" name="NewURL" size="40"
value="http://"></font></p>
<p>  </p>
<table width="700" border="0" cellspacing="10" cellpadding="1"><tr><td width="251">
<div align="right"><input type="submit" name="send" value="Send Report"></div></td>
<td width="196"> </td><td width="207">
<div align="left"><input type="reset" name="clear" value="Clear Form"></div></td></tr>
<tr colspan=3><td colspan=3>
<table width="500" border="0" height="2" align="center" cellpadding="0" cellspacing="0"
bgcolor="#000000"><tr><td><font size="1" color="#000000">.</font></td></tr></table>
</td></tr>
<tr><td colspan=3><div align="center">
<font face="Arial, Helvetica, sans-serif" size="1"><b>http://</b></font><br><font size="2"> 
<font face="Arial, Helvetica, sans-serif" size="1"><b>&copy; 2001</b></font></font>
<font face="Arial, Helvetica, sans-serif" size="2"><a href="mailto:">
<b><font size="1">Contact Webmaster</font></b></a></font></div></td></tr>
</table></form>
</body>
</html>
```

Report a Broken Link or Problem — Perl Script

```perl
#!/usr/local/bin/perl

# ************************************************
# ABOVE is where you MUST specify the path to your
# perl interpreter on your Web server.
# Replace /usr/local/bin/perl with your path.
# ************************************************

if ($ENV{'REQUEST_METHOD'}eq"GET"){$buffer = $ENV{'QUERY_STRING'};}
    elsif($ENV{'REQUEST_METHOD'}eq"POST"){
        read(STDIN,$buffer,$ENV{'CONTENT_LENGTH'});
    }
$bufferb = $buffer;
#separate the name of the input from its value.
@forminputs = split(/&/, $bufferb);

foreach $forminput (@forminputs)
{
    #separate the name of the input from its value
    ($name, $value) = split(/=/, $forminput);

    #Un-Webify plus signs and %-encoding
    $value =~ tr/+/ /;
    $value =~ s/%([a-fA-F0-9][a-fA-F0-9])/pack("C", hex($1))/eg;

    #stick them in the in array
    $in{$name} = $value;
}
print "Content-type: text/html\n\n";

##############################################################
# ABOVE is the required header for a perl script           #
##############################################################


################################################################
# (Below) Email received by library containing user-entered information #
################################################################


# ************************************************
# Here's where you MUST specify the path to your
# email program (probably sendmail) ON your Web server.
# Replace /usr/sbin/sendmail with your path.
# ************************************************
```

```
open (LMAIL, "l/usr/sbin/sendmail -t");
print LMAIL ("To: $in{LibraryEmail}\n");

print LMAIL ("From: $in{CampusEmail}\n");
print LMAIL ("Subject: $in{Form} - patron submission\n");

print LMAIL ("-------------------\nPatron information\n\n");
print LMAIL ("Name:\n $in{Name}\n\n");
print LMAIL ("Department / Major:\n $in{Department}\n\n");
print LMAIL ("Campus Address:\n $in{CampusAddress}\n\n");
print LMAIL ("Campus Email:\n $in{CampusEmail}\n\n");
print LMAIL ("Campus Phone:\n $in{CampusPhone}\n\n");
print LMAIL ("Other Phone:\n $in{OtherPhone}\n\n");
print LMAIL ("Status:\n $in{Status}\n\n");

print LMAIL ("------------------\nSubmitted information \n\n");

print LMAIL ("Specific Web page where the problem exists:\n $in{SpecificPage}\n\n");
print LMAIL ("Type of problem:\n $in{TypeOfProblem}\n\n");
print LMAIL ("Description of the problem:\n $in{Description}\n\n");
print LMAIL ("Current broken URL:\n $in{BrokenURL}\n\n");
print LMAIL ("Correct URL:\n $in{NewURL}\n\n");

print LMAIL ("\n.\n");

###########################################################
# Email received by the user confirming form submission #
###########################################################

# ***********************************************
# Here's where you MUST specify the path to your
# email program ON your Web server.
# Replace /usr/sbin/sendmail with your path.
# ***********************************************

open (MAIL, "l/usr/sbin/sendmail -t");

# ***********************************************
# Here's where you MAY customize the email
# response to the user. You may change any wording
# on the form.
# ***********************************************

print MAIL<<toEnd;
To: $in{CampusEmail}
```

From: $in{LibraryEmail}
Subject: $in{Form}

Thanks for letting us know about a broken link or other problem with our Web site.\n\n
We will get it fixed as soon as we can.

toEnd
    print MAIL ("\n.\n");

```
###################################################
# Screen response to user after submitting the form  #
###################################################
```

print ("<html><head><title>$in{Form}</title></head>");
print ("<body bgcolor=\"ffffff\">");

```
# ************************************************
# Here's where you MAY change the screen response
# the user sees after submitting the form. You may
# change any wording between the quotation marks.
# ************************************************
```

print ("Thanks for letting us know about a broken link or other problem with our Web site.<p>
We will get it fixed as soon as we can.");

```
# ************************************************
# Here's where you MAY change the name of the link
# back to your main page. You may replace Return
# to our main page with your own wording.
# ************************************************
```

print ("<p> <a href=$in{LibraryURL}>Return to our main page.</a> ");
print ("</body></html>");

Library Web Site Survey

We'd like to know what you think of our library's Web site. Please complete this brief survey to help us create the best possible Web site for the campus community.

You and the Library's Web Site

How many times have you used the library's Web site in the last 30 days? ▢

How did you find out / hear about the library's Web site?

- ○ Friend / colleague / faculty
- ○ Link from another Web site
- ○ Library publications
- ○ Campus publications
- ○ Library staff member
- ○ Other

While using the library's Web site you usually find...

- ○ More than you expected to find
- ○ Some things you expected to find
- ○ Nothing you expected to find
- ○ Exactly what you expected to find
- ○ A few things you expected to find

When you need help using the library's Web site what do you do?

- ○ Ask a staff member
- ○ Use online help screens
- ○ Refer to printed documentation
- ○ Quit using the Web site
- ○ Ask a friend
- ○ Don't ask for help

Web Site Content

Which sections / pages of the library's Web site do you use most often?

▢

What do you like the *most* about the library's Web site?

▢

What do you like the *least* about the library's Web site?

▢

What makes the library's Web site difficult to use?

▢

What new links / information would you like to see added to our Web site?

▢

Grade the Library's Web Site

(1-poor 2-fair 3-good 4-very good 5-excellent)

	1	2	3	4	5
Organization of information	O	O	O	O	O
Value of information	O	O	O	O	O
Ability to Navigate	O	O	O	O	O
Value of links	O	O	O	O	O
Currency of links	O	O	O	O	O
Visual appeal	O	O	O	O	O
Page load times	O	O	O	O	O
Sufficient on-line help	O	O	O	O	O
Ability to provide feedback / comments	O	O	O	O	O
Overall rating	O	O	O	O	O

Name (last, first middle)

Department / Major

Campus e-mail

Campus phone

Status

O Freshman   O Sophomore   O Junior   O Senior

O Grad Student   O Faculty   O Staff   O Other

[Send Survey]   [Clear Survey]

Library Web Site Survey — HTML Form

```
<html>
<head><title>Library Web Site Survey</title></head>
<body bgcolor="#FFFFFF">
<table width="700" border="0" height="85" bgcolor="#000000">
<tr valign="middle" align="center"><td>
<p>
<font halign=center color="#FFFFFF" face="Arial, Helvetica, sans-serif" size="5">
<b><i><font size="+3">Library Web Site Survey</font></i></b></font></p>
</td></tr></table>
<form method="post" action="http://www.yourLibrary.edu/cgi-bin/alw4.pl"><p> </p>
<p>
<font face="Arial, Helvetica, sans-serif" size="2"><b>We'd like to know what you think of our library's Web site.
Please complete this brief survey <br> to help us create the best possible Web site for the campus community.
</b></font></p>
<p> </p>
<input type="hidden" name="LibraryEmail" value="you@yourLibrary.edu">
<input type="hidden" name="LibraryURL" value="http://www.yourLibrary.edu">
<input type="hidden" name="Form" value="Library Web Site Survey">
<p></p>
<p>
<b><font face="Arial, Helvetica, sans-serif" size="3">You and the Library's Web Site</font></b></p>
<p> <font face="Arial, Helvetica, sans-serif" size="2"><b>How many times have you used the library's Web site
in the last 30 days?</b><font size="3"> <input type="text" name="TimesVisited" size="5"></font>
</font></p>
<p>
<font face="Arial, Helvetica, sans-serif" size="2"><b>How did you find out / hear about the library's Web
site?<br></b></font>
<table width="550" border="0" cellspacing="0" cellpadding="0">
<tr><td width="218">
<font face="Arial, Helvetica, sans-serif" size="2"><b><font face="Arial, Helvetica, sans-serif" size="2"><input
type="radio" name="FindOut" value="Friend / colleague / faculty"></font></b><font face= "Arial, Helvetica, sans-
serif" size="2">Friend / colleague / faculty</font></font></td>
<td width="161">
<font face= "Arial, Helvetica, sans-serif" size="2"><input type="radio" name="FindOut" value="Library
publications">Library publications</font></td>
<td width="171">
<font face= "Arial, Helvetica, sans-serif" size="2"><input type="radio" name="FindOut" value="Library staff
members">Library staff member</font></td></tr>
<tr><td width="218">
<font face= "Arial, Helvetica, sans-serif" size="2"><input type="radio" name="FindOut" value="Link from another
Web site">Link from another Web site</font></td>
<td width="161">
<font face= "Arial, Helvetica, sans-serif" size="2"><input type="radio" name="FindOut" value="Campus
```

publications">Campus publications</font></td>
<td width="171">
<font face= "Arial, Helvetica, sans-serif" size="2"><input type="radio" name="FindOut" value="Other"> Other
</font></td></tr></table>
<p>
<font face="Arial, Helvetica, sans-serif" size="2">While using the library's Web site you usually find...
</font>
<table width="550" border="0" cellspacing="0" cellpadding="0">
<tr><td width="248">
<font face="Arial, Helvetica, sans-serif" size="2"><input type="radio" name="IFound" value="More than you
expected to find"></font><font face="Arial, Helvetica, sans-serif" size="2">More than you expected to find
</font></td>
<td width="302">
<font face="Arial, Helvetica, sans-serif" size="2"><input type="radio" name="IFound" value="Exactly what you
expected to find">Exactly what you expected to find</font></td></tr>
<tr><td width="248">
<font face="Arial, Helvetica, sans-serif" size="2"><input type="radio" name="IFound" value="Some things you
expected to find">Some things you expected to find</font></td>
<td width="302">
<font face="Arial, Helvetica, sans-serif" size="2"><input type="radio" name="IFound" value="A few things you
expected to find">A few things you expected to find</font></td></tr>
<tr><td width="248">
<font face="Arial, Helvetica, sans-serif" size="2"><input type="radio" name="IFound" value="Nothing you
expected to find">Nothing you expected to find</font></td><td width="302"> </td></tr></table>
<p>
<font face="Arial, Helvetica, sans-serif" size="2">When you need help using the library's Web site what do
you do?
</font>
<table width="550" border="0" cellspacing="0" cellpadding="0">
<tr><td width="176"><font face="Arial, Helvetica, sans-serif" size="2"><input type="radio" name="HelpDo"
value="Ask a staff member">Ask a staff member</font></td>
<td width="224">
<font face= "Arial, Helvetica, sans-serif" size="2"><input type="radio" name="HelpDo" value="Refer to printed
documentation">Refer to printed documentation</font></td>
<td width="150">
<font face= "Arial, Helvetica, sans-serif" size="2"><input type="radio" name="HelpDo" value="Ask a friend">Ask
a friend</font></td></tr>
<tr><td width="176">
<font face= "Arial, Helvetica, sans-serif" size="2"><input type="radio" name="HelpDo" value="Use online help
screens">Use online help screens</font></td>
<td width="224">
<font face= "Arial, Helvetica, sans-serif" size="2"><input type="radio" name="HelpDo" value="Quit using the
Web site">Quit using the Web site</font></td>
<td width="150">
<font face= "Arial, Helvetica, sans-serif" size="2"><input type="radio" name="HelpDo" value="Don't ask for
help">Don't ask for help</font></td></tr><table>

```
<p> </p>
<p>
<b><font face="Arial, Helvetica, sans-serif" size="3">Web Site Content</font></b></p>
<p>
<font face="Arial, Helvetica, sans-serif" size="2"><b>Which sections / pages of the library's Web site do you use
most often? </b><br><font face="Arial, Helvetica, sans-serif" size="3"><textarea name= "Features" cols="40"
rows="2"></textarea></font><br></font></p>
<p>
<font face="Arial, Helvetica, sans-serif" size="2"><b>What do you like the <i>most</i> about the library's Web
site? <br></b><font face="Arial, Helvetica, sans-serif" size="3"><textarea name= "Most" cols="40" rows="2">
</textarea></font></font></p>
<p>
<font face="Arial, Helvetica, sans-serif" size="2"><b>What do you like the <i>least</i> about the library's Web
site? <br></b><font face="Arial, Helvetica, sans-serif" size="3"><textarea name= "Least" cols="40" rows="2">
</textarea></font></font></p>
<p>
<font face="Arial, Helvetica, sans-serif" size="2"><b>What makes the library's Web site difficult to use?<br>
</b><font face="Arial, Helvetica, sans-serif" size="3"><textarea name="Difficult" cols="40" rows="2">
</textarea></font></font></p>
<p>
font face="Arial, Helvetica, sans-serif" size="2"><b>What new links / information would you like to see added to
our Web site?<br></b><font face="Arial, Helvetica, sans-serif" size="3"><textarea name="Added" cols="40"
rows="2"></textarea></font></font></p>
<p> </p>
<p>
<b><font face="Arial, Helvetica, sans-serif" size="3">Grade the Library's Web Site</font><br>
<br></b><font face="Arial, Helvetica, sans-serif" size="1">(1-poor   2-fair
   3-good   4-very good   5-excellent) \
</font><br>
<table width="422" border="0">
<tr align="center">
<td> </td>
<td><font face="Arial, Helvetica, sans-serif" size="1"><b>1</b></font></td>
<td><font face="Arial, Helvetica, sans-serif" size="1"><b>2</b></font></td>
<td><font face="Arial, Helvetica, sans-serif" size="1"><b>3</b></font></td>
<td><font face="Arial, Helvetica, sans-serif" size="1"><b>4</b></font></td>
<td><font face="Arial, Helvetica, sans-serif" size="1"><b>5</b></font></td>
</tr>
<tr><td><font face="Arial, Helvetica, sans-serif" size="2">Organization of information</font></td>
<td><input type="radio" name="Organized" value="poor"></td>
<td><input type="radio" name="Organized" value="fair"></td>
<td><input type="radio" name="Organized" value="good"></td>
<td><input type="radio" name="Organized" value="very good"></td>
<td><input type="radio" name="Organized" value="excellent"></td>
</tr>
```

```
<tr><td><font face="Arial, Helvetica, sans-serif" size="2">Value of information</font></td>
<td><input type="radio" name="Writing" value="poor"></td>
<td><input type="radio" name="Writing" value="fair"></td>
<td><input type="radio" name="Writing" value="good"></td>
<td><input type="radio" name="Writing" value="very good"></td>
<td><input type="radio" name="Writing" value="excellent"></td>
</tr>
<tr><td><font face="Arial, Helvetica, sans-serif" size="2">Ability to Navigate</font></td>
<td><input type="radio" name="Moving" value="poor"></td>
<td><input type="radio" name="Moving" value="fair"></td>
<td><input type="radio" name="Moving" value="good"></td>
<td><input type="radio" name="Moving" value="very good"></td>
<td><input type="radio" name="Moving" value="excellent"></td>
</tr>
<tr><td><font face="Arial, Helvetica, sans-serif" size="2">Value of links</font></td>
<td><input type="radio" name="Important" value="poor"></td>
<td><input type="radio" name="Important" value="fair"></td>
<td><input type="radio" name="Important" value="good"></td>
<td><input type="radio" name="Important" value="very good"></td>
<td><input type="radio" name="Important" value="excellent"></td>
</tr>
<tr><td><font face="Arial, Helvetica, sans-serif" size="2">Currency of links</font></td>
<td><input type="radio" name="UpToDate" value="poor"></td>
<td><input type="radio" name="UpToDate" value="fair"></td>
<td><input type="radio" name="UpToDate" value="good"></td>
<td><input type="radio" name="UpToDate" value="very good"></td>
<td><input type="radio" name="UpToDate" value="excellent"></td>
</tr>
<tr><td><font face="Arial, Helvetica, sans-serif" size="2">Visual appeal </font></td>
<td><input type="radio" name="Visual" value="poor"></td>
<td><input type="radio" name="Visual" value="fair"></td>
<td><input type="radio" name="Visual" value="good"></td>
<td><input type="radio" name="Visual" value="very good"></td>
<td><input type="radio" name="Visual" value="excellent"></td>
</tr>
<tr><td><font face="Arial, Helvetica, sans-serif" size="2">Page load times</font></td>
<td><input type="radio" name="Web" value="poor"></td>
<td><input type="radio" name="Web" value="fair"></td>
<td><input type="radio" name="Web" value="good"></td>
<td><input type="radio" name="Web" value="very good"></td>
<td><input type="radio" name="Web" value="excellent"></td>
</tr>
<tr><td><font face="Arial, Helvetica, sans-serif" size="2">Sufficient on-line help </font></td>
<td><input type="radio" name="Help" value="poor"></td>
<td><input type="radio" name="Help" value="fair"></td>
```

```
<td><input type="radio" name="Help" value="good"></td>
<td><input type="radio" name="Help" value="very good"></td>
<td><input type="radio" name="Help" value="excellent"></td>
</tr>
<tr><td><font face="Arial, Helvetica, sans-serif" size="2">Ability to provide feedback / comments</font></td>
<td><input type="radio" name="Feedback" value="poor"></td>
<td><input type="radio" name="Feedback" value="fair"></td>
<td><input type="radio" name="Feedback" value="good"></td>
<td><input type="radio" name="Feedback" value="very good"></td>
<td><input type="radio" name="Feedback" value="excellent"></td>
</tr>
<tr><td><font face="Arial, Helvetica, sans-serif" size="2"><b>Overall rating</b></font></td>
<td><input type="radio" name="Overall" value="poor"></td>
<td><input type="radio" name="Overall" value="fair"></td>
<td><input type="radio" name="Overall" value="good"></td>
<td><input type="radio" name="Overall" value="very good"></td>
<td><input type="radio" name="Overall" value="excellent"></td>
</tr></table>
<p> <font face="Arial, Helvetica, sans-serif" size="2"><br></font> </p>
<table width="500" border="0" cellspacing="4" cellpadding="1"><tr>
<td width="257">
<b><font face="Arial, Helvetica, sans-serif" size="2">Name </font></b><font face="Arial, Helvetica, sans-serif" size="1"> (last, first middle)</font><br><font face="Arial, Helvetica, sans-serif" size="2"><input type="text" name="Name" size="25"></font></td>
<td width="227">
<b><font face="Arial, Helvetica, sans-serif" size="2">Department / Major<br></font></b><font face="Arial, Helvetica, sans-serif" size="2"><input type="text" name="Department" size="25">
</font></td></tr>
<tr><td width="257">
<b><font face="Arial, Helvetica, sans-serif" size="2">Campus e-mail<br></font></b><font face="Arial, Helvetica, sans-serif" size="2"><input type="text" name="CampusEmail" size="25"></font></td>
<td width="227">
<b><font face="Arial, Helvetica, sans-serif" size="2">Campus phone </font></b><br>nt face="Arial, Helvetica, sans-serif" size="2"><input type="text" name="CampusPhone2" size="25"></font></td></tr></table>
<p>
<b><font face="Arial, Helvetica, sans-serif" size="2">Status</font></b><table width="550" border="0" cellspacing="0" cellpadding="0">
<tr><td width="126" height="13">
<font face="Arial, Helvetica, sans-serif" size="2"><input type="radio" name="Status" value="Freshman">Freshman</font></td>
<td width="117" height="13">
<font face="Arial, Helvetica, sans-serif" size="2"><input type="radio" name="Status" value="Sophomore">Sophomore</font></td>
<td width="87" height="13">
<font face="Arial, Helvetica, sans-serif" size="2"><input type="radio" name="Status" value="Junior">Junior
```

```
</font></td>
<td width="202" height="13">
<font face="Arial, Helvetica, sans-serif" size="2"><input type="radio" name="Status" value="Senior">Senior
</font></td></tr>
<tr><td width="126" height="9">
<font face="Arial, Helvetica, sans-serif" size="2"><input type="radio" name="Status"
value="Graduate Student">Grad Student</font></td>
<td width="117" height="9">
<font face="Arial, Helvetica, sans-serif" size="2"><input type="radio" name="Status" value="Faculty">Faculty
</font></td>
<td width="87" height="9">
<font face="Arial, Helvetica, sans-serif" size="2"><input type="radio" name="Status" value="Staff">Staff
</font></td>
<td width="202" height="9">
<font face="Arial, Helvetica, sans-serif" size="2"><input type="radio" name="Status" value="Other">Other
</font></td></tr></table>
<font face="Arial, Helvetica, sans-serif" size="2">
<p>  </p>
<table width="700" border="0" cellspacing="10" cellpadding="1">
<tr><td width="226">
<div align="right"><input type="submit" name="send" value="Send Survey"></div></td>
<td width="207"> </td>
<td width="221">
<div align="left"><input type="reset" name="clear" value="Clear Survey"></div></td></tr>
<tr colspan=3><td colspan=3>
 <table width="500" border="0" height="2" align="center" cellpadding="0" cellspacing="0"
bgcolor="#000000"><tr><td><font size="1" color="#000000">.</font></td></tr></table></td>    </tr>
<tr><td colspan=3><div align="center">
<font face="Arial, Helvetica, sans-serif" size="1"><b>http://</b></font><br><font size="2">  
<font face="Arial, Helvetica, sans-serif" size="1"><b>&copy; 2001</b></font></font>
<font face="Arial, Helvetica, sans-serif" size="2"><a href="mailto:">
<b><font size="1">Contact Webmaster</font></b></a> </font></div></td></tr>
</table></font></form>
<body>
</html>
```

Library Web Site Survey — Perl Script

```perl
#!/usr/local/bin/perl

# **************************************************
# ABOVE is where you MUST specify the path to your
# perl interpreter on your Web server.
# Replace /usr/local/bin/perl with your path.
# **************************************************

if ($ENV{'REQUEST_METHOD'}eq"GET"){$buffer = $ENV{'QUERY_STRING'};}
    elsif($ENV{'REQUEST_METHOD'}eq"POST"){
        read(STDIN,$buffer,$ENV{'CONTENT_LENGTH'});
    }
$bufferb = $buffer;
#separate the name of the input from its value.
@forminputs = split(/&/, $bufferb);

foreach $forminput (@forminputs)
{
    #separate the name of the input from its value
    ($name, $value) = split(/=/, $forminput);

    #Un-Webify plus signs and %-encoding
    $value =~ tr/+/ /;
    $value =~ s/%([a-fA-F0-9][a-fA-F0-9])/pack("C", hex($1))/eg;

    #stick them in the in array
    $in{$name} = $value;
}
print "Content-type: text/html\n\n";


##############################################################
# ABOVE is the required header for a perl script          #
##############################################################


###################################################################
# (Below) Email received by library containing user-entered information #
###################################################################


# **************************************************
# Here's where you MUST specify the path to your
# email program (probably sendmail) ON your Web server.
# Replace /usr/sbin/sendmail with your path.
# **************************************************
```

```
open (LMAIL, "l/usr/sbin/sendmail -t");
print LMAIL ("To: $in{LibraryEmail}\n");
print LMAIL ("From: $in{CampusEmail}\n");
print LMAIL ("Subject: $in{Form} - patron submission\n");

print LMAIL ("------------------\nPatron information\n\n");
print LMAIL ("Name:\n $in{Name}\n\n");
print LMAIL ("Department / Major:\n $in{Department}\n\n");
print LMAIL ("Campus Email:\n $in{CampusEmail}\n\n");
print LMAIL ("Campus Phone:\n $in{CampusPhone}\n\n");
print LMAIL ("Status:\n $in{Status}\n\n");

print LMAIL ("------------------\nSubmitted information \n\n");

print LMAIL ("How many times I have visited the library's Web site in the last 30 days:\n $in{TimesVisited}\n\n");
print LMAIL ("How I heard about the Web site:\n $in{FindOut}\n\n");
print LMAIL ("When using the site I found:\n $in{IFound}\n\n");
print LMAIL ("When I need help with the Web site I:\n $in{HelpDo}\n\n");
print LMAIL ("Sections / pages I use most often:\n $in{Features}\n\n");
print LMAIL ("What I like most about the library's Web site:\n $in{Most}\n\n");
print LMAIL ("What I like least about the library's Web site:\n $in{Least}\n\n");
print LMAIL ("What I find difficult to use on the Web site:\n $in{Difficult}\n\n");
print LMAIL ("What I would like to see added to the Web site:\n $in{Added}\n\n");

print LMAIL ("Library Web site grades\n\n");
print LMAIL ("Organization of information:\t $in{Organized}\n");
print LMAIL ("Value of information:\t $in{Writing}\n");
print LMAIL ("Ability to navigate:\t $in{Moving}\n");
print LMAIL ("Value of links:\t $in{Important}\n");
print LMAIL ("Currency of links:\t $in{UpToDate}\n");
print LMAIL ("Visual appeal:\t $in{Visual}\n");
print LMAIL ("Page load times:\t $in{Web}\n");
print LMAIL ("Sufficient on-line help:\t $in{Help}\n");
print LMAIL ("Ability to provide feedback / comments:\t $in{Feedback}\n");
print LMAIL ("OVERALL RATING:\t $in{Overall}\n");

print LMAIL ("\n.\n");


##################################################
# Email received by the user confirming form submission #
##################################################


# ************************************************
# Here's where you MUST specify the path to your
# email program ON your Web server.
```

```
# Replace /usr/sbin/sendmail with your path.
# **********************************************

open (MAIL, "l/usr/sbin/sendmail -t");


# **********************************************
# Here's where you MAY customize the email
# response to the user. You may change any wording
# on the form.
# **********************************************

print MAIL<<toEnd;
To: $in{CampusEmail}
From: $in{LibraryEmail}
Subject: $in{Form}

Thanks for taking the time to fill out our Web Site Survey.\n\n
We will use your input to help us improve our Web site and its content.

toEnd
    print MAIL ("\n.\n");


#################################################
# Screen response to user after submitting the form  #
#################################################

print ("<html><head><title>Library Web Site Survey Submitted</title></head>");
print ("<body bgcolor=\"ffffff\">");


# **********************************************
# Here's where you MAY change the screen response
# the user sees after submitting the form. You may
# change any wording between the quotation marks.
# **********************************************

print ("Thanks for taking the time to fill out our Web Site Survey.<p>
We will use your input to help us improve our Web site and its content.");


# **********************************************
# Here's where you MAY change the name of the link
# back to your main page. You may replace Return
# to our main page with your own wording.
# **********************************************

print ("<p><center><a href=$in{LibraryURL}>Return to our main page.</a></center>");
print ("</body></html>");
```

Group 5 — Collection Development Forms / Surveys

In this section you'll find one Web-based form which allows faculty, students, and staff to suggest books, videos, DVDs, audiotapes, CDs, etc. that they'd like to see your library purchase.

Library Purchase Request

Make it simple for faculty, staff, and students to suggest a book, videocassette, DVD, audiotape, or CD that they want you to purchase for the library collection. All they have to do is fill out the item's title, author/ artist, publication information, and why they think your library should purchase it and e-mail it to your acquisitions staff. Staff can contact patrons via e-mail or phone if your library decides to purchase the item. Put a link to this form on your homepage or library collections page.

Library Purchase Request

If you'd like the library to purchase a book, reference resource, newspaper, journal, DVD, etc. fill out the form below with the title, author, publication information, and why you think we should purchase it. We'll contact you via e-mail or phone if we purchase it.

Name (last, first middle)

Department / Major

Campus address

Campus e-mail

Campus phone

Fax / Other phone

Status

- ○ Freshman
- ○ Sophomore
- ○ Junior
- ○ Senior
- ○ Grad Student
- ○ Faculty
- ○ Staff
- ○ Other

Material type

- ○ Book
- ○ Reference resource
- ○ Journal / Newspaper
- ○ CD-ROM
- ○ Online database
- ○ Thesis / Dissertation
- ○ Video / DVD
- ○ Audio / CD
- ○ Microfilm / fiche
- ○ Other (please specify)

Title

Author / Editor / Artist (last, first)

Edition

ISBN number

Publisher

Date of publication

Cited in

If a Journal / Newspaper also include...

Journal / Newspaper title

[   ]

Volume number   **ISSN number**

[   ]   [   ]

Cited in

[   ]

Priority (faculty only)

○ Rush   ○ Course reserve   ○ Course-related   ○ Professional research

○ Other (please specify) [   ]

I need the item before (specify date)

[   ]   ○ Anytime is fine

I think that the library should purchase this item because...

[   ]

Special instructions (eg. rush order, course reserve)

[   ]

If we purchase the item, would you like us to hold / notify you?   ○ Yes   ○ No

[Send Request]   [Clear Form]

Library Purchase Request — HTML Form

```
<html>
<head><title>Library Purchase Request</title></head>
<body bgcolor="#FFFFFF">
<table width="700" border="0" bordercolor="000000" height="85" bgcolor="#000000">
<tr valign="middle" align="center"><td>
<p>
<font halign=center color="#FFFFFF" face="Arial, Helvetica, sans-serif" size="+3">
<b><i>Library Purchase Request</i></b></font></p>
</td></tr></table>
<form method="post" action="http://www.yourLibrary.edu/cgi-bin/aa1.pl"><p> </p>
<p>
<font face="Arial, Helvetica, sans-serif" size="2"><b>If you'd like the library to purchase a book, reference
resource, newspaper, journal, DVD, etc. fill out the <br>form below with the title, author, publication information,
and why you think we should purchase it. <br> We'll contact you via e-mail or phone if we purchase it. </b>
</font></p>
<p> </p>
<input type="hidden" name="LibraryEmail" value="you@yourLibrary.edu">
<input type="hidden" name="LibraryURL" value="http://www.yourLibrary.edu">
<input type="hidden" name="Form" value="Library Purchase Request">
<p></p>
<table width="500" border="0" cellspacing="4" cellpadding="1"><tr><td width="257">
<b><font face="Arial, Helvetica, sans-serif" size="2">Name </font></b><font face="Arial, Helvetica, sans-
serif" size="1"> (last, first middle)</font><br><font face="Arial, Helvetica, sans-serif" size="2"><input
type="text" name="Name" size="25"></font></td>
<td width="227">
<b><font face="Arial, Helvetica, sans-serif" size="2">Department / Major<br></font></b><font face="Arial,
Helvetica, sans-serif" size="2"><input type="text" name="Department" size="25"></font> </td></tr>
<tr><td width="257">
<b><font face="Arial, Helvetica, sans-serif" size="2">Campus address<br></font></b><font face="Arial,
Helvetica, sans-serif" size="2"><input type="text" name="CampusAddress" size="25"></font></td>
<td width="227">
<b><font face="Arial, Helvetica, sans-serif" size="2">Campus e-mail<br></font></b><font face="Arial, Helvetica,
sans-serif" size="2"><input type="text" name="CampusEmail" size="25"></font></td></tr>
<tr><td width="257">
<b><font face="Arial, Helvetica, sans-serif" size="2">Campus phone</font></b><br><font face="Arial, Helvetica,
sans-serif" size="2"><input type="text" name="CampusPhone" size="25"></font></td>
<td width="227">
<b><font face="Arial, Helvetica, sans-serif" size="2">Fax / Other phone<br></font></b><font face="Arial,
Helvetica, sans-serif" size="2"><input type="text" name="OtherPhone" size="25"></font></td> </tr> </table>
<p><b><font face="Arial, Helvetica, sans-serif" size="2">Status</font></b>
<table width="550" border="0" cellspacing="0" cellpadding="0"><tr>
<td width="126" height="13">
<font face="Arial, Helvetica, sans-serif" size="2"><input type="radio" name="Status" value=
```

"Freshman"> Freshman</font></td>
<td width="117" height="13">
<font face="Arial, Helvetica, sans-serif" size="2"><input type="radio" name="Status" value=
"Sophomore">Sophomore</font></td>
<td width="87" height="13">
<font face="Arial, Helvetica, sans-serif" size="2"><input type="radio" name="Status" value= "Junior">Junior
</font></td>
<td width="202" height="13">
<font face="Arial, Helvetica, sans-serif" size="2"><input type="radio" name="Status" value= "Senior">Senior
</font></td></tr>
<tr><td width="126" height="9">
<font face="Arial, Helvetica, sans-serif" size="2"><input type="radio" name="Status" value=
"Graduate Student">Grad Student</font></td>
<td width="117" height="9">
<font face="Arial, Helvetica, sans-serif" size="2"><input type="radio" name="Status" value=" Faculty">Faculty
</font></td>
<td width="87" height="9">
<font face="Arial, Helvetica, sans-serif" size="2"><input type="radio" name="Status" value=" Staff">Staff
</font></td>
<td width="202" height="9">
<font face="Arial, Helvetica, sans-serif" size="2"><input type="radio" name="Status" value=" Other">Other
</font></td></tr></table>
<p>
<font face="Arial, Helvetica, sans-serif" size="2">Material type</font>
<table width="550" bor-
der="0" cellspacing="0" cellpadding="0"><tr>
<td width="133">
<font face="Arial, Helvetica, sans-serif" size="2"><input type="radio" name="Material" value="Book"> Book
</font></td>
<td width="154">
<font face="Arial, Helvetica, sans-serif" size="2"><input type="radio" name="Material" value="Reference
resource">Reference resource</font></td>
<td width="154">
<font face="Arial, Helvetica, sans-serif" size="2"><input type="radio" name="Material" value="Journal /
Newspaper">Journal / Newspaper</font></td>
<td width="109">
<font face="Arial, Helvetica, sans-serif" size="2"><input type="radio" name="Material" value="CD-ROM">CD-
ROM"></font></td></tr>
<tr>
<td width="133">
<font face="Arial, Helvetica, sans-serif" size="2"><input type="radio" name="Material" value="Online
databases">Online database</font></td>
<td width="154">
<font face="Arial, Helvetica, sans-serif" size="2"><input type="radio" name="Material" value="Thesis /
Dissertation">Thesis / Dissertation</font></td>
<td width="154">

```
<font face="Arial, Helvetica, sans-serif" size="2"><input type="radio" name="Material" value="Video /
DVD">Video / DVD</font></td>
<td width="109">
<font face="Arial, Helvetica, sans-serif" size="2"><input type="radio" name="Material" value="Book">Audio /
CD"></font></td></tr>
<tr><td width="133">
<font face="Arial, Helvetica, sans-serif" size="2"><input type="radio" name="Material" value="Microfilm /
fiche">Microfilm / fiche</font></td>
<td colspan="3">
<font face="Arial, Helvetica, sans-serif" size="2"><input type="radio" name="Material" value="Other">Other
 <font face="Arial, Helvetica, sans-serif" size="1">(please specify)</font> <font size="3">  <input
type="text" name="OtherType" size="20"></font></font></td></tr></table>
<p>
<font face="Arial, Helvetica, sans-serif" size="2"><b>Title</b><br><font size="3"><input type="text"
name="Title" size="40"></font></font></p>
<p>
<font face="Arial, Helvetica, sans-serif" size="2"><b>Author / Editor / Artist </b> 
<font size="1">(last, first)</font><br><font size="3"><input type="text" name="Author" size="40">
</font></font></p>
<table width="209" border="0"><tr>
<td width="92">
<font face="Arial, Helvetica, sans-serif" size="2"><b>Edition</b><br><font size="3"><input type="text"
name="Edition" size="10"></font></font></td>
<td width="107">
<font face="Arial, Helvetica, sans-serif" size="2"><b>ISBN number</b><br><font size="3"><input type="text"
name="ISBN" size="10"></font></font>
</td></tr></table>
<p>
<font face="Arial, Helvetica, sans-serif" size="2"><b>Publisher </b><br><font size="3"><input type="text"
name="Publisher" size="40"></font></font></p>
<p>
<font face="Arial, Helvetica, sans-serif" size="2"><b>Date of publication</b><br><font size="3"><input type=
"text" name="PublisherDate" size="40"></font></font></p>
<p>
<font face="Arial, Helvetica, sans-serif" size="2"><b>Cited in</b><br><font size="3"><input type="text"
name="CitedIn" size="40"></font></font></p>
<p> </p>
<p> <font face="Arial, Helvetica, sans-serif" size="3"><b>If a Journal / Newspaper also include... </b></font>
</p>
<p>
<font face="Arial, Helvetica, sans-serif" size="2"><b>Journal / Newspaper title</b><br><font size= "3"><input
type="text" name="MagName" size="40"></font> </font> </p>
<table width="363" border="0" cellspacing="0" cellpadding="0"><tr>
<td width="213">
<font face="Arial, Helvetica, sans-serif" size="2"><b>Volume number</b><br><font size="3">
```

```
<input type="text" name="VolNum" size="20">
</font></font></td>
<td width="150">
<font face="Arial, Helvetica, sans-serif" size="2"><b>ISSN number </b><br><font size="3">
<input type="text" name="ISSN" size="10"></font></font>
</td></tr></table>
<p><font face="Arial, Helvetica, sans-serif" size="2"><b>Cited in</b><br><font size="3">
<input type="text" name="CitedInMag" size="40"></font></font></p>
<p> </p>
<p>
<b><font face="Arial, Helvetica, sans-serif" size="2">Priority </font></b><font face="Arial, Helvetica, sans-
serif" size="1"> (faculty only)</font><br><font face="Arial, Helvetica, sans-serif" size="2">
<input type="radio" name="Priority" value="Rush">Rush   
<input type="radio" name="Priority" value="Course reserve">Course reserve   
<input type="radio" name="Priority" value="Course-related">Course-related  
<input type="radio" name="Priority" value="Professional research">Professional research    
<br>
<input type="radio" name="Priority" value="Other">Other</font>
<font face="Arial, Helvetica, sans-serif" size="1">(please specify)  <font size="3">
<input type="text" name="PriorityO" size="10"></font></font><br></p>
<p>
<font face="Arial, Helvetica, sans-serif" size="2"><b>I need the item before<font size="1"> 
</font></b><font face="Arial, Helvetica, sans-serif" size="1"> (specify date)</font><br>
<font size="3">
<input type="text" name="NeedBefore" size="15">     </font>
<input type="radio" name="TimeIssue" value="Time is not an issue">Anytime is fine</font></p>
<p>
<font face="Arial, Helvetica, sans-serif" size="2"><b>I think that the library should purchase this item be-
cause...</b><br>
<font size="3" face="Arial, Helvetica, sans-serif"><textarea name="ReasonToBuy" cols="40" rows="2">
</textarea></font></font><br>
</p>
<p><font face="Arial, Helvetica, sans-serif" size="2"><b>Special instructions</b>  <font
size="1"> (eg. rush order, </font><font size="1">course reserve)</font><br><font size="3" face="Arial,
Helvetica, sans-serif"><textarea name="SpecialInstr" cols="40" rows="2"></textarea>
</font></font></p>
<p>
<b><font face="Arial, Helvetica, sans-serif" size="2">If we purchase the item, would you like us to hold / notify
you?</font></b><font face="Arial, Helvetica, sans-serif" size="2"> 
<input type="radio" name="Hold" value="Yes">Yes    
<input type="radio" name="Hold" value="No">No</font></p>
<p> </p>
<table width="700" border="0" cellspacing="10" cellpadding="1"><tr><td width="242">
<div align="right"><input type="submit" name="send" value="Send Request"></div></td>
<td width="205"> </td><td width="207">
```

```
<div align="left"><input type="reset" name="clear" value="Clear Form"></div></td></tr>
<tr colspan=3><td colspan=3><table width="500" border="0" height="2" align="center" cellpadding="0"
cellspacing="0" bgcolor="#000000" bordercolor="000000"><tr><td><font size="1" color="#000000"> .</font>
</td></tr></table>
</td></tr>
<tr><td colspan=3><div align="center">
<font face="Arial, Helvetica, sans-serif" size="1"><b>http://</b></font><br> 
<font face="Arial, Helvetica, sans-serif" size="1"><b>&copy; 2001</b></font></font>
<font face="Arial, Helvetica, sans-serif" size="2"><a href="mailto: ">
<b><font size="1">Contact Webmaster</font></b></a></div></td></tr>
</table></form>
</body>
</html>
```

Library Purchase Request — Perl Script

```perl
#!/usr/local/bin/perl

# **************************************************
# ABOVE is where you MUST specify the path to your
# perl interpreter on your Web server.
# Replace /usr/local/bin/perl with your path.
# **************************************************

if ($ENV{'REQUEST_METHOD'}eq"GET"){$buffer = $ENV{'QUERY_STRING'};}
    elsif($ENV{'REQUEST_METHOD'}eq"POST"){
        read(STDIN,$buffer,$ENV{'CONTENT_LENGTH'});
    }
$bufferb = $buffer;
#separate the name of the input from its value.
@forminputs = split(/&/, $bufferb);

foreach $forminput (@forminputs)
{
    #separate the name of the input from its value
    ($name, $value) = split(/=/, $forminput);

    #Un-Webify plus signs and %-encoding
    $value =~ tr/+/ /;
    $value =~ s/%([a-fA-F0-9][a-fA-F0-9])/pack("C", hex($1))/eg;

    #stick them in the in array
    $in{$name} = $value;
}
print "Content-type: text/html\n\n";

############################################################
# ABOVE is the required header for a perl script          #
############################################################


##############################################################
# (Below) Email received by library containing user-entered information #
##############################################################


# **************************************************
# Here's where you MUST specify the path to your
# email program (probably sendmail) ON your Web server.
# Replace /usr/sbin/sendmail with your path.
# **************************************************
```

```
open (LMAIL, "l/usr/sbin/sendmail -t");
print LMAIL ("To: $in{LibraryEmail}\n");
print LMAIL ("From: $in{CampusEmail}\n");
print LMAIL ("Subject: $in{Form} - patron submission\n");

print LMAIL ("-------------------\nPatron information\n\n");
print LMAIL ("Name:\n $in{Name}\n\n");
print LMAIL ("Department / Major:\n $in{Department}\n\n");
print LMAIL ("Campus Address:\n $in{CampusAddress}\n\n");
print LMAIL ("Campus Email:\n $in{CampusEmail}\n\n");
print LMAIL ("Campus Phone:\n $in{CampusPhone}\n\n");
print LMAIL ("Other Phone:\n $in{OtherPhone}\n\n");
print LMAIL ("Status:\n $in{Status}\n\n");

print LMAIL ("-------------------\nSubmitted information \n\n");
print LMAIL ("Material type:\n $in{Material}\n\n");
print LMAIL ("Other material type:\n $in{OtherType}\n\n");
print LMAIL ("Title:\n $in{Title}\n\n");
print LMAIL ("Author / Editor / Artist:\n $in{Author}\n\n");
print LMAIL ("Edition:\n $in{Edition}\n\n");
print LMAIL ("ISBN number:\n $in{ISBN}\n\n");
print LMAIL ("Publisher:\n $in{Publisher}\n\n");
print LMAIL ("Date of publication:\n $in{PublisherDate}\n\n");
print LMAIL ("Cited in:\n $in{CitedIn}\n\n");
print LMAIL ("Journal / Newspaper title:\n $in{JournalNewsTitle}\n\n");
print LMAIL ("Volume number:\n $in{VolNum}\n\n");
print LMAIL ("ISSN number:\n $in{ISSN}\n\n");
print LMAIL ("Cited in:\n $in{CitedInMag}\n\n");
print LMAIL ("Priority:\n $in{Priority}\n\n");
print LMAIL ("Other priority:\n $in{PriorityO}\n\n");
print LMAIL ("I need this item before:\n $in{NeedBefore} $in{TimeIssue}\n\n");
print LMAIL ("I think the library should purchase this item because:\n $in{ReasonToBuy}\n\n");
print LMAIL ("Special instructions:\n $in{SpecialInstr}\n\n");
print LMAIL ("If we purchase this item, would you like to be notified?\n $in{Notify} \n\n");

print LMAIL ("\n.\n");


#########################################################
# Email received by the user confirming form submission #
#########################################################


# ************************************************
# Here's where you MUST specify the path to your
# email program ON your Web server.
# Replace /usr/sbin/sendmail with your path.
# ************************************************
#
```

```
open (MAIL, "l/usr/sbin/sendmail -t");

# **********************************************
# Here's where you MAY customize the email
# response to the user. You may change any wording
# of the message.
# **********************************************

print MAIL<<toEnd;
To: $in{CampusEmail}
From: $in{LibraryEmail}
Subject: $in{Form}

Thanks for suggesting that we purchase a new item for our collection.\n\n
We are always looking for new resources to enrich our collections.

toEnd
    print MAIL ("\n.\n");

######################################################
# Screen response to user after submitting the form  #
######################################################

print ("<html><head><title>$in{Form}</title></head>");
print ("<body bgcolor=\"ffffff\">");

# **********************************************
# Here's where you MAY change the screen response
# the user sees after submitting the form. You may
# change any wording between the quotation marks.
# **********************************************

print ("Thanks for suggesting that we purchase a new item for our collection.<p>
We are always looking for new resources to enrich our collections.
");

# **********************************************
# Here's where you MAY change the name of the link
# back to your main page. You may replace Return
# to our main page with your own wording.
# **********************************************

print ("<p><center><a href=$in{LibraryURL}>Return to our main page.</a></center>");
print ("</body></html>");
```

Group 6 — InterLibrary Loan Forms

In this section you'll find two Web-based forms. The first enables faculty and students to send a request to your InterLibrary Loan staff, indicating not only the books and articles they want/need, but which library resources they've already checked before filling out the form. The second form enables faculty and students to send your ILL staff an e-mail request to renew their ILL materials.

InterLibrary Loan Request
If students or faculty members need the library to try to get a book, magazine, or newspaper article, or any other resource for them via InterLibrary Loan, they can fill out the information provided on the form and send an e-mail request to one of your ILL staff members. You can contact them via e-mail or phone if you can obtain the item for them and when they'll be able to pick it up.

InterLibrary Loan Renewal
If faculty or students have received a book, magazine, newspaper article, or any other resource via InterLibrary Loan and they need/want to renew it, all they have to do is fill out the form below.

InterLibrary Loan Request

If you'd like the library to obtain a book, magazine/newspaper article, or any other resource for you via InterLibrary loan, fill out the form below with the item or article title, author or artist, and publication and magazine/newspaper information. We'll contact you via e-mail or phone if we can obtain it for you and when you'll be able to pick it up.

Name (last, first middle)

Department / Major

Campus address

Campus e-mail

Campus phone

Fax / Other phone

Status

- ○ Freshman
- ○ Sophomore
- ○ Junior
- ○ Senior
- ○ Grad Student
- ○ Faculty
- ○ Staff
- ○ Other

Type of loan

- ○ Book / Book chapter
- ○ Journal article
- ○ Newspaper article
- ○ Thesis / Dissertation
- ○ Other (please specify)

What library resources have you already checked / used?

- ○ Online catalog
- ○ Reference materials
- ○ Books
- ○ CD-ROMs
- ○ Journal articles
- ○ Newspaper articles
- ○ On-line databases
- ○ Other (please specify)

Title

Author / Editor / Artist (last, first)

Edition   **ISBN number**

Publisher

Date of publication

Cited in

[   ]

If a Journal / Newspaper article also include...

Journal / Newspaper title

[   ]

Issue date   **Volume number**   **Issue number**   **ISSN number**

[   ]   [   ]   [   ]   [   ]

Cited in

[   ]

Priority (faculty only)

○ Rush   ○ Course reserve   ○ Course-related   ○ Professional research

○ Other (please specify) [   ]

I need the item before (specify date)

[   ]   ○ Anytime is fine

If there is a charge associated with the loan...

○ Don't process this request, notify me   ○ Go ahead with the loan if less than $[   ]

Warning concerning copyright restrictions

☐ I agree to comply with these restrictions

[Send Request]   [Clear Form]

InterLibrary Loan Request — HTML Form

```
<html>
<head><title>InterLibrary Loan Request</title></head>
<body bgcolor="#FFFFFF">
<table width="700" border="0" height="85" bgcolor="#000000">
<tr valign="middle" align="center"><td>
<p>
<font halign=center color="#FFFFFF" face="Arial, Helvetica, sans-serif" size="+3">
<b><i>InterLibrary Loan Request</i></b></font></p>
</td></tr></table>
<form method="post" action="http://www.yourLibrary.edu/cgi-bin/ail1.pl"><p> </p>
<p>
<font face="Arial, Helvetica, sans-serif" size="2"><b>If you'd like the library to obtain a book, magazine/newspa-
per article, or any other resource for <br>you via InterLibrary loan, fill out the form below with the item or article
title, author or artist, and <br>publication and magazine/ newspaper information. We'll contact you via e-mail or
phone if we <br>can obtain it for you and when you'll be able to pick it up.</b></font></p>
<p> </p>
<input type="hidden" name="LibraryEmail" value="you@yourLibrary.edu">
<input type="hidden" name="LibraryURL" value="http://www.yourLibrary.edu">
<input type="hidden" name="Form" value="InterLibrary Loan Request">
<p></p>
<table width="500" border="0" cellspacing="4" cellpadding="1"><tr>
<td width="257"> <b><font face="Arial, Helvetica, sans-serif" size="2">Name </font></b> <font
face="Arial, Helvetica, sans-serif" size="1"> (last, first middle)</font><br><font face="Arial, Helvetica,
sans-serif" size="2"><input type="text" name="Name" size="25"></font></td>
<td width="227">
<b><font face="Arial, Helvetica, sans-serif" size="2">Department / Major<br></font></b><font face="Arial,
Helvetica, sans-serif" size="2"><input type="text" name="Department" size="25">
</font></td></tr>
<tr><td width="257">
<b><font face="Arial, Helvetica, sans-serif" size="2">Campus address<br></font></b><font face="Arial,
Helvetica, sans-serif" size="2"><input type="text" name="CampusAddress" size="25"></font></td>
<td width="227">
<b><font face="Arial, Helvetica, sans-serif" size="2">Campus e-mail<br></font></b><font face="Arial, Helvetica,
sans-serif" size="2"><input type="text" name="CampusEmail" size="25"></font></td></tr>
<tr><td width="257">
<b><font face="Arial, Helvetica, sans-serif" size="2">Campus phone</font></b><br><font face="Arial, Helvetica,
sans-serif" size="2"><input type="text" name="CampusPhone" size="25"></font></td>
<td width="227">
<b><font face="Arial, Helvetica, sans-serif" size="2">Fax / Other phone<br></font></b><font face="Arial,
Helvetica, sans-serif" size="2"><input type="text" name="OtherPhone" size="25">
</font></td></tr></table>
<p>
<b><font face="Arial, Helvetica, sans-serif" size="2">Status</font></b><table width="550" border="0"
```

```
cellspacing="0" cellpadding="0">
<tr><td width="126" height="13">
<font face="Arial, Helvetica, sans-serif" size="2"><input type="radio" name="Status"
value="Freshman">Freshman</font></td>
<td width="117" height="13">
<font face="Arial, Helvetica, sans-serif" size="2"><input type="radio" name="Status"
value="Sophomore">Sophomore</font></td>
<td width="87" height="13">
<font face="Arial, Helvetica, sans-serif" size="2"><input type="radio" name="Status" value="Junior">Junior
</font></td>
<td width="202" height="13">
<font face="Arial, Helvetica, sans-serif" size="2"><input type="radio" name="Status" value="Senior">Senior
</font></td></tr>
<tr><td width="126" height="9">
<font face="Arial, Helvetica, sans-serif" size="2"><input type="radio" name="Status"
value="Graduate Student">Grad Student</font></td>
<td width="117" height="9">
<font face="Arial, Helvetica, sans-serif" size="2"><input type="radio" name="Status" value="Faculty">Faculty
</font></td>
<td width="87" height="9">
<font face="Arial, Helvetica, sans-serif" size="2"><input type="radio" name="Status" value="Staff">Staff
</font></td>
<td width="202" height="9">
<font face="Arial, Helvetica, sans-serif" size="2"><input type="radio" name="Status" value="Other">Other
</font></td></tr></table>
<p>
<b><font face="Arial, Helvetica, sans-serif" size="2">Type of loan<br></font></b><font face="Arial, Helvetica,
sans-serif" size="2">
<input type="radio" name="MaterialType" value="Book">Book / Book chapter    
<input type="radio" name="MaterialType" value="Journal article">Journal article    
<input type="radio" name="MaterialType" value="Newspaper article">Newspaper  article  
<input type="radio" name="MaterialType" value="Thesis / Dissertation">Thesis / Dissertation
   <br>
<input type="radio" name="MaterialType" value="Other">Other</font><font face="Arial, Helvetica, sans-serif"
size="1">(please specify)<font size="3">  <input type="text" name="OtherMatType" size="10"></font>
</font>
<p>
<b><font face="Arial, Helvetica, sans-serif" size="2">What library resources have you already checked /
used?<br></font></b><table width="600" border="0" cellspacing="0" cellpadding="0"><tr>
<td width="159">
<font face="Arial, Helvetica, sans-serif" size="2"><input type="radio" name="Sources" value="Online
catalog">Online catalog</font></td>
<td width="182">
<font face="Arial, Helvetica, sans-serif" size="2"><input type="radio" name="Sources" value="Reference
materials">Reference materials</font></td>
```

```
<td width="132">
<font face="Arial, Helvetica, sans-serif" size="2"><input type="radio" name="Sources" value="Books"> Books
</font></td>
<td width="127">
<font face="Arial, Helvetica, sans-serif" size="2"><input type="radio" name="Sources" value="CD-ROMs">CD-
ROMs</font></td></tr>
<tr><td width="159">
<font face="Arial, Helvetica, sans-serif" size="2"><input type="radio" name="Sources" value="Journal
articles">Journal articles</font></td>
<td width="182">
<font face="Arial, Helvetica, sans-serif" size="2"><input type="radio" name="Sources" value="Newspaper
articles">Newspaper articles</font></td>
<td colspan="2">
<font face="Arial, Helvetica, sans-serif" size="2"><input type="radio" name="Sources" value="On-line indexes /
databases">On-line databases</font></td></tr>
<tr><td colspan="4">
<font face="Arial, Helvetica, sans-serif" size="2"><input type="radio" name="Sources" value="Other"> Other
</font><font face="Arial, Helvetica, sans-serif" size="1">(please specify)  <font size="3"> <input
type="text" name="OtherResUsed" size="10"></font></font></td></tr></table>
<p>
<font face="Arial, Helvetica, sans-serif" size="2"><b>Title</b><br><font size="3"><input type="text"
name="Title" size="40"></font></font></p>
<p>
<font face="Arial, Helvetica, sans-serif" size="2"><b>Author / Editor / Artist </b>  <font
size="1">(last, first)</font><br><font size="3"><input type="text" name="Author" size="40"></font> </font>
</p><table width="209" border="0">
<tr><td width="92">
<font face="Arial, Helvetica, sans-serif" size="2"><b>Edition</b><br><font size="3"><input type="text"
name="Edition" size="10"></font></font></td>
<td width="107">
<font face="Arial, Helvetica, sans-serif" size="2"><b>ISBN number</b> <br><font size="3">
<input type="text" name="ISBN" size="10">/font></font></td></tr></table>
<p>
<font face="Arial, Helvetica, sans-serif" size="2"><b>Publisher </b><br><font size="3">
 <input type="text" name="Publisher" size="40"></font></font></p>
<p>
<font face="Arial, Helvetica, sans-serif" size="2"><b>Date of publication</b><br><font size="3">
<input type="text" name="PublisherDate" size="40"></font></font></p>
<p>
<font face="Arial, Helvetica, sans-serif" size="2"><b>Cited in</b><br><font size="3"><input type="text"
name="CitedIn" size="40">/font></font></p>
<p> </p>
<p>
<font face="Arial, Helvetica, sans-serif" size="3"><b>If a Journal / Newspaper article also include... </b>
</font></p>
```

```
<p>
<font face="Arial, Helvetica, sans-serif" size="2"><b>Journal / Newspaper title</b><br><font size="3"><input
type="text" name="MagName" size="40"></font> /font></p>
<table width="600" border="0" cellspacing="0" cellpadding="0">
<tr><td width="117" height="11">
<font face="Arial, Helvetica, sans-serif" size="2"><b>Issue date</b><br><font size="3"><input type="text"
name="IssueDate" size="10"></font></font></td>
<td width="120" height="11">
<font face="Arial, Helvetica, sans-serif" size="2"><b>Volume number</b><br><font size="3"><input type="text"
name="VolNum" size="10"></font></font></td>
<td width="102" height="11">
<font face="Arial, Helvetica, sans-serif" size="2"><b>Issue number</b><br><font size="3"><input type="text"
name="IssueNum" size="10"></font></font></td>
<td width="261" height="11">
<font face="Arial, Helvetica, sans-serif" size="2"><b>ISSN number</b><br><font size="3"><input type="text"
name="ISSN" size="10">/font></font></td></tr></table>
<p>
<font face="Arial, Helvetica, sans-serif" size="2"><b>Cited in</b><br><font size="3"><input type="text"
name="CitedInMag" size="40"></font></font></p>
<p>
<b><font face="Arial, Helvetica, sans-serif" size="2">Priority </font></b><font face="Arial, Helvetica, sans-
serif" size="1"> (faculty only)</font><br><font face="Arial, Helvetica, sans-serif" size="2">
<input type="radio" name="Priority" value="Rush">Rush   
<input type="radio" name="Priority" value="Course reserve">Course reserve   
<input type="radio" name="Priority" value="Course-related">Course-related  
<input type="radio" name="Priority" value="Professional research">Professional research    
<br>
<input type="radio" name="Priority" value="Other">Other</font><font face="Arial, Helvetica, sans-serif"
size="1">(please specify)   <font size="3"><input type="text" name="PriorityO" size="10"> </font>
</font><br></p>
<p>
<font face="Arial, Helvetica, sans-serif" size="2"><b>I need the item before<font size="1"> 
</font></b><font face="Arial, Helvetica, sans-serif" size="1"> (specify date)</font><br>
<font size="3"><input type="text" name="NeedBefore" size="15">    
 </font><input type="radio" name="TimeIssue" value="Time is not an issue">Anytime is fine</font></p>
<p>
<font face="Arial, Helvetica, sans-serif" size="2"><b>If there is a charge associated with the loan...</b><br>
<input type="radio" name="Charge" value="Don't process this request, notify me">Don't process this request,
notify me    
<input type="radio" name="Charge" value="Go ahead if less than I specify">Go ahead with the loan if less than
<font size="3">   <input type="text" name="Max" value="$" size="5">
</font></font><br>
</p><p> </p><p>
<b><font face="Arial, Helvetica, sans-serif" size="2">Warning concerning copyright restrictions </font></b>
</p><p>
```

```
<font face="Arial, Helvetica, sans-serif" size="1">The copyright law of the United States (Title 17, United States
Code) governs the making of photocopies or other reproductions <br>of copyrighted material. Under certain
conditions specified in the law, libraries and archives are authorized to furnish a photocopy <br>or other repro-
duction. One of these specified conditions is that the photocopy or other reproduction is not to be &quot;used for
any <br>purpose other than private study, scholarship, or research.&quot; If a user makes a request for, or later
uses, a photocopy or other <br>reproduction for purposes in excess of &quot;fair use&quot;, that user may be
liable for copyright infringement. This institution reserves<br>the right to refuse to accept a copying order if, in its
judgement, fulfillment of the order would involve violation of copyright law.</font><br></p>
<p>
                
                
       
<input type="checkbox" name="Agree" value="I agree"><!-- input type="hidden" name="Agree" -->
<font face="Arial, Helvetica, sans-serif" size="2">I agree to comply with these restrictions</font>
</p><p> </p>
<table width="700" border="0" cellspacing="10" cellpadding="1"><tr><td width="249">
<div align="right"><input type="submit" name="send" value="Send Request"></div></td><td
width="198"> </td><td width="207">
<div align="left"><input type="reset" name="clear" value="Clear Form"></div></td></tr>
<tr colspan=3><td colspan=3>
<table width="500" border="0" height="2" align="center" cellpadding="0" cellspacing="0"
bgcolor="#000000"><tr><td><font size="1" color="#000000">.</font></td></tr></table>
</td></tr>
<tr><td colspan=3><div align="center">
<font face="Arial, Helvetica, sans-serif" size="1"><b>http://</b></font><br> 
<font face="Arial, Helvetica, sans-serif" size="1"><b>&copy; 2001</b></font>
<font face="Arial, Helvetica, sans-serif" size="2"><a href="mailto:">
<b><font size="1">Contact Webmaster</font></b></a></font></div></td></tr>
</table></form>
</body>
</html>
```

InterLibrary Loan Request — Perl Script

```perl
#!/usr/local/bin/perl

# **************************************************
# ABOVE is where you MUST specify the path to your
# perl interpreter on your Web server.
# Replace /usr/local/bin/perl with your path.
# **************************************************

if ($ENV{'REQUEST_METHOD'}eq"GET"){$buffer = $ENV{'QUERY_STRING'};}
    elsif($ENV{'REQUEST_METHOD'}eq"POST"){
        read(STDIN,$buffer,$ENV{'CONTENT_LENGTH'});
    }
$bufferb = $buffer;
#separate the name of the input from its value.
@forminputs = split(/&/, $bufferb);

foreach $forminput (@forminputs)
{
        #separate the name of the input from its value
        ($name, $value) = split(/=/, $forminput);

        #Un-Webify plus signs and %-encoding
        $value =~ tr/+/ /;
        $value =~ s/%([a-fA-F0-9][a-fA-F0-9])/pack("C", hex($1))/eg;

        #stick them in the in array
        $in{$name} = $value;
}
print "Content-type: text/html\n\n";

##############################################################
# ABOVE is the required header for a perl script            #
##############################################################


##################################################################
# (Below) Email received by library containing user-entered information #
##################################################################


# ***********************************************
# Here's where you MUST specify the path to your
# email program (probably sendmail) ON your Web server.
# Replace /usr/sbin/sendmail with your path.
```

```
# ***************************************************

open (LMAIL, "I/usr/sbin/sendmail -t");
print LMAIL ("To: $in{LibraryEmail}\n");

print LMAIL ("From: $in{CampusEmail}\n");
print LMAIL ("Subject: $in{Form} - patron submission\n");
print LMAIL ("------------------\nPatron information\n\n");
print LMAIL ("Name:\n $in{Name}\n\n");
print LMAIL ("Department / Major:\n $in{Department}\n\n");
print LMAIL ("Campus Address:\n $in{CampusAddress}\n\n");
print LMAIL ("Campus Email:\n $in{CampusEmail}\n\n");
print LMAIL ("Campus Phone:\n $in{CampusPhone}\n\n");
print LMAIL ("Other Phone:\n $in{OtherPhone}\n\n");
print LMAIL ("Status:\n $in{Status}\n\n");

print LMAIL ("------------------\nSubmitted information \n\n");

print LMAIL ("Type of loan:\n $in{MaterialType}\n\n");
print LMAIL ("Other type:\n $in{OtherMatType}\n\n");
print LMAIL ("Sources I have already checked:\n $in{Sources}\n\n");
print LMAIL ("Other sources used:\n $in{OtherResUsed}\n\n");
print LMAIL ("Title:\n $in{Title}\n\n");
print LMAIL ("Author / Editor / Artist:\n $in{Author}\n\n");
print LMAIL ("Edition:\n $in{Edition}\n\n");
print LMAIL ("ISBN number:\n $in{ISBN}\n\n");
print LMAIL ("Publisher:\n $in{Publisher}\n\n");
print LMAIL ("Date of publication:\n $in{PublisherDate}\n\n");
print LMAIL ("Cited in:\n $in{CitedIn}\n\n");
print LMAIL ("Journal / Newspaper article\n");
print LMAIL ("Journal / Newspaper title:\n $in{MagName}\n\n");
print LMAIL ("Issue date:\n $in{IssueDate}\n\n");
print LMAIL ("Volume number:\n $in{VolNum}\n\n");
print LMAIL ("Issue number:\n $in{IssueNum}\n\n");
print LMAIL ("ISSN number:\n $in{ISSN}\n\n");
print LMAIL ("Cited in:\n $in{CitedInMag}\n\n");
print LMAIL ("Priority:\n $in{Priority}\n\n");
print LMAIL ("Other priority:\n $in{PriorityO}\n\n");
print LMAIL ("I need this item before:\n $in{NeedBefore} $in{TimeIssue}\n\n");
print LMAIL ("If there is a charge associated with the loan:\n $in{Charge}\n\n");
print LMAIL ("Specified amount:\n $in{Max}\n\n");
print LMAIL ("I agree:\n $in{Agree}\n\n");
print LMAIL ("\n.\n");
```

```
######################################################
# Email received by the user confirming form submission #
######################################################


# **********************************************
# Here's where you MUST specify the path to your
# email program ON your Web server.
# Replace /usr/sbin/sendmail with your path.
# **********************************************

open (MAIL, "l/usr/sbin/sendmail -t");


# **********************************************
# Here's where you MAY customize the email
# response to the user. You may change any wording
# on the form.
# **********************************************

print MAIL<<toEnd;
To: $in{CampusEmail}
From: $in{LibraryEmail}
Subject: $in{Form}

Thanks for submitting an InterLibrary Loan request.\n\n
A librarian will contact you in the next couple of days to let you know if we will be able to obtain the item for you.
toEnd
    print MAIL ("\n.\n");


######################################################
# Screen response to user after submitting the form  #
######################################################

print ("<html><head><title>$in{Form}</title></head>");
print ("<body bgcolor=\"ffffff\">");


# **********************************************
# Here's where you MAY change the screen response
# the user sees after submitting the form. You may
# change any wording between the quotation marks.
# **********************************************

print ("Thanks for submitting an InterLibrary Loan request.<p>
A librarian will contact you in the next couple of days to let you know if we will be able to obtain the item for
you.");
```

```
# ***************************************************
# Here's where you MAY change the name of the link
# back to your main page. You may replace Return
# to our main page with your own wording.
# ***************************************************

print ("<p><center><a href=$in{LibraryURL}>Return to our main page.</a></center>");
print ("</body></html>");
```

InterLibrary Loan Renewal

If you've received a book, bound journal volume, or any other resource via InterLibrary Loan, and you need/want to renew it, fill out the form below. We'll contact you via e-mail or phone to let you know if we can renew the item for you.

Name (last, first middle)

Department / Major

Campus address

Campus e-mail

Campus phone

Fax / Other phone

Status

- ○ Freshman
- ○ Sophomore
- ○ Junior
- ○ Senior
- ○ Grad Student
- ○ Faculty
- ○ Staff
- ○ Other

Call number

Title

Author / Editor / Artist (last, first)

Original due date

Due date requested

Comments / Special instructions

Send Request   Clear Form

InterLibrary Loan Renewal — HTML Form

```
<html>
<head><title>InterLibrary Loan Renewal</title>
</head>
<body bgcolor="#FFFFFF">
<table width="700" border="0" height="85" bgcolor="#000000">
<tr valign="middle" align="center"><td>
<p>
<font halign=center color="#FFFFFF" face="Arial, Helvetica, sans-serif" size="+3"> <b><i>InterLibrary Loan
Renewal</i></b></font></p>
</td></tr></table>
<form method="post" action="http://www.yourLibrary.edu/cgi-bin/ail2.pl"><p> </p>
<p>
<font face="Arial, Helvetica, sans-serif" size="2"><b>If you've received a book, bound journal volume, or any
other resource via InterLibrary Loan, <br>and you need/want to renew it, fill out the form below. We'll contact you
via e-mail or phone<br>to let you know if we can renew the item for you.</b></font></p>
<p> </p>
<input type="hidden" name="LibraryEmail" value="you@yourLibrary.edu">
<input type="hidden" name="LibraryURL" value="http://www.yourLibrary.edu">
<input type="hidden" name="Form" value="InterLibrary Loan Renewal"><p></p>
<p></p>
<table width="500" border="0" cellspacing="4" cellpadding="1">
<tr><td width="257">
<b><font face="Arial, Helvetica, sans-serif" size="2">Name </font></b><font face="Arial, Helvetica, sans-
serif" size="1"> (last, first middle)</font><br><font face="Arial, Helvetica, sans-serif" size="2"><input
type="text" name="Name" size="25"></font></td>
<td width="227">
<b><font face="Arial, Helvetica, sans-serif" size="2">Department / Major<br></font></b><font face="Arial,
Helvetica, sans-serif" size="2"><input type="text" name="Department" size="25">
</font></td></tr>
<tr><td width="257">
<b><font face="Arial, Helvetica, sans-serif" size="2">Campus address<br></font></b><font face="Arial,
Helvetica, sans-serif" size="2"><input type="text" name="CampusAddress" size="25"></font></td>
<td width="227">
<b><font face="Arial, Helvetica, sans-serif" size="2">Campus e-mail<br></font></b><font face="Arial, Helvetica,
sans-serif" size="2"><input type="text" name="CampusEmail" size="25"></font></td></tr>
<tr><td width="257">
<b><font face="Arial, Helvetica, sans-serif" size="2">Campus phone</font></b><br><font face="Arial, Helvetica,
sans-serif" size="2"><input type="text" name="CampusPhone" size="25"></font></td>
<td width="227">
<b><font face="Arial, Helvetica, sans-serif" size="2">Fax / Other phone<br></font></b><font face="Arial,
Helvetica, sans-serif" size="2"><input type="text" name="OtherPhone" size="25">
</font></td></tr></table>
<p>
```

```
<b><font face="Arial, Helvetica, sans-serif" size="2">Status</font></b><table width="550" border="0"
cellspacing="0" cellpadding="0">
<tr><td width="126" height="13">
<font face="Arial, Helvetica, sans-serif" size="2"><input type="radio" name="Status"
value="Freshman">Freshman</font></td>
<td width="117" height="13">
<font face="Arial, Helvetica, sans-serif" size="2"><input type="radio" name="Status"
value="Sophomore">Sophomore</font></td>
<td width="87" height="13">
<font face="Arial, Helvetica, sans-serif" size="2"><input type="radio" name="Status" value="Junior">Junior
</font></td>
<td width="202" height="13">
<font face="Arial, Helvetica, sans-serif" size="2"><input type="radio" name="Status" value="Senior">Senior
</font></td></tr>
<tr><td width="126" height="9">
<font face="Arial, Helvetica, sans-serif" size="2"><input type="radio" name="Status"
value="Graduate Student">Grad Student</font></td>
<td width="117" height="9">
<font face="Arial, Helvetica, sans-serif" size="2"><input type="radio" name="Status" value="Faculty">Faculty
</font></td>
<td width="87" height="9">
<font face="Arial, Helvetica, sans-serif" size="2"><input type="radio" name="Status" value="Staff">Staff
</font></td>
<td width="202" height="9"><font face="Arial, Helvetica, sans-serif" size="2"><input type="radio"
name="Status" value="Other">Other</font></td></tr></table>
<p>
<font face="Arial, Helvetica, sans-serif" size="2"><b>Call number</b><br><font size="3"><input type="text"
name="CallNumber" size="40"></font></font></p>
<p>
<font face="Arial, Helvetica, sans-serif" size="2"><b>Title</b><br><font size="3"><input type="text"
name="Title" size="40"></font></font></p>
<p>
<font face="Arial, Helvetica, sans-serif" size="2"><b>Author / Editor / Artist</b> <font face="Arial,
Helvetica, sans-serif" size="1"> (last, first)</font><br><font size="3"><input type="text" name="Author"
size="40"></font></font> </p>
<table width="320" border="0">
<tr><td width="137">
<font face="Arial, Helvetica, sans-serif" size="2"><b>Original due date</b><br><font size="3">
<input type="text" name="OriginalDueDate" size="10"></font></font></td>
<td width="173">
<font face="Arial, Helvetica, sans-serif" size="2"><b>Due date requested</b><br><font size="3">
<input type="text" name="NewDueDate" size="10"></font></font></td></tr></table>
<p>
<font face="Arial, Helvetica, sans-serif" size="2"><b>Comments / Special instructions</b><br><font
size="3"><textarea name="Comments" cols="40" rows="2"></textarea></font></font></p>
```

```
<p> </p>
<table width="700" border="0" cellspacing="10" cellpadding="1"><tr><td width="236">
<div align="right"><input type="submit" name="send" value="Send Request"></div></td>
<td width="211"> </td><td width="207">
<div align="left"><input type="reset" name="clear" value="Clear Form"></div></td></tr>
<tr colspan=3><td colspan=3>
<table width="500" border="0" height="2" align="center" cellpadding="0" cellspacing="0"
bgcolor="#000000"><tr> <td><font size="1" color="#000000">.</font></td></tr></table>
</td></tr>
<tr><td colspan=3><div align="center">
<font face="Arial, Helvetica, sans-serif" size="1"><b>http://</b></font><br><font size="2"> 
<font face="Arial, Helvetica, sans-serif" size="1"><b>&copy; 2001</b></font></font>
<font face="Arial, Helvetica, sans-serif" size="2"><a href="mailto:">
<b><font size="1">Contact Webmaster</font></b></a></font></div></td></tr>
</table></form>
</body>
</html>
```

InterLibrary Loan Renewal — Perl Script

```perl
#!/usr/local/bin/perl

# **************************************************
# ABOVE is where you MUST specify the path to your
# perl interpreter on your Web server.
# Replace /usr/local/bin/perl with your path.
# **************************************************

if ($ENV{'REQUEST_METHOD'}eq"GET"){$buffer = $ENV{'QUERY_STRING'};}
    elsif($ENV{'REQUEST_METHOD'}eq"POST"){
        read(STDIN,$buffer,$ENV{'CONTENT_LENGTH'});
    }
$bufferb = $buffer;
#separate the name of the input from its value.
@forminputs = split(/&/, $bufferb);

foreach $forminput (@forminputs)
{
    #separate the name of the input from its value
    ($name, $value) = split(/=/, $forminput);

    #Un-Webify plus signs and %-encoding
    $value =~ tr/+/ /;
    $value =~ s/%([a-fA-F0-9][a-fA-F0-9])/pack("C", hex($1))/eg;

    #stick them in the in array
    $in{$name} = $value;
}
print "Content-type: text/html\n\n";

################################################################
# ABOVE is the required header for a perl script            #
################################################################


####################################################################
# (Below) Email received by library containing user-entered information #
####################################################################


# **************************************************
# Here's where you MUST specify the path to your
# email program (probably sendmail) ON your Web server.
# Replace /usr/sbin/sendmail with your path.
# **************************************************
```

```
open (LMAIL, "I/usr/sbin/sendmail -t");
print LMAIL ("To: $in{LibraryEmail}\n");

print LMAIL ("From: $in{CampusEmail}\n");
print LMAIL ("Subject: $in{Form} - patron submission\n");

print LMAIL ("------------------\nPatron information\n\n");
print LMAIL ("Name:\n $in{Name}\n\n");
print LMAIL ("Department / Major:\n $in{Department}\n\n");
print LMAIL ("Campus Address:\n $in{CampusAddress}\n\n");
print LMAIL ("Campus Email:\n $in{CampusEmail}\n\n");
print LMAIL ("Campus Phone:\n $in{CampusPhone}\n\n");
print LMAIL ("Other Phone:\n $in{OtherPhone}\n\n");
print LMAIL ("Status:\n $in{Status}\n\n");

print LMAIL ("------------------\nSubmitted information \n\n");

print LMAIL ("Call number:\n $in{CallNumber}\n\n");
print LMAIL ("Title:\n $in{Title}\n\n");
print LMAIL ("Author / Editor / Artist:\n $in{Author}\n\n");

print LMAIL ("Original due date:\n $in{OriginalDueDate}\n\n");
print LMAIL ("Requested due date:\n $in{NewDueDate}\n\n");
print LMAIL ("Comments / Special instructions:\n $in{Comments}\n\n");

print LMAIL ("\n.\n");

#########################################################
# Email received by the user confirming form submission #
#########################################################


# ************************************************
# Here's where you MUST specify the path to your
# email program ON your Web server.
# Replace /usr/sbin/sendmail with your path.
# ************************************************


open (MAIL, "I/usr/sbin/sendmail -t");

# ************************************************
# Here's where you MAY customize the email
# response to the user. You may change any wording
# on the form.
# ************************************************
```

```
print MAIL<<toEnd;
To: $in{CampusEmail}
From: $in{LibraryEmail}
Subject: $in{Form}

Thanks for submitting an InterLibrary Loan renewal request.\n\n
A librarian will contact you in the next couple of days to let you know if we are able to renew the item for you.

toEnd
    print MAIL ("\n.\n");


####################################################
# Screen response to user after submitting the form  #
####################################################

print ("<html><head><title>$in{Form}</title></head>");
print ("<body bgcolor=\"ffffff\">");


# ************************************************
# Here's where you MAY change the screen response
# the user sees after submitting the form. You may
# change any wording between the quotation marks.
# ************************************************

print ("Thanks for submitting an InterLibrary Loan renewal request.<p>
A librarian will contact you in the next couple of days to let you know if we are able to renew the item for you.");


# ************************************************
# Here's where you MAY change the name of the link
# back to your main page. You may replace Return
# to our main page with your own wording.
# ************************************************

print ("<p><center><a href=$in{LibraryURL}>Return to our main page.</a></center>");
print ("</body></html>");
```

Group 7 — Circulation Forms

In this section you'll find four forms. The first two forms allow patrons to apply for a library card, put a hold on an item, recall an item that has been checked out by another patron, and renew a book that has been checked out. The third form allows patrons to submit information to your circulation/stacks staff about library materials they can't locate. The last form lets faculty send course reserve requests to library staff via e-mail.

Library Card Application

Whether students or faculty are new to your campus or haven't found the time to come to the library to get a library card, now they can apply for one online. When their card is ready to pick up at the circulation desk, you can contact patrons via e-mail or phone to let them know where to pick up their new library card. Be sure to put a link to this form on your circulation page.

Hold / Recall / Renew

Students, faculty, and staff can use this form to extend the due date of an item they've already checked out, to ask that an item checked out by another library patron be returned to the library so that they can use it, or to place a hold on an item that has been returned or is about to be returned by another library patron. You can contact patrons via e-mail or phone to let them know when they can pick up the item or when a renewed item is due. Put a link to this form on all of your circulation pages.

Missing Item Report

Make it simple for students, staff, and faculty to inform you when an item can't be located. You can contact patrons via e-mail or phone if you locate the item. If you can't locate it, you can notify patrons via phone or e-mail if you'll borrow the item from InterLibrary Loan or purchase a replacement copy. Place a link to this form on your homepage, your circulation page, and your library collections pages.

Course Reserve Request form

Each academic year faculty members place hundreds of books and journal articles on course reserve. Make the process simpler for faculty (and your staff) by placing a link to this online form on your circulation Web page so that faculty can e-mail you their requests for the materials they want you to put on reserve for their students.

Library Card Application

Whether you're new to campus or haven't had time to come to the library to get a library card, you can now apply for one online. We'll send you an e-mail message or call you to let you know when your library card is ready to pick up at the circulation desk.

Name (last, first middle)

Department / Major

Campus address

Campus e-mail

Campus phone

Fax / Other phone

Status

○ Freshman   ○ Sophomore   ○ Junior   ○ Senior
○ Grad Student   ○ Faculty   ○ Staff   ○ Other

Student ID number

Date of birth

(mm/dd/yyyy)

I will abide by all library rules and regulations. I will fully compensate the library for delinquent, lost, or damaged items checked out with my library card.

☐ I agree with the above statements

[Send Application]   [Clear Form]

Library Card Application — HTML Form

```
<html>
<head><title>Library Card Application</title></head>
<body bgcolor="#FFFFFF">
<table width="700" border="0" height="85" bgcolor="#000000">
<tr valign="middle" align="center"><td>
<p><font halign=center color="#FFFFFF" face="Arial, Helvetica, sans-serif" size="+3"> <b><i>Library Card
Application</i></b></font></p>
</td></tr></table>
<form method="post" action="http://www.yourLibrary.edu/cgi-bin/ac1.pl"><p> </p>
<p>
<font face="Arial, Helvetica, sans-serif" size="2"><b>Whether you're new to campus or haven't had time to come
to the library to get a library card, <br>you can now apply for one online. We'll send you an e-mail message or call
you to let you know <br>when your library card is ready to pick up at the circulation desk.</b></font></p>
<p> </p>
<input type="hidden" name="LibraryEmail" value="you@yourLibrary.edu">
<input type="hidden" name="LibraryURL" value="http://www.yourLibrary.edu">
<input type="hidden" name="Form" value="Library Card Application">
<p></p>
<table width="500" border="0" cellspacing="4" cellpadding="1">
<tr>
<td width="257">
<b><font face="Arial, Helvetica, sans-serif" size="2">Name </font></b><font face="Arial, Helvetica, sans-
serif" size="1"> (last, first middle)</font><br><font face="Arial, Helvetica, sans-serif" size="2"><input
type="text" name="Name" size="25"></font></td>
<td width="227">
<b><font face="Arial, Helvetica, sans-serif" size="2">Department / Major<br></font></b><font face= "Arial,
Helvetica, sans-serif" size="2"><input type="text" name="Department" size="25"></font></td></tr>
<tr><td width="257">
<b><font face="Arial, Helvetica, sans-serif" size="2">Campus address<br></font></b><font face="Arial,
Helvetica, sans-serif" size="2"><input type="text" name="CampusAddress" size="25"></font></td>
<td width="227">
<b><font face="Arial, Helvetica, sans-serif" size="2">Campus e-mail<br></font></b><font face="Arial, Helvetica,
sans-serif" size="2"><input type="text" name="CampusEmail" size="25"></font></td></tr>
<tr><td width="257">
<b><font face="Arial, Helvetica, sans-serif" size="2">Campus phone</font></b><br><font face="Arial, Helvetica,
sans-serif" size="2"><input type="text" name="CampusPhone" size="25"></font></td>
<td width="227">
<b><font face="Arial, Helvetica, sans-serif" size="2">Fax / Other phone<br></font></b><font face="Arial,
Helvetica, sans-serif" size="2"><input type="text" name="OtherPhone" size="25"></font>
</td></tr><table>
<p>
<b><font face="Arial, Helvetica, sans-serif" size="2">Status</font></b><table width="550" border="0"
cellspacing="0" cellpadding="0">
```

```
<tr><td width="126" height="13">
<font face="Arial, Helvetica, sans-serif" size="2"><input type="radio" name="Status" value=
"Freshman">Freshman</font></td>
<td width="117" height="13">
<font face="Arial, Helvetica, sans-serif" size="2"><input type="radio" name="Status" value=
"Sophomore">Sophomore</font></td>
<td width="87" height="13">
<font face="Arial, Helvetica, sans-serif" size="2"> <input type="radio" name="Status" value= "Junior">Junior
</font></td>
<td width="202" height="13">
<font face="Arial, Helvetica, sans-serif" size="2"><input type="radio" name="Status" value= "Senior">Senior
</font></td></tr>
<tr><td width="126" height="9">
<font face="Arial, Helvetica, sans-serif" size="2"><input type="radio" name="Status" value=
"Graduate Student">Grad Student</font></td>
<td width="117" height="9">
<font face="Arial, Helvetica, sans-serif" size="2"><input type="radio" name="Status" value= "Faculty">Faculty
</font></td>
<td width="87" height="9">
<font face="Arial, Helvetica, sans-serif" size="2"><input type="radio" name="Status" value= "Staff">Staff
</font></td>
<td width="202" height="9">
<font face="Arial, Helvetica, sans-serif" size="2"><input type="radio" name="Status" value= "Other">Other
</font></td></tr></table>
<p>
<b><font face="Arial, Helvetica, sans-serif" size="2">Student ID number   
  </font></b><br><font face="Arial, Helvetica, sans-serif" size="3"><input type="text" name="ID"
size="15">  </font>
<p>
<b><font face="Arial, Helvetica, sans-serif" size="2">Date of birth</font></b><br>
<font face="Arial, Helvetica, sans-serif" size="3"><input type="text" name="DateOfBirth" size="15">
   <font face="Arial, Helvetica, sans-serif" size="1">(mm/dd/yyyy)</font>  
  </font>
<p>
<b><font face="Arial, Helvetica, sans-serif" size="2">I will abide by all library rules and regulations. I will fully
compensate the library for delinquent,<br>lost, or damaged items checked out with my library card.</font></b>
</p><p>
              
               
         
<input type="checkbox" name="Agreement" value="I agree"><! -- input type="hidden" name= "Agreement" --
><font face="Arial, Helvetica, sans-serif" size="2">I agree with the above statements </font></p>
<p> </p>
<table width="700" border="0" cellspacing="10" cellpadding="1"><tr><td width="269">
<div align="right"><input type="submit" name="send" value="Send Application"></div></td>
```

```
<td width="178"> </td><td width="207">
<div align="left"><input type="reset" name="clear" value="Clear Form"></div></td></tr>
<tr colspan=3><td colspan=3>
<table width="500" border="0" height="2" align="center" cellpadding="0" cellspacing="0"
bcolor="#000000"><tr><td><font size="1" color="#000000">.</font></td></tr></table>
</td></tr>
<tr><td colspan=3><div align="center">
<font face="Arial, Helvetica, sans-serif" size="1"><b>http://</b></font><br><font size="2"> 
<font face="Arial, Helvetica, sans-serif" size="1"><b>&copy; 2001</b></font></font>
<font face="Arial, Helvetica, sans-serif" size="2"><a href="mailto: ">
<b><font size="1">Contact Webmaster</font></b></a></font></div></td></tr>
</table></form>
</body>
</html>
```

Library Card Application — Perl Script

```perl
#!/usr/local/bin/perl

# ************************************************
# ABOVE is where you MUST specify the path to your
# perl interpreter on your Web server.
# Replace /usr/local/bin/perl with your path.
# ************************************************

if ($ENV{'REQUEST_METHOD'}eq"GET"){$buffer = $ENV{'QUERY_STRING'};}
    elsif($ENV{'REQUEST_METHOD'}eq"POST"){
        read(STDIN,$buffer,$ENV{'CONTENT_LENGTH'});
    }
$bufferb = $buffer;
#separate the name of the input from its value.
@forminputs = split(/&/, $bufferb);

foreach $forminput (@forminputs)
{
     #separate the name of the input from its value
     ($name, $value) = split(/=/, $forminput);

     #Un-Webify plus signs and %-encoding
     $value =~ tr/+/ /;
     $value =~ s/%([a-fA-F0-9][a-fA-F0-9])/pack("C", hex($1))/eg;

     #stick them in the in array
     $in{$name} = $value;
}
print "Content-type: text/html\n\n";

###############################################################
# ABOVE is the required header for a perl script        #
###############################################################


###################################################################
# (Below) Email received by library containing user-entered information #
###################################################################


# ************************************************
# Here's where you MUST specify the path to your
# email program (probably sendmail) ON your Web server.
# Replace /usr/sbin/sendmail with your path.
# ************************************************
```

```
open (LMAIL, "I/usr/sbin/sendmail -t");
print LMAIL ("To: $in{LibraryEmail}\n");

print LMAIL ("From: $in{CampusEmail}\n");
print LMAIL ("Subject: $in{Form} - patron submission\n");

print LMAIL ("------------------\nPatron information\n\n");
print LMAIL ("Name:\n $in{Name}\n\n");
print LMAIL ("Department / Major:\n $in{Department}\n\n");
print LMAIL ("Campus Address:\n $in{CampusAddress}\n\n");
print LMAIL ("Campus Email:\n $in{CampusEmail}\n\n");
print LMAIL ("Campus Phone:\n $in{CampusPhone}\n\n");
print LMAIL ("Other Phone:\n $in{OtherPhone}\n\n");
print LMAIL ("Status:\n $in{Status}\n\n");
print LMAIL ("Student ID number:\n $in{ID}\n\n");
print LMAIL ("Date of birth:\n $in{DateOfBirth}\n\n");
print LMAIL ("Employer / school name:\n $in{Employer}\n\n");
print LMAIL ("I agree:\n $in{Agreement}\n\n");

print LMAIL ("\n.\n");

#######################################################
# Email received by the user confirming form submission #
#######################################################

# ***********************************************
# Here's where you MUST specify the path to your
# email program ON your Web server.
# Replace /usr/sbin/sendmail with your path.
# ***********************************************

open (MAIL, "I/usr/sbin/sendmail -t");

# ***********************************************
# Here's where you MAY customize the email
# response to the user. You may change any wording
# on the form.
# ***********************************************

print MAIL<<toEnd;
To: $in{CampusEmail}
From: $in{LibraryEmail}
Subject: $in{Form}

Thanks for applying for a library card \n\n
```

A librarian will contact you in the next couple of days to let you know when your card will be ready to pick up, where you can pick it up, and what ID you need to bring along with you.

```
toEnd
    print MAIL ("\n.\n");


######################################################
# Screen response to user after submitting the form  #
######################################################

print ("<html><head><title>$in{Form}</title></head>");
print ("<body bgcolor=\"ffffff\">");


# ************************************************
# Here's where you MAY change the screen response
# the user sees after submitting the form. You may
# change any wording between the quotation marks.
# ************************************************

print ("Thanks for applying for a library card <p>
A librarian will contact you in the next couple of days to let you know when your card will be ready to pick up,
where you can pick it up, and what ID you need to bring along with you.");


# ************************************************
# Here's where you MAY change the name of the link
# back to your main page. You may replace Return
# to our main page with your own wording.
# ************************************************

print ("<p><center><a href=$in{LibraryURL}>Return to our main page.</a></center>");
print ("</body></html>");
```

Hold / Recall / Renew

Use this form to place a HOLD on an item that has been returned, or is about to be returned by a student or faculty member, to RECALL an item currently checked out, or to RENEW an item you've checked out from the library. We'll contact you via e-mail or phone to let you know when the item is due, or when you can pick the item up at the library.

Name (last, first middle)

Department / Major

Campus address

Campus e-mail

Campus phone

Fax / Other phone

Status

○ Freshman ○ Sophomore ○ Junior ○ Senior

○ Grad Student ○ Faculty ○ Staff ○ Other

Material type

○ Book ○ Journal issue / vol ○ Thesis / Dissertation ○ CD-ROM

○ Video / DVD ○ Audio / CD ○ Microfilm / fiche

○ Other (please specify)

Type of request

○ Hold ○ Recall ○ Renew

Call number

Title

Author / Editor / Artist (last, first)

Hold / Recall

I need the item before (specify date)

○ Anytime is fine

Priority

○ Course reading   ○ Course-related   ○ Research

○ Other (please specify) [＿＿＿＿＿]

Comments / special requests

[＿＿＿＿＿＿＿＿＿＿＿]

Renew

Original due date   **Due date requested**

[＿＿＿＿＿]   [＿＿＿＿＿]

Please renew

○ Only the item listed above   ○ All materials checked out   ○ Only overdue materials

Comments / special requests

[＿＿＿＿＿＿＿＿＿＿＿]

[Send Request]   [Clear Form]

Hold / Recall / Renew — HTML Form

```
<html>
<head><title>Hold / Recall / Renew</title></head>
<body bgcolor="#FFFFFF">
<table width="700" border="0" height="85" bgcolor="#000000">
<tr valign="middle" align="center"><td>
<p>
<font halign=center color="#FFFFFF" face="Arial, Helvetica, sans-serif" size="+3">
<b><i>Hold / Recall / Renew</i></b></font></p>
</td></tr></table>
<form method="post" action="http://www.yourLibrary.edu/cgi-bin/ac2.pl"><p> </p>
<p>
<font face="Arial, Helvetica, sans-serif" size="2"><b>Use this form to place a HOLD on an item that has been
returned, or is about to be returned by a student or <br>faculty member, to RECALL an item currently checked
out, or to RENEW an item you've checked out <br>from the library. We'll contact you via e-mail or phone to let
you know when the item is due, or when <br>you can pick the item up at the library. </b></font></p>
<p> </p>
<input type="hidden" name="LibraryEmail" value="you@yourLibrary.edu">
<input type="hidden" name="LibraryURL" value="http://www.yourLibrary.edu">
<input type="hidden" name="Form" value="Hold / Recall / Renew">
<p></p>
<table width="500" border="0" cellspacing="4" cellpadding="1">
<tr>
<td width="257">
<b><font face="Arial, Helvetica, sans-serif" size="2">Name </font></b><font face="Arial, Helvetica, sans-
serif" size="1"> (last, first middle)</font><br><font face="Arial, Helvetica, sans-serif" size="2"><input
type="text" name="Name" size="25"></font></td>
<td width="227">
<b><font face="Arial, Helvetica, sans-serif" size="2">Department / Major<br></font></b><font face= "Arial,
Helvetica, sans-serif" size="2"><input type="text" name="Department" size="25"> </font></td></tr>
<tr><td width="257">
<b><font face="Arial, Helvetica, sans-serif" size="2">Campus address<br></font></b><font face="Arial,
Helvetica, sans-serif" size="2"><input type="text" name="CampusAddress" size="25"></font></td>
<td width="227">
<b><font face="Arial, Helvetica, sans-serif" size="2">Campus e-mail<br></font></b><font face="Arial, Helvetica,
sans-serif" size="2"><input type="text" name="CampusEmail" size="25"></font></td></tr>
<tr><td width="257">
<b><font face="Arial, Helvetica, sans-serif" size="2">Campus phone</font></b><br><font face="Arial, Helvetica,
sans-serif" size="2"><input type="text" name="CampusPhone" size="25"></font></td>
<td width="227">
<b><font face="Arial, Helvetica, sans-serif" size="2">Fax / Other phone<br></font></b><font face="Arial,
Helvetica, sans-serif" size="2"><input type="text" name="OtherPhone" size="25"></font></td></tr> </table>
<p><b><font face="Arial, Helvetica, sans-serif" size="2">Status</font></b> <table width="550" border="0"
cellspacing="0" cellpadding="0">
```

```
<tr><td width="126" height="13">
<font face="Arial, Helvetica, sans-serif" size="2"><input type="radio" name="Status" value=
"Freshman">Freshman</font></td>
<td width="117" height="13">
<font face="Arial, Helvetica, sans-serif" size="2"><input type="radio" name="Status" value=
"Sophomore">Sophomore</font></td>
<td width="87" height="13">
<font face="Arial, Helvetica, sans-serif" size="2"><input type="radio" name="Status" value= "Junior">Junior
</font></td>
<td width="202" height="13">
<font face="Arial, Helvetica, sans-serif" size="2"><input type="radio" name="Status" value=
"Senior">Senior</font></td></tr>
<tr><td width="126" height="9">
<font face="Arial, Helvetica, sans-serif" size="2"><input type="radio" name="Status" value=
"Graduate Student">Grad Student</font></td>
<td width="117" height="9">
<font face="Arial, Helvetica, sans-serif" size="2"><input type="radio" name="Status" value=
"Faculty">Faculty</font></td>
<td width="87" height="9">
<font face="Arial, Helvetica, sans-serif" size="2"><input type="radio" name="Status" value=
"Staff">Staff</font></td>
<td width="202" height="9">
<font face="Arial, Helvetica, sans-serif" size="2"><input type="radio" name="Status" value=
"Other">Other</font></td></tr></table>
<p>
<b><font face="Arial, Helvetica, sans-serif" size="2">Material type</font></b><table width="548" border="0"
cellspacing="0" cellpadding="0">
<tr><td width="143">
<font face="Arial, Helvetica, sans-serif" size="2"><input type="radio" name="Material" value="Book">
Book</font></td>
<td width="149">
<font face="Arial, Helvetica, sans-serif" size="2"><input type="radio" name="Material" value="Journal
issue">Journal issue / vol</font></td>
<td width="146">
<font face="Arial, Helvetica, sans-serif" size="2"><input type="radio" name="Material" value="Thesis /
Dissertation">Thesis / Dissertation</font></td>
<td width="110">
<font face="Arial, Helvetica, sans-serif" size="2"><input type="radio" name="Material" value="CD-ROM">CD-
ROM</font></td></tr>
<tr><td width="143" height="15">
<font face="Arial, Helvetica, sans-serif" size="2"><input type="radio" name="Material" value="Video /
DVD">Video / DVD</font></td>
<td width="149" height="15">
<font face="Arial, Helvetica, sans-serif" size="2"><input type="radio" name="Material" value="Audio / CD">Audio
/ CD </font></td>
```

```
<td width="146" height="15">
<font face="Arial, Helvetica, sans-serif" size="2"><input type="radio" name="Material" value="Microfilm /
fiche">Microfilm / fiche</font></td>
<td width="110" height="15"><font face="Arial, Helvetica, sans-serif" size="2"></font></td></tr>
<tr><td colspan="3">
<font face="Arial, Helvetica, sans-serif" size="2"><input type="radio" name="Material" value="Other">
Other <b><font face="Arial, Helvetica, sans-serif" size="2"> </font></b><font face="Arial, Helvetica, sans-
serif" size="1">(please specify)</font>    <font size="3"><input type="text" name="OtherType"
size="20"></font></font></td>
<td width="110"></td></tr></table>
<p>
<font face="Arial, Helvetica, sans-serif" size="2"><b>Type of request<br></b>
<input type="radio" name="TypeOfRequest" value="Hold">Hold    
<input type="radio" name="TypeOfRequest" value="Recall">Recall   
<input type="radio" name="TypeOfRequest" value="Renew">Renew</font>
<p>
<font face="Arial, Helvetica, sans-serif" size="2"><b>Call number</b><br><font size="3"><input type="text"
name="CallNumber" size="40"></font></font></p>
<p>
<font face="Arial, Helvetica, sans-serif" size="2"><b>Title</b><br><font size="3"><input type="text"
name="Title" size="40"></font></font></p>
<p>
<font face="Arial, Helvetica, sans-serif" size="2"><b>Author / Editor / Artist </b>  <font
size="1">(last, first)</font><br><font size="3"><input type="text" name="Author" size="40"> </font></font></p>
<p> </p><p>
<b><font face="Arial, Helvetica, sans-serif" size="3">Hold / Recall</font></b></p>
<p>
<font face="Arial, Helvetica, sans-serif" size="2"><b>I need the item before </b> <font face="Arial,
Helvetica, sans-serif" size="1"> (specify date)</font><br><font size="3"><input type="text"
name="NeedBefore" size="15">      </font>
<font face="Arial, Helvetica, sans-serif" size="1"><input type="radio" name="TimeIssue" value="Time is not an
issue"></font>Anytime is fine</font></p>
<p>
<b><font face="Arial, Helvetica, sans-serif" size="2">Priority<br></font></b><font face="Arial, Helvetica, sans-
serif" size="2">
<input type="radio" name="Priority" value="Course reading">Course reading   
<input type="radio" name="Priority" value="Course-related">Course-related  
<input type="radio" name="Priority" value="Research">Research    <br>
<input type="radio" name="Priority" value="Other">Other</font><font face="Arial, Helvetica, sans-serif"
size="1">(please specify)<font size="3">   input type="text" name="PriorityO" size="10"></font>
</font></p>
<p>
<font face="Arial, Helvetica, sans-serif" size="2"><b>Comments / special requests</b><br><font size="3">
<textarea name="Comments" cols="40" rows="2"></textarea></font></font></p>
<p> </p>
```

```
<p>
<b><font face="Arial, Helvetica, sans-serif" size="3">Renew</font></b></p><table width="320" border="0">
<tr><td width="137">
<font face="Arial, Helvetica, sans-serif" size="2"><b>Original due date</b><br><font size="3">
<input type="text" name="OriginalDueDate" size="10"></font></font></td>
<td width="173">
<font face="Arial, Helvetica, sans-serif" size="2"><b>Due date requested</b><br><font size="3">
<input type="text" name="NewDueDate" size="10"></font></font></td></tr></table>
<p>
<b><font face="Arial, Helvetica, sans-serif" size="2">Please renew<br></font></b><font face="Arial, Helvetica,
sans-serif" size="2">
<input type="radio" name="Renew" value="Only the item listed above">Only the item listed
above   
<input type="radio" name="Renew" value="All materials checked out">All materials checked
out   
<input type="radio" name="Renew" value="Only overdue materials">Only overdue materials 
   <br>
</font></p>
<p>
<font face="Arial, Helvetica, sans-serif" size="2"><b>Comments / special requests</b><br><font
size="3"><textarea name="RenewComments" cols="40" rows="2"></textarea></font></font><br></p>
<p> </p>
<table width="700" border="0" cellspacing="10" cellpadding="1"><tr><td width="241">
<div align="right"><input type="submit" name="send" value="Send Request"></div></td>
<td width="206"> </td><td width="207">
<div align="left"><input type="reset" name="clear" value="Clear Form"></div></td></tr>
<tr colspan=3><td colspan=3>
<table width="500" border="0" height="2" align="center" cellpadding="0" cellspacing="0"
bgcolor="#000000"><tr><td><font size="1" color="#000000">.</font></td></tr></table>
</td></tr>
<tr><td colspan=3><div align="center">
<font face="Arial, Helvetica, sans-serif" size="1"><b>http:// </b></font><br><font size="2">  
<font face="Arial, Helvetica, sans-serif" size="1"><b>&copy;2001</b></font></font>
<font face="Arial, Helvetica, sans-serif" size="2"><a href="mailto: ">
<b><font size="1">Contact Webmaster</font></b></a></font></div></td></tr>
</table></form>
</body>
</html>
```

Hold / Recall / Renew — Perl Script

```perl
#!/usr/local/bin/perl

# ************************************************
# ABOVE is where you MUST specify the path to your
# perl interpreter on your Web server.
# Replace /usr/local/bin/perl with your path.
# ************************************************

if ($ENV{'REQUEST_METHOD'}eq"GET"){$buffer = $ENV{'QUERY_STRING'};}
    elsif($ENV{'REQUEST_METHOD'}eq"POST"){
        read(STDIN,$buffer,$ENV{'CONTENT_LENGTH'});
    }
$bufferb = $buffer;
#separate the name of the input from its value.
@forminputs = split(/&/, $bufferb);

foreach $forminput (@forminputs)
{
    #separate the name of the input from its value
    ($name, $value) = split(/=/, $forminput);

    #Un-Webify plus signs and %-encoding
    $value =~ tr/+/ /;
    $value =~ s/%([a-fA-F0-9][a-fA-F0-9])/pack("C", hex($1))/eg;

    #stick them in the in array
    $in{$name} = $value;
}
print "Content-type: text/html\n\n";

############################################################
# ABOVE is the required header for a perl script          #
############################################################


###################################################################
# (Below) Email received by library containing user-entered information #
###################################################################


# ************************************************
# Here's where you MUST specify the path to your
# email program (probably sendmail) ON your Web server.
# Replace /usr/sbin/sendmail with your path.
# ************************************************
```

```perl
open (LMAIL, "l/usr/sbin/sendmail -t");
print LMAIL ("To: $in{LibraryEmail}\n");

print LMAIL ("From: $in{CampusEmail}\n");
print LMAIL ("Subject: $in{Form} - patron submission\n");

print LMAIL ("-------------------\nPatron information\n\n");
print LMAIL ("Name:\n $in{Name}\n\n");
print LMAIL ("Department / Major:\n $in{Department}\n\n");
print LMAIL ("Campus Address:\n $in{CampusAddress}\n\n");
print LMAIL ("Campus Email:\n $in{CampusEmail}\n\n");
print LMAIL ("Campus Phone:\n $in{CampusPhone}\n\n");
print LMAIL ("Other Phone:\n $in{OtherPhone}\n\n");
print LMAIL ("Status:\n $in{Status}\n\n");
print LMAIL ("------------------\nSubmitted information \n\n");
print LMAIL ("Material type:\n $in{Material}\n\n");
print LMAIL ("Other type:\n $in{OtherType}\n\n");
print LMAIL ("Type of request:\n $in{TypeOfRequest}\n\n");
print LMAIL ("Call number:\n $in{CallNumber}\n\n");
print LMAIL ("Title:\n $in{Title}\n\n");
print LMAIL ("Author / Editor / Artist:\n $in{Author}\n\n");
print LMAIL ("Hold / Recall\n");
print LMAIL ("I need this item before:\n $in{NeedBefore} $in{TimeIssue}\n\n");
print LMAIL ("Priority:\n $in{Priority}\n\n");
print LMAIL ("Other Priority:\n $in{PriorityO}\n\n");
print LMAIL ("Comments / Special requests:\n $in{Comments}\n\n");
print LMAIL ("Renew\n");
print LMAIL ("Original due date:\n $in{OriginalDueDate}\n\n");
print LMAIL ("Requested due date:\n $in{NewDueDate}\n\n");
print LMAIL ("Please renew:\n $in{Renew}\n\n");
print LMAIL ("Comments / special requests:\n $in{RenewComments}\n\n");

print LMAIL ("\n.\n");


############################################################
# Email received by the user confirming form submission #
############################################################


# ************************************************
# Here's where you MUST specify the path to your
# email program ON your Web server.
# Replace /usr/sbin/sendmail with your path.
# ************************************************


open (MAIL, "l/usr/sbin/sendmail -t");
```

```
# *********************************************
# Here's where you MAY customize the email
# response to the user. You may change any wording
# on the form.
# *********************************************

print MAIL<<toEnd;
To: $in{CampusEmail}
From: $in{LibraryEmail}
Subject: $in{Form}

Thanks for submitting a hold, recall, renew request. \n\n
A librarian will contact you in the next couple of days to let you know when we might have the item ready for you
to pick up.

toEnd
    print MAIL ("\n.\n");


##################################################
# Screen response to user after submitting the form  #
##################################################

print ("<html><head><title>$in{Form}</title></head>");
print ("<body bgcolor=\"ffffff\">");


# *********************************************
# Here's where you MAY change the screen response
# the user sees after submitting the form. You may
# change any wording between the quotation marks.
# *********************************************

print ("Thanks for submitting a hold, recall, renew request. <p>
A librarian will contact you in the next couple of days to let you know when we might have the item ready for you
to pick up.");


# *********************************************
# Here's where you MAY change the name of the link
# back to your main page. You may replace Return
# to our main page with your own wording.
# *********************************************

print ("<p><center><a href=$in{LibraryURL}>Return to our main page.</a></center>");
print ("</body></html>");
```

Missing Item Report

Please let us know if you can't locate an item. We'll contact you via e-mail or phone if we locate it. If we can't, we'll contact you via e-mail or phone if we can get the item for you via InterLibrary Loan or if we'll purchase a replacement copy.

Name (last, first middle)

Department / Major

Campus address

Campus e-mail

Campus phone

Fax / Other phone

Status

○ Freshman   ○ Sophomore   ○ Junior   ○ Senior
○ Grad Student   ○ Faculty   ○ Staff   ○ Other

Where have you already checked / looked for the item? (select all that apply)

○ On-line catalog   ○ Shelves   ○ Journal / Newspaper holdings   ○ Circulation staff

Material type

○ Book   ○ Journal issue / article   ○ Newspaper issue / article
○ Thesis / Dissertation   ○ Video / DVD   ○ Audio / CD
○ Microfilm / fiche   ○ Other (please specify)

Call number

Title

Author / Editor / Artist (last, first)

I need the item before (specify date)

○ Anytime is fine

Priority

○ Course reading   ○ Course-related   ○ Research
○ Other (please specify)

If we locate the item, would you like us to hold the item for you? ○ Yes   ○ No

[Send Report]   [Clear Form]

Missing Item Report — HTML Form

```
<html>
<head><title>Missing Item Report</title></head>
<body bgcolor="#FFFFFF">
<table width="700" border="0" height="85" bgcolor="#000000">
<tr valign="middle" align="center"><td>
<p>
<font halign=center color="#FFFFFF" face="Arial, Helvetica, sans-serif" size="+3"> <b><i>Missing Item Report</i></b></font></p>
</td></tr></table>
<form method="post" action="http://www.yourLibrary.edu/cgi-bin/ac3.pl"><p> </p>
<p>
<font face="Arial, Helvetica, sans-serif" size="2"><b>Please let us know if you can't locate an item. We'll contact you via e-mail or phone if we locate it. <br> If we can't, we'll contact you via e-mail or phone if we can get the item for you via InterLibrary Loan <br> or if we'll purchase a replacement copy. </b></font></p>
<p> </p>
<input type="hidden" name="LibraryEmail" value="you@yourLibrary.edu">
<input type="hidden" name="LibraryURL" value="http://www.yourLibrary.edu">
<input type="hidden" name="Form" value="Missing Item Report">
<p></p>
<table width="500" border="0" cellspacing="4" cellpadding="1"><tr>
<td width="257">
<b><font face="Arial, Helvetica, sans-serif" size="2">Name </font></b><font face="Arial, Helvetica, sans-serif" size="1"> (last, first middle)</font><br><font face="Arial, Helvetica, sans-serif" size="2"><input type="text" name="Name" size="25"></font></td>
<td width="227">
<b><font face="Arial, Helvetica, sans-serif" size="2">Department / Major<br></font></b><font face="Arial, Helvetica, sans-serif" size="2"><input type="text" name="Department" size="25">
</font></td></tr>
<tr><td width="257">
<b><font face="Arial, Helvetica, sans-serif" size="2">Campus address<br></font></b><font face="Arial, Helvetica, sans-serif" size="2"><input type="text" name="CampusAddress" size="25"></font></td>
<td width="227">
<b><font face="Arial, Helvetica, sans-serif" size="2">Campus e-mail<br></font></b><font face="Arial, Helvetica, sans-serif" size="2"><input type="text" name="CampusEmail" size="25">
</font></td></tr>
<tr><td width="257">
<b><font face="Arial, Helvetica, sans-serif" size="2">Campus phone</font></b><br><font face="Arial, Helvetica, sans-serif" size="2"><input type="text" name="CampusPhone" size="25">
</font></td>
<td width="227">
<b><font face="Arial, Helvetica, sans-serif" size="2">Fax / Other phone<br></font></b><font face="Arial, Helvetica, sans-serif" size="2"><input type="text" name="OtherPhone" size="25">
</font></td></tr></table>
```

```
<p>
<b><font face="Arial, Helvetica, sans-serif" size="2">Status</font></b><table width="550" border="0"
cellspacing="0" cellpadding="0"><tr>
<td width="126" height="13">
<font face="Arial, Helvetica, sans-serif" size="2"><input type="radio" name="Status"
value="Freshman">Freshman</font></td>
<td width="117" height="13">
<font face="Arial, Helvetica, sans-serif" size="2"><input type="radio" name="Status"
value="Sophomore">Sophomore</font></td>
<td width="87" height="13">
<font face="Arial, Helvetica, sans-serif" size="2"><input type="radio" name="Status" value="Junior">Junior
</font></td>
<td width="202" height="13">
<font face="Arial, Helvetica, sans-serif" size="2"><input type="radio" name="Status" value="Senior">Senior
</font></td></tr>
<tr><td width="126" height="9">
<font face="Arial, Helvetica, sans-serif" size="2"><input type="radio" name="Status"
value="Graduate Student">Grad Student</font></td>
<td width="117" height="9">
<font face="Arial, Helvetica, sans-serif" size="2"><input type="radio" name="Status" value="Faculty">Faculty
</font></td>
<td width="87" height="9">
<font face="Arial, Helvetica, sans-serif" size="2"><input type="radio" name="Status" value="Staff">Staff
</font></td>
<td width="202" height="9">
<font face="Arial, Helvetica, sans-serif" size="2"><input type="radio" name="Status" value="Other">Other
</font></td></tr></table>
<p>
<b><font face="Arial, Helvetica, sans-serif" size="2">Where have you already checked / looked for the item?
</font></b><font face="Arial, Helvetica, sans-serif" size="1">   
(select all that apply)</font><br><font face="Arial, Helvetica, sans-serif" size="2">
<input type="radio" name="S" value="I've checked the on-line catalog">On-line catalog    
<input type="radio" name="OC" value="I've checked shelves">Shelves    
<input type="radio" name="MN" value="I've checked journal or newspaper holdings">Journal / Newspaper
holdings   
<input type="radio" name="CD" value="I've checked with the circ. staff">Circulation staff</font>
<p>
<b><font face="Arial, Helvetica, sans-serif" size="2">Material type<br></font></b>
<table width="548" border="0" cellspacing="0" cellpadding="0">
<tr><td width="128">
<font face="Arial, Helvetica, sans-serif" size="2"><input type="radio" name="Material" value="Book">Book
</font></td>
<td width="157">
<font face="Arial, Helvetica, sans-serif" size="2"><input type="radio" name="Material" value="Journal issue /
article">Journal issue / article</font></td>
```

```
<td width="182">
<font face="Arial, Helvetica, sans-serif" size="2"><input type="radio" name="Material" value="Newspaper issue /
article">Newspaper issue / article</font></td></tr>
<tr><td width="128" height="15">
<font face="Arial, Helvetica, sans-serif" size="2"><input type="radio" name="Material" value="Thesis /
Dissertation">Thesis / Dissertation</font></td>
<td width="157" height="15">
<font face="Arial, Helvetica, sans-serif" size="2"><input type="radio" name="Material" value="Video /
DVD">Video / DVD</font></td>
<td width="182" height="15">
<font face="Arial, Helvetica, sans-serif" size="2"><input type="radio" name="Material" value="Book"> Audio /
CD</font></td></tr>
<tr><td colspan="1">
<font face="Arial, Helvetica, sans-serif"><input type="radio" name="Material" value="Microfilm / fiche"><font
size="2">Microfilm / fiche</font></font></td>
<td colspan="2">
<font face="Arial, Helvetica, sans-serif"><input type="radio" name="Material" value="Other">
<font size="2">Other</font>  <font size="1">(please specify)  </font></font><font
size="3"><input type="text" name="OtherType" size="20">  </font></td></tr> </table>
<p>
<font face="Arial, Helvetica, sans-serif" size="2"><b>Call number</b><br><font size="3"><input type="text"
name="CallNumber" size="40"></font></font></p>
<p>
<font face="Arial, Helvetica, sans-serif" size="2"><b>Title</b></font><font face="Arial, Helvetica, sans-serif"
size="3"><br><input type="text" name="Title" size="40"></font></p>
<p>
<font face="Arial, Helvetica, sans-serif" size="2"><b>Author / Editor / Artist </b> <font face="Arial,
Helvetica, sans-serif" size="1"> (last, first)</font><br><font size="3"><input type="text" name="Author"
size="40"></font></font></p>
<p>
<font face="Arial, Helvetica, sans-serif" size="2"><b>I need the item before<font size="1"> 
</font></b><font face="Arial, Helvetica, sans-serif" size="1"> (specify date)</font><br>
<font size="3"><input type="text" name="NeedBefore" size="15">      </font>
<font face="Arial, Helvetica, sans-serif" size="1"><input type="radio" name="Deadline" value="Time is not an
issue"></font>Anytime is fine</font>
<p>
<b><font face="Arial, Helvetica, sans-serif" size="2">Priority<br></font></b>
<font face="Arial, Helvetica, sans-serif" size="2">
<input type="radio" name="Priority" value="Course reading">Course reading    
<input type="radio" name="Priority" value="Course-related">Course-related  
<input type="radio" name="Priority" value="Research">Research    <br>
<input type="radio" name="Priority" value="Other">Other</font> <font face="Arial, Helvetica, sans-serif"
size="1">(please specify)<font size="3">   <input type="text" name="PriorityO" size="10"></font>
</font>
<p>
```

```
<b><font face="Arial, Helvetica, sans-serif" size="2">If we locate the item, would you like us to hold the item for
you?  </font></b><font face="Arial, Helvetica, sans-serif" size="2"> 
<input type="radio" name="LocateAndHold" value="Yes">Yes    
<input type="radio" name="LocateAndHold" value="No">No</font><br></p>
<p> </p>
<table width="700" border="0" cellspacing="10" cellpadding="1"><tr><td width="217">
<div align="right"><input type="submit" name="send" value="Send Report"></div></td>
<td width="230"> </td>
<td width="207"><div align="left"><input type="reset" name="clear" value="Clear Form">
</div></td></tr><tr colspan=3><td colspan=3>
<table width="500" border="0" height="2" align="center" cellpadding="0" cellspacing="0"
bgcolor="#000000"><tr><td><font size="1" color="#000000">.</font></td></tr></table>
</td></tr>
<tr><td colspan=3><div align="center">
<font face="Arial, Helvetica, sans-serif" size="1"><b>http://</b></font><br><font size="2"> 
<font face="Arial, Helvetica, sans-serif" size="1"><b>&copy; 2001</b></font></font>
<font face="Arial, Helvetica, sans-serif" size="2"><a href="mailto:">
<b><font size="1">Contact Webmaster</font></b></a></font></div></td></tr>
</table></form>
</body>
</html>
```

Missing Item Report — Perl Script

```perl
#!/usr/local/bin/perl


# **************************************************
# ABOVE is where you MUST specify the path to your
# perl interpreter on your Web server.
# Replace /usr/local/bin/perl with your path.
# **************************************************

if ($ENV{'REQUEST_METHOD'}eq"GET"){$buffer = $ENV{'QUERY_STRING'};}
    elsif($ENV{'REQUEST_METHOD'}eq"POST"){
        read(STDIN,$buffer,$ENV{'CONTENT_LENGTH'});
    }
$bufferb = $buffer;
#separate the name of the input from its value.
@forminputs = split(/&/, $bufferb);

foreach $forminput (@forminputs)
{
        #separate the name of the input from its value
        ($name, $value) = split(/=/, $forminput);

        #Un-Webify plus signs and %-encoding
        $value =~ tr/+/ /;
        $value =~ s/%([a-fA-F0-9][a-fA-F0-9])/pack("C", hex($1))/eg;

        #stick them in the in array
        $in{$name} = $value;
}
print "Content-type: text/html\n\n";


#################################################################
# ABOVE is the required header for a perl script          #
#################################################################


#####################################################################
# (Below) Email received by library containing user-entered information #
#####################################################################


# **************************************************
# Here's where you MUST specify the path to your
# email program (probably sendmail) ON your Web server.
# Replace /usr/sbin/sendmail with your path.
# **************************************************
```

```
open (LMAIL, "l/usr/sbin/sendmail -t");
print LMAIL ("To: $in{LibraryEmail}\n");

print LMAIL ("From: $in{CampusEmail}\n");
print LMAIL ("Subject: $in{Form} - patron submission\n");

print LMAIL ("------------------\nPatron information\n\n");
print LMAIL ("Name:\n $in{Name}\n\n");
print LMAIL ("Department / Major:\n $in{Department}\n\n");
print LMAIL ("Campus Address:\n $in{CampusAddress}\n\n");
print LMAIL ("Campus Email:\n $in{CampusEmail}\n\n");
print LMAIL ("Campus Phone:\n $in{CampusPhone}\n\n");
print LMAIL ("Other Phone:\n $in{OtherPhone}\n\n");
print LMAIL ("Status:\n $in{Status}\n\n");

print LMAIL ("------------------\nSubmitted information \n\n");

print LMAIL ("I have already checked these resources:\n $in{OC}, $in{S}, $in{MN}, $in{CD}\n\n");
print LMAIL ("Material type:\n $in{Material}\n\n");
print LMAIL ("Other type:\n $in{OtherType}\n\n");
print LMAIL ("Call number:\n $in{CallNumber}\n\n");
print LMAIL ("Title:\n $in{Title}\n\n");
print LMAIL ("Author / Editor / Artist:\n $in{Author}\n\n");
print LMAIL ("I need this item before:\n $in{NeedBefore} $in{Deadline}\n\n");
print LMAIL ("Priority:\n $in{Priority}\n\n");
print LMAIL ("Other priority:\n $in{PriorityO}\n\n");
print LMAIL ("Do you want us to hold the item if located?\n $in{LocateAndHold}\n\n");

print LMAIL ("\n.\n");


##########################################################
# Email received by the user confirming form submission #
##########################################################


# ************************************************
# Here's where you MUST specify the path to your
# email program ON your Web server.
# Replace /usr/sbin/sendmail with your path.
# ************************************************

open (MAIL, "l/usr/sbin/sendmail -t");

# ************************************************
# Here's where you MAY customize the email
# response to the user. You may change any wording
```

```
# on the form.
# ************************************************

print MAIL<<toEnd;
To: $in{CampusEmail}
From: $in{LibraryEmail}
Subject: $in{Form}

Thanks for taking the time to let us know that an item is missing.\n\n
We will contact you as soon as we either locate the item or decide to purchase a replacement copy.

toEnd
    print MAIL ("\n.\n");


####################################################
# Screen response to user after submitting the form  #
####################################################

print ("<html><head><title>$in{Form}</title></head>");
print ("<body bgcolor=\"ffffff\">");


# ************************************************
# Here's where you MAY change the screen response
# the user sees after submitting the form. You may
# change any wording between the quotation marks.
# ************************************************

print ("Thanks for taking the time to let us know that an item is missing.<p>
We will contact you as soon as we either locate the item or decide to purchase a replacement copy.");


# ************************************************
# Here's where you MAY change the name of the link
# back to your main page. You may replace Return
# to our main page with your own wording.
# ************************************************

print ("<p><center><a href=$in{LibraryURL}>Return to our main page.</a></center>");
print ("</body></html>");
```

Course Reserve Request

Faculty only

Fill out the form below to let us know which library materials you will be putting on class reserve for the coming semester. Please submit course reserve requests as soon as possible. We may have to recall items checked out to students/faculty or search for items that we cannot immediately locate.

Name (last, first middle)

Department / Major

Campus address

Campus e-mail

Campus phone

Fax / Other phone

Course title

Course number

Section number

Number of students

Semester / Quarter

Loan period

Books

Call Number

Title

Author

Edition

Pages

Call Number

Title

Author

Edition

Pages

Call Number

Title

Author

Edition

Pages

Journal / Newspaper articles

Journal / Newspaper title

Article title

Author

Volume number

Issue number   **Issue date**   **Pages**

Journal / Newspaper title

Article title

Author

Volume number

Issue number   **Issue date**   **Pages**

Journal / Newspaper title

Article title

Author

Volume number

Issue number   **Issue date**   **Pages**

[Send Request]   [Clear Form]

Course Reserve Request — HTML Form

```
<html>
<head><title>Course Reserve Request</title></head>
<body bgcolor="#FFFFFF">
<table width="700" border="0" height="85" bgcolor="#000000">
<tr valign="middle" align="center">
<td>
<p>
<font halign=center color="#FFFFFF" face="Arial, Helvetica, sans-serif" size="+3"><b><i> Course Reserve
Request</i></b></font></p>
</td></tr></table>
<form method="post" action="http://www.yourLibrary.edu/cgi-bin/aor1.pl"><p> </p>
<p>
<font face="Arial, Helvetica, sans-serif" size="2"><font size="4"><b><font size="3"><i>Faculty only</i>
</font></b></font></font></p>
<p>
<font face="Arial, Helvetica, sans-serif" size="2"><b>Fill out the form below to let us know which library materials
you will be putting on class reserve for <br>the coming semester. Please submit course reserve requests as soon
as possible. We may have to <br>recall items checked out to students/faculty or search for items that we cannot
immediately locate.</b></font></p>
<p> </p>
<input type="hidden" name="LibraryEmail" value="you@yourLibrary.edu">
<input type="hidden" name="LibraryURL" value="http://www.yourLibrary.edu">
<input type="hidden" name="Form" value="Comments, Suggestions"><p></p>
<p></p>
<table width="500" border="0" cellspacing="4" cellpadding="1">
<tr><td width="257">
<b><font face="Arial, Helvetica, sans-serif" size="2">Name </font></b><font face="Arial, Helvetica, sans-
serif" size="1"> (last, first middle)</font><br><font face="Arial, Helvetica, sans-serif" size="2"><input
type="text" name="Name" size="25"></font></td>
<td width="227">
<b><font face="Arial, Helvetica, sans-serif" size="2">Department / Major<br></font></b><font face="Arial,
Helvetica, sans-serif" size="2"><input type="text" name="Department" size="25"></font> </td></tr>
<tr><td width="257">
<b><font face="Arial, Helvetica, sans-serif" size="2">Campus address<br></font></b><font face="Arial,
Helvetica, sans-serif" size="2"><input type="text" name="CampusAddress" size="25"></font></td>
<td width="227"> <b><font face="Arial, Helvetica, sans-serif" size="2">Campus e-mail<br>
</font></b><font face="Arial, Helvetica, sans-serif" size="2"><input type="text" name="CampusEmail"
size="25"></font></td></tr>
<tr><td width="257">
<b><font face="Arial, Helvetica, sans-serif" size="2">Campus phone</font></b><br><font face="Arial, Helvetica,
sans-serif" size="2"><input type="text" name="CampusPhone" size="25"></font></td>
<td width="227">
```

```
<b><font face="Arial, Helvetica, sans-serif" size="2">Fax / Other phone<br></font></b><font face="Arial,
Helvetica, sans-serif" size="2"><input type="text" name="OtherPhone" size="25"></font></td></tr> </
table><br>
<br>
<table width="500" border="0" cellspacing="0" cellpadding="0">
<tr><td width="257">
<b><font face="Arial, Helvetica, sans-serif" size="2">Course title</font></b><br><font face="Arial, Helvetica,
sans-serif" size="3"><input type="text" name="CTitle" size="25"></font></td>
<td width="227">
<b><font face="Arial, Helvetica, sans-serif" size="2">Course number <br></font></b><font face="Arial,
Helvetica, sans-serif" size="3"><input type="text" name="CNum" size="25"></font></td></tr>
<tr><td width="257">
<b><font face="Arial, Helvetica, sans-serif" size="2">Section number <br></font></b><font face="Arial,
Helvetica, sans-serif" size="3"><input type="text" name="SNum" size="25"></font></td>
<td width="227">
<b><font face="Arial, Helvetica, sans-serif" size="2">Number of students<br></font></b><font ace="Arial,
Helvetica, sans-serif" size="3"><input type="text" name="NumOfS" size="25"></font></td></tr>
<tr><td width="257">
<b><font face="Arial, Helvetica, sans-serif" size="2">Semester / Quarter<br></font></b><font face="Arial,
Helvetica, sans-serif" size="3"><input type="text" name="Semester" size="25"></font></td>
<td width="227">
<b><font face="Arial, Helvetica, sans-serif" size="2">Loan period <br></font></b><font face="Arial, Helvetica,
sans-serif" size="3"><input type="text" name="Loan" size="25"></font></td></tr></table><br>
<p>
<font size="3" face="Arial, Helvetica, sans-serif"><b>Books</b></font></p>
<table width="600" border="0" cellspacing="0" cellpadding="0">
<tr><td width="168">
<font face="Arial, Helvetica, sans-serif" size="2"><b>Call Number</b><br><font size="3"><input type="text"
name="CallNum" size="20"></font></font></td>
<td colspan="2">
<font face="Arial, Helvetica, sans-serif" size="2"><b>Title</b><br><font size="3"><input type="text"
name="Title" size="20"></font></font></td></tr>]
<tr><td width="168">
<font face="Arial, Helvetica, sans-serif" size="2"><b>Author</b><br><font size="3"><input type="text"
name="Author" size="20"></font></font></td>
<td colspan="1" width="97">
<font face="Arial, Helvetica, sans-serif" size="2"><b>Edition</b><br><font size="3"><input type="text"
name="Edition" size="10"></font></font></td>
<td width="335">
<font face="Arial, Helvetica, sans-serif" size="2"><b>Pages </b><br><font face="Arial, Helvetica, sans-serif"
size="3"><input type="text" name="Pages" size="10"></font></font></td></tr></table><br>
<br> <table width="600" border="0" cellspacing="0" cellpadding="0">
<tr><td width="168">
<font face="Arial, Helvetica, sans-serif" size="2"><b>Call Number</b><br><font size="3"><input type="text"
name="CallNum2" size="20"></font></font></td>
```

```
<td colspan="2">
<font face="Arial, Helvetica, sans-serif" size="2"><b>Title</b><br><font size="3"><input type="text"
name="Title2" size="20"></font></font></td></tr>
<tr><td width="168">
<font face="Arial, Helvetica, sans-serif" size="2"><b>Author</b><br><font size="3"><input type="text"
name="Author3" size="20"></font></font></td>
<td colspan="1" width="97">
<font face="Arial, Helvetica, sans-serif" size="2"><b>Edition</b><br><font size="3"><input type="text"
name="Edition2" size="10"></font></font></td>
<td width="335">
<font face="Arial, Helvetica, sans-serif" size="2"><b>Pages</b><br><font size="3"> </font><font face="Arial,
Helvetica, sans-serif" size="3"><input type="text" name="Pages2" size="10"></font> </font></td></tr></
table><br>
<br><table width="600" border="0" cellspacing="0" cellpadding="0">
<tr><td width="168">
<font face="Arial, Helvetica, sans-serif" size="2"><b>Call Number</b><br><font size="3"><input type="text"
name="CallNum3" size="20"></font></font></td>
<td colspan="2">
<font face="Arial, Helvetica, sans-serif" size="2"><b>Title</b><br><font size="3"><input type="text"
name="Title3" size="20"></font></font></td></tr>
<tr><td width="168">
<font face="Arial, Helvetica, sans-serif" size="2"><b>Author</b><br><font size="3"><input type="text"
name="Author4" size="20"></font></font></td>
<td colspan="1" width="97">
<font face="Arial, Helvetica, sans-serif" size="2"><b>Edition</b><br><font size="3"><input type="text"
name="Edition3" size="10"></font></font></td>
<td width="335">
<font face="Arial, Helvetica, sans-serif" size="2"><b>Pages</b><br><font face="Arial, Helvetica, sans-serif"
size="3"><input type="text" name="Pages3" size="10"></font></font></td></tr></table>
<p><br></p>
<p>
<font size="3" face="Arial, Helvetica, sans-serif"><b>Journal / Newspaper articles</b></font></p><table
width="600" border="0" cellspacing="0" cellpadding="0"><tr>
<td width="172">
<font face="Arial, Helvetica, sans-serif" size="2"><b>Journal / Newspaper title</b><br><font size="3">
<input type="text" name="TitleJ" size="20"></font></font></td>
<td width="428">
<font face="Arial, Helvetica, sans-serif" size="2"><b>Article title</b><br><font size="3"><input type="text"
name="ArtTit" size="25"></font></font></td></tr>
<tr><td width="172">
<font face="Arial, Helvetica, sans-serif" size="2"><b>Author</b><br><font size="3"><input type="text"
name="Author2" size="20"></font></font></td>
<td width="428">
<font face="Arial, Helvetica, sans-serif" size="2"><b>Volume number</b><br><font size="3"><input type="text"
name="VolNum" size="25"></font></font></td></tr></table>
```

```
<table width="500" border="0" cellspacing="0" cellpadding="0">
<tr><td width="101">
font face="Arial, Helvetica, sans-serif" size="2"><b>Issue number</b><br><font size="3"><input type="text"
name="IssueNum" size="10"></font></font></td>
<td width="99">
<font face="Arial, Helvetica, sans-serif" size="2"><b>Issue date</b><br><font size="3"><input type="text"
name="IssueDate" size="10"></font></font></td>
<td width="300">
<font face="Arial, Helvetica, sans-serif" size="2"><b>Pages</b><br><font size="3"><input type="text"
name="PagesJ" size="10"></font></font></td></tr></table><br>
<br><table width="600" border="0" cellspacing="0" cellpadding="0">
<tr><td width="172">
<font face="Arial, Helvetica, sans-serif" size="2"><b>Journal / Newspaper title</b><br><font size="3">
<input type="text" name="TitleJ2" size="20"></font></font></td>
<td width="428">
<font face="Arial, Helvetica, sans-serif" size="2"><b>Article title</b><br><font size="3"><input type="text"
name="ArtTit2" size="25"></font></font></td></tr>
<tr><td width="172">
<font face="Arial, Helvetica, sans-serif" size="2"><b>Author</b><br><font size="3"><input type="text"
name="Author22" size="20"></font></font></td>
<td width="428">
<font face="Arial, Helvetica, sans-serif" size="2"><b>Volume number</b><br><font size="3"><input type="text"
name="VolNum2" size="25"></font></font></td></tr></table>
<table width="500" border="0" cellspacing="0" cellpadding="0">
<tr><td width="101"><font face="Arial, Helvetica, sans-serif" size="2"><b>Issue number</b><br>
<font size="3"><input type="text" name="IssueNum2" size="10"></font></font></td>
<td width="99">
<font face="Arial, Helvetica, sans-serif" size="2"><b>Issue date</b><br><font size="3"><input type="text"
name="IssueDate2" size="10"></font></font></td>
<td width="300">
<font face="Arial, Helvetica, sans-serif" size="2"><b>Pages</b><br><font size="3"><input type="text"
name="PagesJ2" size="10"></font></font></td></tr></table><br>
<br><table width="600" border="0" cellspacing="0" cellpadding="0">
<tr><td width="172">
<font face="Arial, Helvetica, sans-serif" size="2"><b>Journal / Newspaper title</b><br><font size="3">
<input type="text" name="TitleJ3" size="20"></font></font></td>
<td width="428">
<font face="Arial, Helvetica, sans-serif" size="2"><b>Article title</b><br><font size="3"><input type="text"
name="ArtTit3" size="25"></font></font></td></tr>
<tr><td width="172">
<font face="Arial, Helvetica, sans-serif" size="2"><b>Author</b><br><font size="3"><input type="text"
name="Author23" size="20"></font></font></td>
<td width="428">
<font face="Arial, Helvetica, sans-serif" size="2"><b>Volume number</b><br><font size="3"><input type="text"
name="VolNum3" size="25"></font></font></td></tr></table>
```

```
<table width="500" border="0" cellspacing="0" cellpadding="0">
<tr><td width="101">
<font face="Arial, Helvetica, sans-serif" size="2"><b>Issue number</b><br><font size="3"><input type="text"
name="IssueNum3" size="10"></font></font></td>
<td width="99">
<font face="Arial, Helvetica, sans-serif" size="2"><b>Issue date</b><br><font size="3"><input type="text"
name="IssueDate3" size="10"></font></font></td>
<td width="300">
<font face="Arial, Helvetica, sans-serif" size="2"><b>Pages</b><br><font size="3"><input type="text"
name="PagesJ3" size="10"></font></font></td></tr></table>
<p> </p>
<table width="700" border="0" cellspacing="10" cellpadding="1"><tr><td width="251">
<div align="right"><input type="submit" name="send" value="Send Request"></div></td>
<td width="196"> </td><td width="207">
<div align="left"><input type="reset" name="clear" value="Clear Form"></div></td></tr>
<tr colspan=3><td colspan=3>
<table width="500" border="0" height="2" align="center" cellpadding="0" cellspacing="0"
bgcolor="#000000"><tr><td><font size="1" color="#000000">.</font></td></tr></table>
</td></tr><tr>
<td colspan=3><div align="center">
<font face="Arial, Helvetica, sans-serif" size="1"><b>http://</b></font><br> 
<font face="Arial, Helvetica, sans-serif" size="1"><b>&copy; 2001</b></font>
<font face="Arial, Helvetica, sans-serif" size="2"><a href="mailto:">
<b><font size="1">Contact Webmaster</font></b></a></font></div></td></tr>
</table></form>
</body>
</html>
```

Course Reserve Request — Perl Script

```perl
#!/usr/local/bin/perl

# **************************************************
# ABOVE is where you MUST specify the path to your
# perl interpreter on your Web server.
# Replace /usr/local/bin/perl with your path.
# **************************************************

if ($ENV{'REQUEST_METHOD'}eq"GET"){$buffer = $ENV{'QUERY_STRING'};}
    elsif($ENV{'REQUEST_METHOD'}eq"POST"){
        read(STDIN,$buffer,$ENV{'CONTENT_LENGTH'});
    }
$bufferb = $buffer;
#separate the name of the input from its value.
@forminputs = split(/&/, $bufferb);

foreach $forminput (@forminputs)
{
    #separate the name of the input from its value
    ($name, $value) = split(/=/, $forminput);

    #Un-Webify plus signs and %-encoding
    $value =~ tr/+/ /;
    $value =~ s/%([a-fA-F0-9][a-fA-F0-9])/pack("C", hex($1))/eg;

    #stick them in the in array
    $in{$name} = $value;
}
print "Content-type: text/html\n\n";


################################################################
# ABOVE is the required header for a perl script          #
################################################################


##################################################################
# (Below) Email received by library containing user-entered information #
##################################################################


# ***********************************************
# Here's where you MUST specify the path to your
# email program (probably sendmail) ON your Web server.
# Replace /usr/sbin/sendmail with your path.
```

```perl
# ***************************************************

open (LMAIL, "l/usr/sbin/sendmail -t");
print LMAIL ("To: $in{LibraryEmail}\n");

print LMAIL ("From: $in{CampusEmail}\n");
print LMAIL ("Subject: $in{Form} - patron submission\n");

print LMAIL ("------------------\nPatron information\n\n");
print LMAIL ("Name:\n $in{Name}\n\n");
print LMAIL ("Department / Major:\n $in{Department}\n\n");
print LMAIL ("Campus Address:\n $in{CampusAddress}\n\n");
print LMAIL ("Campus Email:\n $in{CampusEmail}\n\n");
print LMAIL ("Campus Phone:\n $in{CampusPhone}\n\n");
print LMAIL ("Other Phone:\n $in{OtherPhone}\n\n");

print LMAIL ("------------------\nSubmitted information \n\n");

print LMAIL ("Course title:\n $in{CTitle}\n\n");
print LMAIL ("Course number:\n $in{CNum} \n\n");
print LMAIL ("Section number:\n $in{SNum}\n\n");
print LMAIL ("Number of student:\n $in{NumOfS}\n\n");
print LMAIL ("Semester / Quarter:\n $in{Semester}\n\n");
print LMAIL ("Loan period:\n $in{Loan}\n\n");

print LMAIL ("Book One\n\n");
print LMAIL ("Call number:\n $in{CallNum}\n\n");
print LMAIL ("Title:\n $in{Title}\n\n");
print LMAIL ("Author:\n $in{Author}\n\n");
print LMAIL ("Edition:\n $in{Edition}\n\n");
print LMAIL ("Pages:\n $in{Pages}\n\n");

print LMAIL ("Book Two\n\n");
print LMAIL ("Call number:\n $in{CallNum2}\n\n");
print LMAIL ("Title:\n $in{Title2}\n\n");
print LMAIL ("Author:\n $in{Author2}\n\n");
print LMAIL ("Edition:\n $in{Edition2}\n\n");
print LMAIL ("Pages:\n $in{Pages2}\n\n");

print LMAIL ("Book Three\n\n");
print LMAIL ("Call number:\n $in{CallNum3}\n\n");
print LMAIL ("Title:\n $in{Title3}\n\n");
print LMAIL ("Author:\n $in{Author3}\n\n");
print LMAIL ("Edition:\n $in{Edition3}\n\n");
print LMAIL ("Pages:\n $in{Pages3}\n\n");
```

```
print LMAIL ("Journal / Newspaper One\n\n");
print LMAIL ("Journal / Newspaper title:\n $in{TitleJ}\n\n");
print LMAIL ("Article title:\n $in{ArtTit}\n\n");
print LMAIL ("Author:\n $in{AuthorJ}\n\n");
print LMAIL ("Volume number:\n $in{VolNum}\n\n");
print LMAIL ("Issue number:\n $in{IssueNum}\n\n");
print LMAIL ("Issue date:\n $in{IssueDate}\n\n");
print LMAIL ("Pages:\n $in{PagesJ}\n\n");

print LMAIL ("Journal / Newspaper Two\n\n");
print LMAIL ("Journal / Newspaper title:\n $in{TitleJ2}\n\n");
print LMAIL ("Article title:\n $in{ArtTit2}\n\n");
print LMAIL ("Author:\n $in{AuthorJ2}\n\n");
print LMAIL ("Volume number:\n $in{VolNum2}\n\n");
print LMAIL ("Issue number:\n $in{IssueNum2}\n\n");
print LMAIL ("Issue date:\n $in{IssueDate2}\n\n");
print LMAIL ("Pages:\n $in{PagesJ2}\n\n");

print LMAIL ("Journal / Newspaper Three\n\n");
print LMAIL ("Journal / Newspaper title:\n $in{TitleJ3}\n\n");
print LMAIL ("Article title:\n $in{ArtTit3}\n\n");
print LMAIL ("Author:\n $in{AuthorJ3}\n\n");
print LMAIL ("Volume number:\n $in{VolNum3}\n\n");
print LMAIL ("Issue number:\n $in{IssueNum3}\n\n");
print LMAIL ("Issue date:\n $in{IssueDate3}\n\n");
print LMAIL ("Pages:\n $in{PagesJ3}\n\n");
print LMAIL ("\n.\n");


#########################################################
# Email received by the user confirming form submission #
#########################################################


# ************************************************
# Here's where you MUST specify the path to your
# email program ON your Web server.
# Replace /usr/sbin/sendmail with your path.
# ************************************************

open (MAIL, "|/usr/sbin/sendmail -t");

# ************************************************
# Here's where you MAY customize the email
# response to the user. You may change any wording
# on the form.
```

```
# **************************************************

print MAIL<<toEnd;
To: $in{CampusEmail}
From: $in{LibraryEmail}
Subject: $in{Form}

Thanks for taking the time to fill out our Course Reserve Request.\n\n
A librarian will be in contact with you shortly.

toEnd
    print MAIL ("\n.\n");


####################################################
# Screen response to user after submitting the form  #
####################################################

print ("<html><head><title>$in{Form}</title></head>");
print ("<body bgcolor=\"ffffff\">");


# **************************************************
# Here's where you MAY change the screen response
# the user sees after submitting the form. You may
# change any wording between the quotation marks.
# **************************************************

print ("Thanks for taking the time to fill out our Course Reserve Request.<p>
A librarian will be in contact with you shortly.");


# **************************************************
# Here's where you MAY change the name of the link
# back to your main page. You may replace Return
# to our main page with your own wording.
# **************************************************

print ("<p><center><a href=$in{LibraryURL}>Return to our main page.</a></center>");
print ("</body></html>");
```

Group 8 — Miscellaneous Forms

In this section you'll find two Web-based forms. The first form will allow faculty members and teaching assistants to reserve a video, DVD, or piece of software, and any related equipment they need. The second form lets students, faculty, and staff give feedback to library administrators on how to improve library services, improve your collections, and to make your library building a more patron-friendly place to study and do research.

Media / Equipment Request form

If your library has purchased DVDs, videos, sound recordings, and software that circulate to faculty and students OR if your library has a collection of AV and computing equipment that it loans out to faculty and teaching assistants, place a link to this form on your media Web page so that faculty can reserve a video and VCR or program and traveling laptop via e-mail.

Strategic Planning Survey

Get student, faculty, and staff input on the materials you should be purchasing, the services you should be providing, and spaces you should be creating/updating in your library. Post this survey periodically on your library's homepage to see how you can do a better job serving your patrons.

Media / Equipment Request

Faculty only

If you would like the library to supply you with AV or computing equipment, a film/video/DVD, or other equipment, fill out the form below. We'll contact you to let you know if we can fulfill your request.

Name (last, first middle)

Department / Major

Campus address

Campus e-mail

Campus phone

Fax / Other phone

Course title

Course number

Section number

Number of students

Date   **Time**   to

Location

Film / Video / DVD

Call number / Catalog number

Title

Equipment

Projectors (eg. LCD, 16mm, overhead, slide)

Video players / recorders (eg. VCR, laserdisk, DVD, camcorder)

Audio players / recorders (eg. CD, cassette, record)

Computing equipment (eg. monitor, disk drives, mouse, networking)

Computer software (eg. browser, word processor)

Misc. equipment (eg. microphone, screen, flip chart)

Comments / Special instructions

Send Request   Clear Form

Media / Equipment Request — HTML Form

```
<html>
<head><title>Media / Equipment Request</title></head>
<body bgcolor="#FFFFFF">
<table width="700" border="0" height="85" bgcolor="#000000">
<tr valign="middle" align="center"><td>
<p>
<font halign=center color="#FFFFFF" face="Arial, Helvetica, sans-serif" size="+3"><b><i>Media / Equipment
Request</i></b></font></p>
</td></tr></table>
<form method="post" action="http://www.yourLibrary.edu/cgi-bin/am3.pl"><p> </p>
<p>
<font face="Arial, Helvetica, sans-serif" size="2"><font size="4"><b><font size="3"><i>Faculty
 only</i></font></b></font></font></p>
<p>
<font face="Arial, Helvetica, sans-serif" size="2"><b>If you would like the library to supply you with AV or com-
puting equipment, a film/video/DVD, or other <br>equipment, fill out the form below. We'll contact you to let you
know if we can fulfill your request.</b></font></p>
<p> </p>
<input type="hidden" name="LibraryEmail" value="you@yourLibrary.edu">
<input type="hidden" name="LibraryURL" value="http://www.yourLibrary.edu">
<input type="hidden" name="Form" value="Comments, Suggestions"><p></p>
<p></p>
<table width="500" border="0" cellspacing="4" cellpadding="1">
<tr><td width="257">
<b><font face="Arial, Helvetica, sans-serif" size="2">Name </font></b><font face="Arial, Helvetica, sans-
serif" size="1"> (last, first middle)</font><br><font face="Arial, Helvetica, sans-serif" size="2"><input
type="text" name="Name" size="25"></font></td>
<td width="227">
<b><font face="Arial, Helvetica, sans-serif" size="2">Department / Major<br></font></b><font face="Arial,
Helvetica, sans-serif" size="2"><input type="text" name="Department" size="25"></font> </td></tr>
<tr><td width="257">
<b><font face="Arial, Helvetica, sans-serif" size="2">Campus address<br></font></b><font face="Arial,
Helvetica, sans-serif" size="2"><input type="text" name="CampusAddress" size="25"></font></td>
<td width="227">
<b><font face="Arial, Helvetica, sans-serif" size="2">Campus e-mail<br></font></b><font face="Arial, Helvetica,
sans-serif" size="2"><input type="text" name="CampusEmail" size="25"></font></td></tr>
<tr><td width="257">
<b><font face="Arial, Helvetica, sans-serif" size="2">Campus phone</font></b><br><font face="Arial, Helvetica,
sans-serif" size="2"><input type="text" name="CampusPhone" size="25"></font></td>
<td width="227">
<b><font face="Arial, Helvetica, sans-serif" size="2">Fax / Other phone<br></font></b><font face="Arial,
Helvetica, sans-serif" size="2"><input type="text" name="OtherPhone" size="25"></font></td></tr>
```

```
</table><br><br>
<table width="500" border="0" cellspacing="0" cellpadding="0">
<tr><td width="257">
<b><font face="Arial, Helvetica, sans-serif" size="2">Course title</font></b><br><font face="Arial, Helvetica,
sans-serif" size="3"><input type="text" name="CTitle" size="25"></font></td>
<td width="227">
<b><font face="Arial, Helvetica, sans-serif" size="2">Course number<br></font></b><font face="Arial, Helvetica,
sans-serif" size="3"><input type="text" name="CNum" size="25"></font></td></tr>
<tr><td width="257">
<b><font face="Arial, Helvetica, sans-serif" size="2">Section number<br></font></b><font face="Arial,
Helvetica, sans-serif" size="3"><input type="text" name="SNum" size="25"></font></td>
<td width="227">
<b><font face="Arial, Helvetica, sans-serif" size="2">Number of students<br></font></b><font face="Arial,
Helvetica, sans-serif" size="3"><input type="text" name="NumOfS" size="25">
</font></td></tr></table>
<p>
<font face="Arial, Helvetica, sans-serif" size="2"><b>Date</b></font><font size="3"><font face="Arial, Helvetica,
sans-serif"><input type="text" name="Date1" size="15"></font>   
 
<font face="Arial, Helvetica, sans-serif" size="2"><b>Time</b></font><font face="Arial, Helvetica, sans-
serif"><input type="text" name="TimeBegin1" size="10"><font size="2"><b>to</b></font><input type="text"
name="TimeEnd1" size="10"></font></font></p>
<p>
<b><font face="Arial, Helvetica, sans-serif" size="2">Location</font></b><font size="3"><font face="Arial,
Helvetica, sans-serif"><input type="text" name="Location" size="13"></font> </font></p>
<p> </p>
<p>
<font size="3" face="Arial, Helvetica, sans-serif"><b>Film / Video / DVD</b></font></p>
<table width="500" border="0" cellspacing="0" cellpadding="0">
<tr><td width="257">
<b><font face="Arial, Helvetica, sans-serif" size="2">Call number / Catalog number</font></b><br>
<font face="Arial, Helvetica, sans-serif" size="2"> <font size="3"><input type="text" name="CallNum"
size="25"></font></font></td>
<td width="227">
<b><font face="Arial, Helvetica, sans-serif" size="2">Title<br></font></b><font face="Arial, Helvetica, sans-serif"
size="2"> <font size="3"><input type="text" name="Title" size="25"></font></font></td></tr>
</table><p> </p>
<p>
<font size="3" face="Arial, Helvetica, sans-serif"><b>Equipment</b></font></p>
<p>
<b><font face="Arial, Helvetica, sans-serif" size="2">Projectors </font></b><font face="Arial, Helvetica,
sans-serif" size="1"> (e.g. LCD, 16mm, overhead, slide)</font><br><font face="Arial, Helvetica, sans-serif"
size="3"><textarea name="Projectors" cols="40" rows="2"></textarea></font>
<p>
<b><font face="Arial, Helvetica, sans-serif" size="2">Video players / recorders </font></b><font
```

```
face="Arial, Helvetica, sans-serif" size="1"> (e.g. VCR, laserdisk, DVD, camcorder)</font><br>    <font
face="Arial, Helvetica, sans-serif" size="3"><textarea name="Video" cols="40" rows="2"> </textarea></font>
<p>
<b><font face="Arial, Helvetica, sans-serif" size="2">Audio players / recorders </font></b><font
face="Arial, Helvetica, sans-serif" size="1"> (e.g. CD, cassette, record)</font><br><font face="Arial,
Helvetica, sans-serif" size="3"><textarea name="Audio" cols="40" rows="2"></textarea></font>
<p>
<b><font face="Arial, Helvetica, sans-serif" size="2">Computing equipment </font></b><font face="Arial,
Helvetica, sans-serif" size="1"> (e.g. monitor, disk drives, mouse, networking)</font> <b><br><font
face="Arial, Helvetica, sans-serif" size="3"><textarea name="CompH" cols="40" rows="2"> </textarea></font>
<p>
<b><font face="Arial, Helvetica, sans-serif" size="2">Computer software </font></b><font face="Arial,
Helvetica, sans-serif" size="1"> (e.g. browser, word processor)</font><br><font face="Arial, Helvetica,
sans-serif" size="3"><textarea name="CompS" cols="40" rows="2"></textarea>
</font>
<p>
<b><font face="Arial, Helvetica, sans-serif" size="2">Misc. equipment </font></b><font face="Arial,
Helvetica, sans-serif" size="1"> (e.g. microphone, screen, flip chart)</font><br><font face="Arial,
Helvetica, sans-serif" size="3"><textarea name="Misc" cols="40" rows="2"></textarea></font>
<p>
<b><font face="Arial, Helvetica, sans-serif" size="2">Comments / Special instructions</font></b><br>
<font face="Arial, Helvetica, sans-serif" size="3"><textarea name="Comments" cols="40" rows="2">
</textarea></font><p> 
<p> 
<table width="700" border="0" cellspacing="10" cellpadding="1"><tr><td width="251">
<div align="right"><input type="submit" name="send" value="Send Request"></div></td>
<td width="196"> </td><td width="207">
<div align="left"><input type="reset" name="clear" value="Clear Form"></div></td></tr>
<tr colspan=3><td colspan=3>
<table width="500" border="0" height="2" align="center" cellpadding="0" cellspacing="0"
bgcolor="#000000"><tr><td><font size="1" color="#000000">.</font></td></tr></table>
</td></tr>
<tr><td colspan=3><div align="center">
<font face="Arial, Helvetica, sans-serif" size="1"><b>http://</b></font><br> 
<font face="Arial, Helvetica, sans-serif" size="1"><b>&copy; 2001</b></font>
<font face="Arial, Helvetica, sans-serif" size="2"><a href="mailto:">
<b><font size="1">Contact Webmaster</font></b></a> </font></div></td></tr>
</table></form>
</body>
</html>
```

Media / Equipment Request — Perl Script

```perl
#!/usr/local/bin/perl

# ***************************************************
# ABOVE is where you MUST specify the path to your
# perl interpreter on your Web server.
# Replace /usr/local/bin/perl with your path.
# ***************************************************

if ($ENV{'REQUEST_METHOD'}eq"GET"){$buffer = $ENV{'QUERY_STRING'};}
     elsif($ENV{'REQUEST_METHOD'}eq"POST"){
         read(STDIN,$buffer,$ENV{'CONTENT_LENGTH'});
     }
$bufferb = $buffer;
#separate the name of the input from its value.
@forminputs = split(/&/, $bufferb);

foreach $forminput (@forminputs)
{
     #separate the name of the input from its value
     ($name, $value) = split(/=/, $forminput);

     #Un-Webify plus signs and %-encoding
     $value =~ tr/+/ /;
     $value =~ s/%([a-fA-F0-9][a-fA-F0-9])/pack("C", hex($1))/eg;

     #stick them in the in array
     $in{$name} = $value;
}
print "Content-type: text/html\n\n";

###############################################################
# ABOVE is the required header for a perl script         #
###############################################################


#################################################################
# (Below) Email received by library containing user-entered information #
#################################################################


# ***************************************************
# Here's where you MUST specify the path to your
# email program (probably sendmail) ON your Web server.
# Replace /usr/sbin/sendmail with your path.
```

```
# ***************************************************

open (LMAIL, "|/usr/sbin/sendmail -t");
print LMAIL ("To: $in{LibraryEmail}\n");
print LMAIL ("From: $in{CampusEmail}\n");
print LMAIL ("Subject: $in{Form} - patron submission\n");

print LMAIL ("------------------\nPatron information\n\n");
print LMAIL ("Name:\n $in{Name}\n\n");
print LMAIL ("Department / Major:\n $in{Department}\n\n");
print LMAIL ("Campus Address:\n $in{CampusAddress}\n\n");
print LMAIL ("Campus Email:\n $in{CampusEmail}\n\n");
print LMAIL ("Campus Phone:\n $in{CampusPhone}\n\n");
print LMAIL ("Other Phone:\n $in{OtherPhone}\n\n");

print LMAIL ("------------------\nSubmitted information \n\n");

print LMAIL ("Course title:\n $in{CTitle}\n\n");
print LMAIL ("Course number:\n $in{CNum} \n\n");
print LMAIL ("Section number:\n $in{SNum}\n\n");
print LMAIL ("Number of students:\n $in{NumOfS}\n\n");

print LMAIL ("Date / Time:\n $in{Date1}, $in{TimeBegin1} to $in{TimeEnd1}\n\n");
print LMAIL ("Location:\n $in{Location}\n\n");
print LMAIL ("Date / time incident occurred:\n $in{Date} / $in{Time}\n\n");
print LMAIL ("Film / Video / DVD\n");
print LMAIL ("Call number / Catalog number:\n $in{CallNum}\n\n");
print LMAIL ("Title:\n $in{Title}\n\n");
print LMAIL ("Equipment\n");
print LMAIL ("Projectors:\n $in{Projectors}\n\n");
print LMAIL ("Video players / recorders:\n $in{Video}\n\n");
print LMAIL ("Audio players / recorders:\n $in{Audio}\n\n");
print LMAIL ("Computing equipment:\n $in{Computing}\n\n");
print LMAIL ("Computer software:\n $in{Computer}\n\n");
print LMAIL ("Misc. Equipment:\n $in{Misc}\n\n");
print LMAIL ("Comments / Special instructions:\n $in{Comments}\n\n");
print LMAIL ("\n.\n");


####################################################
# Email received by the user confirming form submission #
####################################################


# ***************************************************
# Here's where you MUST specify the path to your
# email program ON your Web server.
```

```
# Replace /usr/sbin/sendmail with your path.
# ***********************************************

open (MAIL, "I/usr/sbin/sendmail -t");

# ***********************************************
# Here's where you MAY customize the email
# response to the user. You may change any wording
# on the form.
# ***********************************************

print MAIL<<toEnd;
To: $in{CampusEmail}
From: $in{LibraryEmail}
Subject: $in{Form}

Thanks for sending us your media / equipment request.\n\n
A librarian will be in contact with you shortly.

toEnd
   print MAIL ("\n.\n");

####################################################
# Screen response to user after submitting the form  #
####################################################

print ("<html><head><title>$in{Form}</title></head>");
print ("<body bgcolor=\"ffffff\">");

# ***********************************************
# Here's where you MAY change the screen response
# the user sees after submitting the form. You may
# change any wording between the quotation marks.
# ***********************************************

print ("Thanks for sending us your media / equipment request.<p>
A librarian will be in contact with you shortly.");

# ***********************************************
# Here's where you MAY change the name of the link
# back to your main page. You may replace Return
# to our main page with your own wording.
# ***********************************************

print ("<p><center><a href=$in{LibraryURL}>Return to our main page.</a></center>");
print ("</body></html>");
```

Strategic Planning Survey

Help us plan the library of the future. Tell us which new library materials we should purchase and which existing materials we should put into storage or discard. Let us know any new library services we should provide and any existing services we might do without. Most importantly, tell us how library staff can better help you and how we can make the inside of the library more user-friendly.

What *new* library materials should the library purchase?

What *existing* materials could we put into storage or discard?

What *new* library services should the library provide?

What *existing* services could we discontinue?

What *new* equipment should the library purchase?

What *existing* equipment could we discard or sell?

What *new* things can staff do to help?

How can we improve the inside of the library?

Is there any other way we can make the library a better place?

Name (last, first middle)

[   ]

Department / Major

[   ]

Campus e-mail

[   ]

Campus phone

[   ]

Status

○ Freshman   ○ Sophomore   ○ Junior   ○ Senior
○ Grad Student   ○ Faculty   ○ Staff   ○ Other

[Send Survey]   [Clear Survey]

Strategic Planning Survey — HTML Form

```
<html>
<head><title>Strategic Planning Survey</title></head>
<body bgcolor="#FFFFFF">
<table width="700" border="0" height="85" bgcolor="#000000">
<tr valign="middle" align="center"><td>
<p>
<font halign=center color="#FFFFFF" face="Arial, Helvetica, sans-serif" size="+3">
<b><i>Strategic Planning Survey</i></b></font></p>
</td></tr></table>
<form method="post" action="http://www.yourLibrary.edu/cgi-bin/am4.pl"><p> </p>
<p>
<font face="Arial, Helvetica, sans-serif" size="2"><b>Help us plan the library of the future. Tell us which new
library materials we should purchase and which <br>existing materials we should put into storage or discard. Let
us know any new library services we should <br>provide and any existing services we might do without. Most
importantly, tell us how library staff can <br>better help you and how we can make the inside of the library more
user-friendly.</b></font></p>
<p> </p>
<input type="hidden" name="LibraryEmail" value="you@yourLibrary.edu">
<input type="hidden" name="LibraryURL" value="http://www.yourLibrary.edu">
<input type="hidden" name="Form" value="Comments, Suggestions"><p></p>
<p></p>
<p>
<b><font face="Arial, Helvetica, sans-serif" size="2">What <i>new</i> library materials should the library pur-
chase?</font></b><br> <font face="Arial, Helvetica, sans-serif" size="3"><textarea name="1" cols="40"
rows="2"></textarea></font>
<p>
<b><font face="Arial, Helvetica, sans-serif" size="2">What <i>existing</i> materials could we put into storage or
discard?</font></b><br><font face="Arial, Helvetica, sans-serif" size="3"><textarea name="2" cols="40"
rows="2"></textarea></font>
<p>
<b><font face="Arial, Helvetica, sans-serif" size="2">What <i>new</i> library services should the library pro-
vide?</font></b><br><font face="Arial, Helvetica, sans-serif" size="3"><textarea name="3" cols="40"
rows="2"></textarea></font>
<p>
<b><font face="Arial, Helvetica, sans-serif" size="2">What <i>existing</i> services could we discontinue?
</font></b><br><font face="Arial, Helvetica, sans-serif" size="3"><textarea name="4" cols="40" rows="2">
</textarea></font>
<p>
<b><font face="Arial, Helvetica, sans-serif" size="2">What <i>new</i> equipment should the library purchase?
</font></b><br><font face="Arial, Helvetica, sans-serif" size="3"><textarea name="5" cols="40" rows="2">
</textarea></font>
<p>
```

```
<b><font face="Arial, Helvetica, sans-serif" size="2">What <i>existing</i> equipment could we discard or sell?
</font></b><br><font face="Arial, Helvetica, sans-serif" size="3"><textarea name="6" cols="40" rows="2">
</textarea></font>
<p>
<b><font face="Arial, Helvetica, sans-serif" size="2">What <i>new</i> things can staff do to help?</font>
</b><br><font face="Arial, Helvetica, sans-serif" size="3"><textarea name="7" cols="40" rows="2">
</textarea></font>
<p>
<b><font face="Arial, Helvetica, sans-serif" size="2">How can we improve the inside of the library?</font>
</b><br><font face="Arial, Helvetica, sans-serif" size="3"><textarea name="8" cols="40" rows="2"></textarea>
</font>
<p></p>
<p>
<b><font face="Arial, Helvetica, sans-serif" size="2">Is there any other way we can make the library a better
place?</font></b><br><font face="Arial, Helvetica, sans-serif" size="3"><textarea name="9" cols="40"
rows="2"></textarea></font>
<p> 
<p> 
<p></p>
<table width="500" border="0" cellspacing="4" cellpadding="1">
<tr>td width="257">
<b><font face="Arial, Helvetica, sans-serif" size="2">Name </font></b><font face="Arial, Helvetica, sans-
serif" size="1"> (last, first middle)</font><br><font face="Arial, Helvetica, sans-serif" size="2"><input
type="text" name="Name" size="25"></font></td>
<td width="227">
<b><font face="Arial, Helvetica, sans-serif" size="2">Department / Major<br></font></b><font face="Arial,
Helvetica, sans-serif" size="2"><input type="text" name="Department" size="25">      </font></td></tr>
<tr><td width="257">
<b><font face="Arial, Helvetica, sans-serif" size="2">Campus e-mail<br></font></b><font face="Arial, Helvetica,
sans-serif" size="2"><input type="text" name="CampusEmail" size="25"></font></td>
<td width="227">
<b><font face="Arial, Helvetica, sans-serif" size="2">Campus phone</font></b><br><font face="Arial, Helvetica,
sans-serif" size="2"><input type="text" name="CampusPhone2" size="25"></font></td></tr></table>
<p>
<b><font face="Arial, Helvetica, sans-serif" size="2">Status</font></b><table width="550" border="0"
cellspacing="0" cellpadding="0">
<tr><td width="126" height="13">
<font face="Arial, Helvetica, sans-serif" size="2"><input type="radio" name="Status"
value="Freshman">Freshman</font></td>
<td width="117" height="13">
<font face="Arial, Helvetica, sans-serif" size="2"><input type="radio" name="Status"
value="Sophomore">Sophomore</font></td>
<td width="87" height="13">
<font face="Arial, Helvetica, sans-serif" size="2"><input type="radio" name="Status" value="Junior">Junior
</font></td>
```

```
<td width="202" height="13">
<font face="Arial, Helvetica, sans-serif" size="2"><input type="radio" name="Status" value="Senior">Senior
</font></td></tr>
<tr><td width="126" height="9">
<font face="Arial, Helvetica, sans-serif" size="2"><input type="radio" name="Status"
value="Graduate Student">Grad Student</font></td>
<td width="117" height="9">
<font face="Arial, Helvetica, sans-serif" size="2"><input type="radio" name="Status"
value="Faculty">Faculty</font></td>
<td width="87" height="9">
<font face="Arial, Helvetica, sans-serif" size="2"><input type="radio" name="Status"
value="Staff">Staff</font></td>
<td width="202" height="9">
<font face="Arial, Helvetica, sans-serif" size="2"><input type="radio" name="Status"
value="Other">Other</font></td></tr></table>
<p> </p>
<table width="700" border="0" cellspacing="10" cellpadding="1"><tr><td width="213">
<div align="right"><input type="submit" name="send" value="Send Survey"></div></td>
<td width="225"> </td><td width="216">
<div align="left"><input type="reset" name="clear" value="Clear Survey"></div></td></tr>
<tr colspan=3><td colspan=3>
<table width="500" border="0" height="2" align="center" cellpadding="0" cellspacing="0"
bgcolor="#000000"><tr><td><font size="1" color="#000000">.</font></td></tr></table>
</td></tr>
<tr><td colspan=3><div align="center">
<font face="Arial, Helvetica, sans-serif" size="1"><b>http://</b></font><br> 
<font face="Arial, Helvetica, sans-serif" size="1"><b>&copy; 2001</b></font>
<font face="Arial, Helvetica, sans-serif" size="2"><a href="mailto:">
<b><font size="1">Contact Webmaster</font></b></a> </font></div></td></tr>
</table></form>
</body>
</html>
```

Strategic Planning Survey — Perl Script

```perl
#!/usr/local/bin/perl

# ************************************************
# ABOVE is where you MUST specify the path to your
# perl interpreter on your Web server.
# Replace /usr/local/bin/perl with your path.
# ************************************************

if ($ENV{'REQUEST_METHOD'}eq"GET"){$buffer = $ENV{'QUERY_STRING'};}
    elsif($ENV{'REQUEST_METHOD'}eq"POST"){
        read(STDIN,$buffer,$ENV{'CONTENT_LENGTH'});
    }
$bufferb = $buffer;
#separate the name of the input from its value.
@forminputs = split(/&/, $bufferb);

foreach $forminput (@forminputs)
{
        #separate the name of the input from its value
        ($name, $value) = split(/=/, $forminput);

        #Un-Webify plus signs and %-encoding
        $value =~ tr/+/ /;
        $value =~ s/%([a-fA-F0-9][a-fA-F0-9])/pack("C", hex($1))/eg;

        #stick them in the in array
        $in{$name} = $value;
}
print "Content-type: text/html\n\n";

################################################################
# ABOVE is the required header for a perl script         #
################################################################


#################################################################
# (Below) Email received by library containing user-entered information #
#################################################################


# ***********************************************
# Here's where you MUST specify the path to your
# email program (probably sendmail) ON your Web server.
# Replace /usr/sbin/sendmail with your path.
```

```
# ****************************************************

open (LMAIL, "I/usr/sbin/sendmail -t");
print LMAIL ("To: $in{LibraryEmail}\n");
print LMAIL ("From: $in{CampusEmail}\n");
print LMAIL ("Subject: $in{Form} - patron submission\n");

print LMAIL ("------------------\nPatron information\n\n");
print LMAIL ("Name:\n $in{Name}\n\n");
print LMAIL ("Department / Major:\n $in{Department}\n\n");
print LMAIL ("Campus Email:\n $in{CampusEmail}\n\n");
print LMAIL ("Campus Phone:\n $in{CampusPhone}\n\n");
print LMAIL ("Status:\n $in{Status}\n\n");

print LMAIL ("------------------\nSubmitted information \n\n");

print LMAIL ("What new materials should the library purchase?\n $in{1}\n\n");
print LMAIL ("What existing materials could we put into storage or discard?\n $in{2} \n\n");
print LMAIL ("What new services should the library provide?\n $in{3}\n\n");
print LMAIL ("What existing services could we discontinue?\n $in{4}\n\n");
print LMAIL ("What new equipment should the library purchase?\n $in{5}\n\n");
print LMAIL ("What existing equipment could we discard or sell?\n $in{6}\n\n");
print LMAIL ("What new things can staff do to help?\n $in{7}\n\n");
print LMAIL ("How can we improve the inside of the library?\n $in{8}\n\n");
print LMAIL ("Is there any other way we can make the library a better place?\n $in{9}\n\n");
print LMAIL ("\n.\n");


##########################################################
# Email received by the user confirming form submission #
##########################################################

# ****************************************************
# Here's where you MUST specify the path to your
# email program ON your Web server.
# Replace /usr/sbin/sendmail with your path.
# ****************************************************

open (MAIL, "I/usr/sbin/sendmail -t");

# ****************************************************
# Here's where you MAY customize the email
# response to the user. You may change any wording
# on the form.
# ****************************************************
```

```
print MAIL<<toEnd;
To: $in{CampusEmail}
From: $in{LibraryEmail}
Subject: $in{Form}

Thanks for completing our Strategic Planning Survey and helping us plan the library of the future.\n\n

toEnd
   print MAIL ("\n.\n");


####################################################
# Screen response to user after submitting the form  #
####################################################


print ("<html><head><title>$in{Form}</title></head>");
print ("<body bgcolor=\"ffffff\">");


# *************************************************
# Here's where you MAY change the screen response
# the user sees after submitting the form. You may
# change any wording between the quotation marks.
# *************************************************

print ("Thanks for completing our Strategic Planning Survey and helping us plan the library of the future.");


# *************************************************
# Here's where you MAY change the name of the link
# back to your main page. You may replace Return
# to our main page with your own wording.
# *************************************************

print ("<p><center><a href=$in{LibraryURL}>Return to our main page.</a></center>");
print ("</body></html>");
```

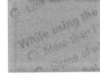

Index

About the Authors

Gail Junion-Metz

As head of her own training and consulting firm, Information Age Consultants, Gail instructs public and school librarians, patrons, teachers, and students of all ages and interests. Gail also likes to write about the Net. She is most widely known for her "Surf For" column, which is featured monthly in *School Library Journal*. Gail has also written a number of Internet books, such as *Internet Coach for Kids: A Guide for Librarians, Teachers, and Parents* and *K–12 Resources on the Internet,* both published by Library Solutions Press. She also co-authored *Using the World Wide Web and Creating Home Pages*: *A How-To-Do-It Manual for Librarians* and *Creating a Power Web Site: HTML, Tables, Imagemaps, Frames and Forms: A book with Web-Enabled CD-ROM,* both published by Neal-Schuman.

Gail holds a Master of Arts degree in Library Science from the University of Wisconsin, Madison. She is happily married to Ray, also a librarian, has a cool step-son Derrek (her current co-author), and lives in Winfield, Pennsylvania, in the heart of Amish country.

Derrek L. Metz

Derrek is in his third year at Bucknell University where he is majoring in Economics and minoring in Computer Science. He has been working with the Internet and creating Web sites since 1995. Derrek currently holds a Web intern coordinator position for the Alumni, Parents, and Volunteers Office at Bucknell, while also creating and maintaining other campus sites. Last summer he interned at Lombard Risk Management in London, serving on their Web marketing team. Derrek has hopes of continuing his research and affiliation with the Internet's application to the financial and business sectors.

How to Launch the CD

Because of the large number of files on the CD and the considerable amount of hard drive space it would take up, we do not recommend that you download the contents of the CD onto your computer. Instead, follow the instructions below to launch the CD from your CD drive any time you want to use it.

Windows Computers

1. Insert the CD into your computer's drive
2. Click on the START button on your taskbar
3. From the START menu, select and click on the RUN option
4. In the RUN box's OPEN: space, type D:/setup.htm then click on the OK button
   (*NOTE:* If your CD drive is not D:/ type the correct drive letter, then type setup.htm)
5. This will automatically launch your default Web browser and load the tutorial

MacIntosh Computers

1. Insert the CD into your computer's drive
2. Locate the CD's icon on your desktop and double click on it
3. In the window that displays, locate and double click on the icon for the *setup.htm* file
4. This will automatically launch your default Web browser and load the tutorial
   (*NOTE:* In some cases your Mac may ask you to select a program to open the file . . . select Internet Explorer or Netscape from the list, then click on the OK button.)